Errand
into
the
Wilderness

PERRY MILLER

ERRAND
INTO
THE
WILDERNESS

THE BELKNAP PRESS OF
HARVARD UNIVERSITY PRESS
Cambridge, Massachusetts

Distributed in Great Britain by Oxford University Press, London

Third Printing, 1970

Library of Congress Catalog Card Number 56–11285

SBN 674–26151–8

Printed in the United States of America

FOR MARK AND MOLLY HOWE

PREFACE

If for twenty-five years a man writes out of steady application to a single theme — if, that is, the theme itself be sufficiently spacious — he discovers that he has wrought out a consistency he could hardly have formulated at the beginning. Not that I have avoided publishing articles, and many sentences, which I wish I had not. I have failed myself much more often than have the scholars I emulate. A few of my more egregious lapses I have silently expunged for this edition. However, certain of my *gaffes* are so much a part of the record that, assuming the record be worth preserving, I let them stand, with prefatory warnings that readers may fully profit by my mistakes.

Omitting, for reasons both of space and policy, works of which I am downright ashamed, along with others that I recast into chapters for either volume of *The New England Mind* (*The Seventeenth Century,* 1939, 1953; *From Colony to Province,* 1952), I here put together those that seem to add up to a rank of spotlights on the massive narrative of the movement of European culture into the vacant wilderness of America.* (Chapter III is an exception, for reasons given in the comments that precede it.)

To the elucidation of this story I, in common with several historians of my generation, have devoted my life; to this investigation, I dedicate what remains of it. These papers, along with three or four books, are all I have yet been able to realize of a determination conceived three decades ago at Matadi on the banks of the Congo. I came there seeking "adventure," jealous of older contemporaries to whom that boon had been offered by the First World War. (Nobody had the prescience to teach me patience, to assure me that I too should have my War.) The adventures that Africa afforded were tawdry enough, but it became the setting for a sudden epiphany (if the word be not too strong) of the pressing necessity for expounding my America to the twentieth century.

Unfortunately (perhaps), such was the nature of the disclosure as to convey an invincible conviction that however valuable as documentation might be the mass of work being accomplished by those I may call "social" historians, they were not getting at the fundamental themes — or anywhere near *the* fundamental theme, assuming that such a theme even exists. I

---

* American scholarship is prone to idolize the footnote. The pieces that require minute annotations are here printed with their appendages, but with the others, since these are arguments rather than monographs, I have omitted the citations.

am the last to decry monographs on stoves or bathtubs, or tax laws, banks, the conduct of presidential elections, or even inventories of artifacts. All this is the warp and woof of American history. Just as we cannot grasp the French Revolution without knowing how the taxes were farmed, nor can we comprehend the Russian without learning as much as we may of the land system, so it is true that the outside world cannot judge America unless it knows about the Wilmot Proviso and the chain store. Even so, I was condemned to another (I do not say a better) sort of quest.

To bring into conjunction a minute event in the history of historiography with a great one: it was given to Edward Gibbon to sit disconsolate amid the ruins of the Capitol at Rome, and to have thrust upon him the "laborious work" of *The Decline and Fall* while listening to barefooted friars chanting responses in the former temple of Jupiter. It was given to me, equally disconsolate on the edge of a jungle of central Africa, to have thrust upon me the mission of expounding what I took to be the innermost propulsion of the United States, while supervising, in that barbaric tropic, the unloading of drums of case oil flowing out of the inexhaustible wilderness of America.

However it came about, the vision demanded of me that I begin at the beginning, not at the beginning of a fall (wherein Gibbon had an artistic advantage, which he improved to the utmost), but at the beginning of a beginning. Once I was back in the security of a graduate school, it seemed obvious that I had to commence with the Puritan migration. (I recognize, and herein pay my tribute to, the priority of Virginia; but what I wanted was a coherence with which I could coherently begin.) One or two of my instructors warned me against throwing my career away: that field, they said, was exhausted, all that wheat had long since been winnowed, there was nothing but chaff remaining. I might have abandoned the mission, persuaded that my voices had misled me, had not Percy Holmes Boynton sustained me. He did this, I now suspect, not so much because he believed that in this area more was needed from scholarship, but simply because he held that a boy should be allowed to do what the boy genuinely, even if misguidedly, is convinced should be done. I attested my debt by dedicating to him *Orthodoxy in Massachusetts*, in 1933; but I could not offer this collection without again, though Boynton is no longer in hearing distance, telling how much I owe him.

Assuredly the works of my senior colleagues, Kenneth Ballard Murdock and Samuel Eliot Morison, with some possible assistance of my own volumes, have shown how stultifying was that conception of Puritan history which had settled like a cloud of patriotic obscurantism over historians of a generation ago. In the 1920's a few strident and derisive voices, such as those of H. L. Mencken and James Truslow Adams, got the vaporous mass to moving. I freely acknowledge the liberation I owe to such violators of the temple, for without them, I and my generation might have lacked the temerity to undertake a fresh and profane examination. I suppose the saddest comment I can make upon the whole enterprise is that, after three decades of endeavor, though we have shaken a few complacencies, we have not arrived at the comprehensive understanding we presumptuously proposed. Hence the exultation I feel at seeing younger scholars — notably Edmund S. Morgan and Bernard Bailyn — coming so grandly along. The one thing I am resolved never to say to a student is that any field of study is exhausted, that all the grain has been threshed. As for that interminable field which may be called the meaning of America, the acreage is immense, and the threshers few. Too often, as in my case, they are sadly deficient in the several skills required for the gigantic labor.

Despite the inadequacies of my technical training, my theme possessed me. What I believe caught my imagination, among the fuel drums, was a realization of the uniqueness of the American experience; even then I could dimly make out the portent for the future of the world, looking upon these tangible symbols of the republic's appalling power. I could see no way of coping with the problem except by going to the beginning. Walt Whitman says, in a somewhat different context, that he commenced his studies, but was never able to get beyond the beginning. Considering that some reviewers have confounded my method with my materials, I may insist that what seized upon me and still directs me is the inner logic of the research. Certainly not — not in any sense — a personal predilection. The beginning I sought was inevitably — being located in the seventeenth century — theological. This was not a fact of my choosing: had the origin been purely economic or imperial, I should have been no less committed to reporting. Since the first articulate body of expression upon which I could get a leverage happened to be a body of Protestant doctrine, I set myself to explore that doctrine in its own terms.

Furthermore, the essence of the challenge was, to change the metaphor, to present these terms, just these and no others, as being comprehensible. I have never entertained the slightest ambition of making these ideas palatable to my contemporaries in any other sense than the historical one. There they are — those with which American thought began. Respect for them is not the same thing as believing in them — as Nathaniel Hawthorne preëminently demonstrated. But historians are apt to slide over these concepts in a shockingly superficial manner simply because they have so little respect for the intellect in general. I have difficulty imagining that anyone can be a historian without realizing that history itself is part of the life of the mind; hence I have been compelled to insist that the mind of man is the basic factor in human history.

There is a disposition among modern publishers, which extends even to university presses, to shy away from the word "essay." To call a collection like this a volume of essays is to curse it with the remembered pomposity of Emerson, the ponderousness of Macaulay. In the world of journalism, the approved noun is "piece." A piece is confessedly a mere exercise, not pretending to pronounce upon the universe. Yet in this usage there is a double implication: while a piece is unpretentious, it secretly prides itself on being workmanlike. And it meets a deadline. Though I have generally manufactured these studies for some sort of deadline, I still enjoy the luxury of revision. Even so, they are not transformed into essays. Wherefore, I am content to offer them, employing a few editorial comments to plead for their general coherence, as a compilation of pieces.

Cambridge, Massachusetts   PERRY MILLER
1 May, 1956

CONTENTS

CHAPTER I

ERRAND INTO THE WILDERNESS

[The title of an election sermon preached in 1670 provided the fitting title for an exhibition of New England imprints at the John Carter Brown Library in Brown University, where I delivered this address on May 16, 1952. Only thereafter did I discover that the Reverend Samuel Danforth had also given me a title.

In his own language, Danforth was trying to do what I too am attempting: to make out some deeper configuration in the story than a mere modification, by obvious and natural necessity, of an imported European culture in adjustment to a frontier. He recognized, as do I, that a basic conditioning factor was the frontier — the wilderness. Even so, the achievement of a personality is not so much the presence of this or that environmental element — no matter how pressing, how terrifying — as the way in which a given personality responds. The real theme is so complex that any simplification does it injustice, though for the sake of communication simplifications are manufactured. Danforth made his simplification by stressing the "errand" more than the "wilderness." So I follow him, and in my context, as in his, "errand" is not a formal thesis but a metaphor.

A metaphor is a vastly different thing from Frederick Jackson Turner's "thesis" that democracy came out of the forest. Happily we no longer are obliged to believe this, although we are ready to recognize, thanks to Turner, that unless we acknowledge the existence of the forest the character of American history is obscure. A newer generation, confessing the importance of Turner's speculations, is concerned with an inherent cultural conflict, in relation to which the forest was, so to speak, as external as the Atlantic Ocean. This ostentatiously simple and monolithic America is in fact a congeries of inner tensions. It has been so from the beginning; it is more so now than at the beginning — as is proved by the frenetic insistence of many Americans that this statement is untrue. Confronted with so gigantic a riddle, the analyst becomes wary of generalizations, though incessantly he strives to comprehend.

In this address, then, I am not thinking, nor in any paper of this volume am I thinking, within the framework of interpretation — the "frontier hypothesis" — that Turner bequeathed us. Immense as is the debt that all seekers after national self-knowledge owe to Turner, we have to insist — at least I do — that he did as much to confuse as to clarify the deepest issue. He worked on the premise — which any Puritan logician (being in this regard a scholastic) could have corrected — that the subject matter of a liberal art determines the form, that the content of a discipline automatically supplies the angle of vision. I might even argue that, by remote implication, the struggle of a Protestant culture in America against its weakening hold on the Puritan insight into this law of the mind, namely, that form controls matter, constitutes one theme of the collection. From Turner's conception of the ruling and compulsive power of the frontier no further avenue could be projected to any cultural synthesis. Ideally, this volume might include a study of Turner as being himself an exemplification — I might more accurately say the foremost victim — of his fallacy, rather than the master of it. However, by now it has become rather the mode to point out the romantic prepossessions of Turner; I mention him not only to salute a great name but also, by calling attention to my dissent from him, to underscore my use of the two concepts, both "errand" and "wilderness," as figures of speech.]

IT was a happy inspiration that led the staff of the John Carter Brown Library to choose as the title of its New England exhibition of 1952 a phrase from Samuel Danforth's election sermon, delivered on May 11, 1670: *A Brief Recognition of New England's Errand into the Wilderness.* It was of course an inspiration, if not of genius at least of talent, for Danforth to invent his title in the first place. But all the election sermons of this period — that is to say, the major expressions of the second generation, which, delivered on these forensic occasions, were in the fullest sense community expression — have interesting titles; a mere listing tells the story of what was happening to the minds and emotions of the New England people: John Higginson's *The Cause of God and His People In New-England* in 1663, William Stoughton's *New England's True Interest, Not to Lie* in 1668, Thomas Shepard's *Eye-Salve* in 1672, Urian Oakes's *New England Pleaded With* in 1673, and, climactically and most explicitly, Increase Mather's *A Discourse Concerning the Danger of Apostasy* in 1677.

All of these show by their title pages alone — and, as those who have looked into them know, infinitely more by their contents — a deep disquietude. They are troubled utterances, worried, fearful. Something has gone wrong. As in 1662 Wigglesworth already was saying in verse, God has a controversy with New England; He has cause to be angry and to punish it because of its innumerable defections. They say, unanimously, that New England was sent on an errand, and that it has failed.

To our ears these lamentations of the second generation sound strange indeed. We think of the founders as heroic men — of the towering stature of Bradford, Winthrop, and Thomas Hooker — who braved the ocean and the wilderness, who conquered both, and left to their children a goodly heritage. Why then this whimpering?

Some historians suggest that the second and third generations suffered a failure of nerve; they weren't the men their fathers had been, and they knew it. Where the founders could range over the vast body of theology and ecclesiastical polity and produce profound works like the treatises of John Cotton or the subtle psychological analyses of Hooker, or even such a gusty though wrongheaded book as Nathaniel Ward's *Simple Cobler*, let alone such lofty and righteaded pleas as Roger Williams' *Bloudy Tenent*, all these children could do was tell each other that they were on probation and that their chances of making good did not seem very promising.

Since Puritan intellectuals were thoroughly grounded in grammar and rhetoric, we may be certain that Danforth was fully aware of the ambiguity concealed in his word "errand." It already had taken on the double meaning which it still carries with us. Originally, as the word first took form in English, it meant exclusively a short journey on which an inferior is sent to convey a message or to perform a service for his superior. In that sense we today speak of an "errand boy"; or the husband says that while in town on his lunch hour, he must run an errand for his wife. But by the end of the Middle Ages, errand developed another connotation: it came to mean the actual business on which the actor goes, the purpose itself, the conscious intention in his mind. In this signification, the runner of the errand is working for himself, is his own boss; the wife, while the husband is away at the office, runs her own errands. Now in the 1660's the problem was this: which had New England originally been — an errand boy or a doer of errands? In which sense had it failed? Had it been despatched for a further purpose, or was it an end in itself? Or had it fallen short not only in one or the other, but in both of the meanings? If so, it was indeed a tragedy, in the primitive sense of a fall from a mighty designation.

If the children were in grave doubt about which had been the original errand — if, in fact, those of the founders who lived into the later period and who might have set their progeny to rights found themselves wondering and confused — there is little chance of our answering clearly. Of course, there is no problem about Plymouth Colony. That is the charm about Plymouth: its clarity. The Pilgrims, as we have learned to call them, were reluctant voyagers; they had never wanted to leave England, but had been obliged to depart because the authorities made life impossible for Separatists. They could, naturally, have stayed at home had they given up being Separatists, but that idea simply did not occur to them. Yet they did not go to Holland as though on an errand; neither can we extract the notion of a mission out of the reasons which, as Bradford tells us, persuaded them to leave Leyden for "Virginia." The war with Spain was about to be resumed, and the economic threat was ominous; their migration was not so much an errand as a shrewd forecast, a plan to get out while the getting was good, lest, should they stay, they would be "intrapped or surrounded by their enemies, so as they should neither be able to fight nor flie." True, once the decision was taken, they congratulated themselves that they might become a means for propagating the gospel in remote parts of the world, and thus of serving as steppingstones to others in the performance of this great work; nevertheless, the substance of their decision was that they "thought it better to dislodge betimes to some place of better advantage and less danger, if any such could be found." The great hymn that Bradford, looking back in his old age, chanted about the landfall is one of the greatest passages, if not the very greatest, in all New England's literature; yet it does not resound with the sense of a mission accomplished — instead, it vibrates with the sorrow and exultation of suffering, the sheer endurance, the pain and the anguish, with the somberness of death faced unflinchingly:

May not and ought not the children of these fathers rightly say: Our fathers were Englishmen which came over this great ocean, and were ready to perish in this wilderness; but they cried unto the Lord, and he heard their voyce, and looked on their adversitie . . . .

We are bound, I think, to see in Bradford's account the prototype of the vast majority of subsequent immigrants — of those Oscar Handlin calls "The Uprooted": they came for better advantage and for less danger, and to give their posterity the opportunity of success.

The Great Migration of 1630 is an entirely other story. True, among the reasons John Winthrop drew up in 1629 to persuade himself and his colleagues that they should commit themselves to the enterprise, the economic motive frankly figures. Wise men thought that England was overpopulated and that the poor would have a better chance in the new land. But Massachusetts Bay was not just an organization of immigrants seeking advantage and opportunity. It had a positive sense of mission — either it was sent on an errand or it had its own intention, but in either case the deed was deliberate. It was an act of will, perhaps of willfulness. These Puritans were not driven out of England (thousands of their fellows stayed and fought the Cavaliers) — they went of their own accord.

So, concerning them, we ask the question, why? If we are not altogether clear about precisely how we should phrase the answer, this is not because they themselves were reticent. They spoke as fully as they knew how, and none more magnificently or cogently than John Winthrop in the midst of the passage itself, when he delivered a lay sermon aboard the flagship *Arbella* and called it "A Modell of Christian Charity." It distinguishes the motives of this great enterprise from those of Bradford's forlorn retreat, and especially from those of the masses who later have come in quest of advancement. Hence, for the student of New England and of America, it is a fact demanding incessant brooding that John Winthrop selected as the "doctrine" of his discourse, and so as the basic proposition to which, it then seemed to him, the errand was committed, the thesis that God had disposed mankind in a hierarchy of social classes, so that "in all times some must be rich, some poor, some highe and eminent in power and dignitie; others mean and in subjeccion." It is as though, preternaturally sensing what the promise of America might come to signify for the rank and file, Winthrop took the precaution to drive out of their heads any notion that in the wilderness the poor and the mean were ever so to improve themselves as to mount above the rich or the eminent in dignity. Were there any who had signed up under the mistaken impression that such was the purpose of their errand, Winthrop told them that, although other peoples, lesser breeds, might come for wealth or pelf, this migration was specifically dedicated to an avowed end that had nothing to do with incomes. We have entered into an explicit covenant with God, "we haue professed to enterprise these Accions vpon these and these ends"; we have drawn up indentures with the Almighty, wherefore if we succeed and do not let ourselves get diverted into making money, He will reward us. Whereas if we fail, if we "fall to embrace this present world and prosecute our carnall intencions, seekeing greate things for our selves and our posterity, the Lord will surely breake out in wrathe against us be revenged of such a periured people and make us knowe the price of the breache of such a Covenant."

Well, what terms were agreed upon in this covenant? Winthrop could say precisely — "It is by a mutuall consent through a specially overruleing providence, and a more than ordinary approbation of the Churches of Christ to seeke out a place of Cohabitation and Consorteshipp under a due forme of Government both civill and ecclesiasticall." If it could be said thus concretely, why should there be any ambiguity? There was no doubt whatsover about what Winthrop meant by a due form of ecclesiastical government: he meant the pure Biblical polity set forth in full detail by the New Testament, that method which later generations, in the days of increasing confusion, would settle down to calling Congregational, but which for Winthrop was no denominational peculiarity but the very essence of organized Christianity. What a due form of civil government meant, therefore, became crystal clear: a political regime, possessing power, which would consider its main function to be the erecting, protecting, and preserving of this form of polity. This due form would have, at the very beginning of its list of responsibilities, the duty of suppressing heresy, of subduing or somehow getting rid of dissenters — of being, in short, deliberately, vigorously, and consistently intolerant.

Regarded in this light, the Massachusetts Bay Company came on an errand in the second and later sense of the word: it was, so to speak, on its own business. What it set out to do was the sufficient reason for its setting out. About this Winthrop seems to be perfectly certain, as he declares specifically what the due forms will be attempting: the end is to improve our lives to do more service to the Lord, to increase the body of Christ, and to preserve our posterity from the corruptions of this evil world, so that they in turn shall work out their salvation under the purity and power of Biblical ordinances. Because the errand was so definable in advance, certain conclusions about the method of conducting it were equally evident: one, obviously, was that those sworn to the covenant should not be allowed to turn aside in a lust for mere physical rewards; but another was, in Winthrop's simple but splendid words, "we must be knit togeher in this worke as one man, wee must entertaine each other in brotherly affection." we must actually delight in each other, "always having before our eyes our Commission and community in the worke, our community as members of the same body." This was to say, were the great purpose kept steadily in mind, if all gazed only at it and strove only for it, then social solidarity (within a scheme of fixed and unalterable class distinctions) would be an automatic consequence. A society despatched upon an errand that is its own reward would want no other rewards: it could go forth to possess a land without ever becoming possessed by it; social gradations would remain eternally what God had originally appointed; there would be no internal contention among groups or interests, and though there would be hard work for everybody, prosperity would be bestowed not as a consequence of labor but as a sign of approval upon the mission itself. For once in the history of humanity (with all its sins), there would be a society so dedicated to a holy cause that success would prove innocent and triumph not raise up sinful pride or arrogant dissension.

Or, at least, this would come about if the people did not deal falsely with God, if they would live up to the articles of their bond. If we do not perform these terms, Winthrop warned, we may expect immediate manifestations of divine wrath; we shall perish out of the land we are crossing the sea to possess. And here in the 1660's and 1670's, all the jeremiads (of which Danforth's is one of the most poignant) are castigations of the people for having defaulted on precisely these articles. They recite the long list of afflictions an angry God had rained upon them, surely enough to prove how abysmally they had deserted the covenant: crop failures, epidemics, grasshoppers, caterpillars, torrid summers, arctic winters, Indian wars, hurricanes, shipwrecks, accidents, and (most grievous of all) unsatisfactory children. The solemn work of the election day, said Stoughton in 1668, is "Foundation-work" — not, that is, to lay a new one, "but to continue, and strengthen, and beautifie, and build upon that which has been laid." It had been laid in the covenant before even a foot was set ashore, and thereon New England should rest. Hence the terms of survival, let alone of prosperity, remained what had first been propounded:

If we should so frustrate and deceive the Lords Expectations, that his Covenant-interest in us, and the Workings of his Salvation be made to cease, then All were lost indeed; Ruine upon Ruine, Destruction upon Destruction would come, until one stone were not left upon another.

Since so much of the literature after 1660 — in fact, just about all of it — dwells on this theme of declension and apostasy, would not the story of New England seem to be simply that of the failure of a mission? Winthrop's dread was realized: posterity had not found their salvation amid pure ordinances but had, despite the ordinances, yielded to the seductions of the good land. Hence distresses were being piled upon them, the slaughter of King Philip's War and now the attack of a profligate king upon the sacred charter. By about 1680, it did in truth seem that shortly no stone would be left upon another, that history would record of New England that the founders had been great men, but that their children and grandchildren progressively deteriorated.

This would certainly seem to be the impression conveyed by the assembled clergy and lay elders who, in 1679, met at Boston in a formal synod, under the leadership of Increase Mather, and there prepared a report on why the land suffered. The result of their deliberation, published under the title *The Necessity of Reformation,* was the first in what has proved to be a distressingly long succession of investigations into the civic health of Americans, and it is probably the most pessimistic. The land was afflicted, it said, because corruption had proceeded apace; assuredly, if the people did not quickly reform, the last blow would fall and nothing but desolation be left. Into what a moral quagmire this dedicated community had sunk, the synod did not leave to imagination; it published a long and detailed inventory of sins, crimes, misdemeanors, and nasty habits, which makes, to say the least, interesting reading.

We hear much talk nowadays about corruption, most of it couched in generalized terms. If we ask our current Jeremiahs to descend to particulars, they tell us that the republic is going on the rocks, or to the dogs, because the wives of politicians aspire to wear mink coats and their husbands take a moderate five per cent cut on certain deals to pay for the garments. The Puritans were devotees of logic, and the verb "methodize" ruled their thinking. When the synod went to work, it had before it a succession of sermons, such as that of Danforth and the other election-day or fast-day orators, as well as such works as Increase Mather's *A Brief History of the Warr With the Indians,* wherein the decimating conflict with Philip was presented as a revenge upon the people for their transgressions. When the synod felt obliged to enumerate the enormities of the land so that the people could recognize just how far short of their errand they had fallen, it did not, in the modern manner, assume that regeneration would be accomplished at the next election by turning the rascals out, but it digested this body of literature; it reduced the contents to method. The result is a staggering compendium of iniquity, organized into twelve headings.

First, there was a great and visible decay of godliness. Second, there were several manifestations of pride — contention in the churches, insubordination of inferiors toward superiors, particularly of those inferiors who had, unaccountably, acquired more wealth than their betters, and, astonishingly, a shocking extravagance in attire, especially on the part of these of the meaner sort, who persisted in dressing beyond their means. Third, there were heretics, especially Quakers and Anabaptists. Fourth, a notable increase in swearing and a spreading disposition to sleep at sermons (these two phenomena seemed basically connected). Fifth, the Sabbath was wantonly violated. Sixth, family government had decayed, and fathers no longer kept their sons and daughters from prowling at night. Seventh, instead of people being knit together as one man in mutual love, they were full of contention, so that lawsuits were on the increase and lawyers were thriving. Under the eighth head, the synod described the sins of sex and alcohol, thus producing some of the juiciest prose of the period: militia days had become orgies, taverns were crowded; women threw temptation in the way of befuddled men by wearing false locks and displaying naked necks and arms "or, which is more abominable, naked Breasts"; there were "mixed Dancings," along with light behavior and "Company-keeping" with vain persons, wherefore the bastardy rate was rising. In 1672, there was actually an attempt to supply Boston with a brothel (it was suppressed, but the synod was bearish about the future). Ninth, New Englanders were betraying a marked disposition to tell lies, especially when selling anything. In the tenth place, the business morality of even the most righteous left everything to be desired: the wealthy speculated in land and raised prices excessively; "Day-Labourers and Mechanicks are unreasonable in their demands." In the eleventh place, the people showed no disposition to reform, and in the twelfth, they seemed utterly destitute of civic spirit.

"The things here insisted on," said the synod, "have been oftentimes mentioned and inculcated by those whom the Lord hath set as Watchmen to the house of Israel." Indeed they had been, and thereafter they continued to be even more inculcated. At the end of the century, the synod's report was serving as a kind of handbook for preachers: they would take some verse of Isaiah or Jeremiah, set up the doctrine that God avenges the iniquities of a chosen people, and then run down the twelve heads, merely bringing the list up to date by inserting the new and still more depraved practices an ingenious people kept on devising. I suppose that in the whole literature of the world, including the satirists of imperial Rome, there is hardly such another uninhibited and unrelenting documentation of a people's descent into corruption.

I have elsewhere endeavored to argue [1] that, while the social or economic historian may read this literature for its contents — and so construct from the expanding catalogue of denunciations a record of social progress — the cultural anthropologist will look slightly askance at these jeremiads; he will exercise a methodological caution about taking them at face value. If you read them all through, the total effect, curiously enough, is not at all depressing: you come to the paradoxical realization that they do not bespeak a despairing frame of mind. There is something of a ritualistic incantation

[1] See *The New England Mind: From Colony to Province* (1952), Chapter II.

about them; whatever they may signify in the realm of theology, in that of psychology they are purgations of soul; they do not discourage but actually encourage the community to persist in its heinous conduct. The exhortation to a reformation which never materializes serves as a token payment upon the obligation, and so liberates the debtors. Changes there had to be: adaptations to environment, expansion of the frontier, mansions constructed, commercial adventures undertaken. These activities were not specifically nominated in the bond Winthrop had framed. They were thrust upon the society by American experience; because they were not only works of necessity but of excitement, they proved irresistible — whether making money, haunting taverns, or committing fornication. Land speculation meant not only wealth but dispersion of the people, and what was to stop the march of settlement? The covenant doctrine preached on the *Arbella* had been formulated in England, where land was not to be had for the taking; its adherents had been utterly oblivious of what the fact of a frontier would do for an imported order, let alone for a European mentality. Hence I suggest that under the guise of this mounting wail of sinfulness, this incessant and never successful cry for repentance, the Puritans launched themselves upon the process of Americanization.

However, there are still more pertinent or more analytical things to be said of this body of expression. If you compare it with the great productions of the founders, you will be struck by the fact that the second and third generations had become oriented toward the social, and only the social, problem; herein they were deeply and profoundly different from their fathers. The finest creations of the founders — the disquisitions of Hooker, Shepard, and Cotton — were written in Europe, or else, if actually penned in the colonies, proceeded from a thoroughly European mentality, upon which the American scene made no impression whatsoever. The most striking example of this imperviousness is the poetry of Anne Bradstreet: she came to Massachusetts at the age of eighteen, already two years married to Simon Bradstreet; there, she says, "I found a new world and new manners, at which my heart rose" in rebellion, but soon convincing herself that it was the way of God, she submitted and joined the church. She bore Simon eight children, and loved him sincerely, as her most charming poem, addressed to him, reveals:

> If ever two were one, then surely we;
> If ever man were loved by wife, then thee.

After the house burned, she wrote a lament about how her pleasant things in ashes lay and how no more the merriment of guests would sound in the hall; but there is nothing in the poem to suggest that the house stood in North Andover or that the things so tragically consumed were doubly precious because they had been transported across the ocean and were utterly irreplaceable in the wilderness. In between rearing children and keeping house she wrote her poetry; her brother-in-law carried the manuscript to London, and there published it in 1650 under the ambitious title, *The Tenth Muse Lately Sprung Up in America.* But the title is the only thing about the volume which shows any sense of America, and that little merely in order to prove that the plantations had something in the way of European wit and learning, that they had not receded into barbarism. Anne's flowers are English flowers, the birds, English birds, and the landscape is Lincolnshire. So also with the productions of immigrant scholarship: such a learned and acute work as Hooker's *Survey of the Summe of Church Discipline,* which is specifically about the regime set up in America, is written entirely within the logical patterns, and out of the religious experience, of Europe; it makes no concession to new and peculiar circumstances.

The titles alone of productions in the next generation show how concentrated have become emotion and attention upon the interest of New England, and none is more revealing than Samuel Danforth's conception of an errand into the wilderness. Instead of being able to compose abstract treatises like those of Hooker upon the soul's preparation, humiliation, or exultation, or such a collection of wisdom and theology as John Cotton's *The Way of Life* or Shepard's *The Sound Believer,* these later saints must, over and over again, dwell upon the specific sins of New England, and the more they denounce, the more they must narrow their focus to the provincial problem. If they write upon anything else, it must be about the halfway covenant and its manifold consequences — a development enacted wholly in this country — or else upon their wars with the Indians. Their range is sadly constricted, but every effort, no matter how brief, is addressed to the persistent question: what is the meaning of this society in the wilderness? If it does not mean what Winthrop said it must mean, what under Heaven is it? Who, they are forever asking themselves, who are we? — and sometimes they are on the verge of saying, who the Devil are we, anyway?

This brings us back to the fundamental ambiguity concealed in the word "errand," that *double entente* of which I am certain Danforth was aware when he published the words that give point to the exhibition. While it was true that in 1630, the covenant philosophy of a special and peculiar bond lifted the migration out of the ordinary realm of nature, provided it with a definite mission which might in the secondary sense be called its errand, there was always present in Puritan thinking the suspicion that God's saints are at best inferiors, despatched by their Superior upon particular assignments. Anyone who has run errands for other people, particularly for people of great importance with many things on their minds, such as army commanders, knows how real is the peril that, by the time he returns with the report of a message delivered or a bridge blown up, the Superior may be interested in something else; the situation at headquarters may be entirely changed, and the gallant errand boy, or the husband who desperately remembered to buy the ribbon, may be told that he is too late. This tragic pattern appears again and again in modern warfare: an agent is dropped by parachute and, after immense hardships, comes back to find that, in the shifting tactical or strategic situations, his contribution is no longer of value. If he gets home in time and his service proves useful, he receives a medal; otherwise, no matter what prodigies he has performed, he may not even be thanked. He has been sent, as the devastating phrase has it, upon a fool's errand, than which there can be a no more shattering blow to self-esteem.

The Great Migration of 1630 felt insured against such treatment from on high by the covenant; nevertheless, the God of the covenant always remained an unpredictable Jehovah, a *Deus Absconditus*. When God promises to abide by stated terms, His word, of course, is to be trusted; but then, what is man that he dare accuse Omnipotence of tergiversation? But if any such apprehension was in Winthrop's mind as he spoke on the *Arbella*, or in the minds of other apologists for the enterprise, they kept it far back and allowed it no utterance. They could stifle the thought, not only because Winthrop and his colleagues believed fully in the covenant, but because they could see in the pattern of history that their errand was not a mere scouting expedition: it was an essential maneuver in the drama of Christendom. The Bay Company was not a battered remnant of suffering Separatists thrown up on a rocky shore; it was an organized task force of Christians, executing a flank attack on the corruptions of Christendom. These Puritans did not flee to America; they went in order to work out that complete reformation which was not yet accomplished in England and Europe, but which would quickly be accomplished if only the saints back there had a working model to guide them. It is impossible to say that any who sailed from Southampton really expected to lay his bones in the new world; were it to come about — as all in their heart of hearts anticipated — that the forces of righteousness should prevail against Laud and Wentworth, that England after all should turn toward reformation, where else would the distracted country look for leadership except to those who in New England had perfected the ideal polity and who would know how to administer it? This was the large unspoken assumption in the errand of 1630: if the conscious intention were realized, not only would a federated Jehovah bless the new land, but He would bring back these temporary colonials to govern England.

In this respect, therefore, we may say that the migration was running an errand in the earlier and more primitive sense of the word — performing a job not so much for Jehovah as for history, which was the wisdom of Jehovah expressed through time. Winthrop was aware of this aspect of the mission — fully conscious of it. "For wee must Consider that wee shall be as a Citty upon a Hill, the eies of all people are upon us." More was at stake than just one little colony. If we deal falsely with God, not only will He descend upon us in wrath, but even more terribly, He will make us "a story and a by-word through the world, wee shall open the mouthes of enemies to speake evill of the wayes of god and all professours for Gods sake." No less than John Milton was New England to justify God's ways to man, though not, like him, in the agony and confusion of defeat but in the confidence of approaching triumph. This errand was being run for the sake of Reformed Christianity; and while the first aim was indeed to realize in America the due form of government, both civil and ecclesiastical, the aim behind that aim was to vindicate the most rigorous ideal of the Reformation, so that ultimately all Europe would imitate New England. If we succeed, Winthrop told his audience, men will say of later plantations, "the lord make it like that of New England." There was an elementary prudence to be observed: Winthrop said that the prayer would arise from subsequent plantations, yet what was England itself but one of God's plantations? In America, he promised, we shall see, or may see, more of God's wisdom, power, and truth "then formerly wee have beene acquainted with." The situation was such that, for the moment, the model had no chance to be exhibited in England; Puritans could talk about it, theorize upon it, but they could not display it, could not prove that it would actually work. But if they had it set up in America — in a bare land, devoid of already established (and corrupt) institutions, empty of bishops and courtiers, where they could start *de novo*, and the eyes of the world were upon it — and if then it performed just as the saints had predicted of it, the Calvinist internationale would know exactly how to go about completing the already begun but temporarily stalled revolution in Europe.[2]

When we look upon the enterprise from this point of view, the psychology of the second and third generations becomes more comprehensible. We realize that the migration was not sent upon its errand in order to found the United States of America, nor even the New England conscience. Actually, it would not perform its errand even when the colonists did erect a due form of government in church and state: what was further required in order for this mission to be a success was that the eyes of the world be kept fixed upon it in rapt attention. If the rest of the world, or at least of Protestantism, looked elsewhere, or turned to another model, or simply got distracted and forgot about New England, if the new land was left with a polity nobody in the great world of Europe wanted — then every success in fulfilling the terms of the covenant would become a diabolical measure of failure. If the due form of government were not everywhere to be saluted, what would New England have upon its hands? How give it a name, this victory nobody could utilize? How provide an identity for something conceived under misapprehensions? How could a universal which turned out to be nothing but a provincial particular be called anything but a blunder or an abortion?

If an actor, playing the leading role in the greatest dramatic spectacle of the century, were to attire himself and put on his make-up, rehearse his lines, take a deep breath, and stride onto the stage, only to find the theater

---

[2] See the perceptive analysis of Alan Heimert (*The New England Quarterly*, XXVI, September 1953) of the ingredients that ultimately went into the Puritans' metaphor of the "wilderness," all the more striking a concoction because they attached no significance a priori to their wilderness destination. To begin with, it was simply a void.

dark and empty, no spotlight working, and himself entirely alone, he would feel as did New England around 1650 or 1660. For in the 1640's, during the Civil Wars, the colonies, so to speak, lost their audience. First of all, there proved to be, deep in the Puritan movement, an irreconcilable split between the Presbyterian and Independent wings, wherefore no one system could be imposed upon England, and so the New England model was unserviceable. Secondly — most horrible to relate — the Independents, who in polity were carrying New England's banner and were supposed, in the schedule of history, to lead England into imitation of the colonial order, betrayed the sacred cause by yielding to the heresy of toleration. They actually welcomed Roger Williams, whom the leaders of the model had kicked out of Massachusetts so that his nonsense about liberty of conscience would not spoil the administrations of charity.

In other words, New England did not lie, did not falter; it made good everything Winthrop demanded — wonderfully good — and then found that its lesson was rejected by those choice spirits for whom the exertion had been made. By casting out Williams, Anne Hutchinson, and the Antinomians, along with an assortment of Gortonists and Anabaptists, into that cesspool then becoming known as Rhode Island, Winthrop, Dudley, and the clerical leaders showed Oliver Cromwell how he should go about governing England. Instead, he developed the utterly absurd theory that so long as a man made a good soldier in the New Model Army, it did not matter whether he was a Calvinist, an Antinomian, an Arminian, an Anabaptist or even — horror of horrors — a Socinian! Year after year, as the circus tours this country, crowds howl with laughter, no matter how many times they have seen the stunt, at the bustle that walks by itself: the clown comes out dressed in a large skirt with a bustle behind; he turns sharply to the left, and the bustle continues blindly and obstinately straight ahead, on the original course. It is funny in a circus, but not in history. There is nothing but tragedy in the realization that one was in the main path of events, and now is sidetracked and disregarded. One is always able, of course, to stand firm on his first resolution, and to condemn the clown of history for taking the wrong turning: yet this is a desolating sort of stoicism, because it always carries with it the recognition that history will never come back to the predicted path, and that with one's own demise, righteousness must die out of the world.

The most humiliating element in the experience was the way the English brethren turned upon the colonials for precisely their greatest achievement. It must have seemed, for those who came with Winthrop in 1630 and who remembered the clarity and brilliance with which he set forth the conditions of their errand, that the world was turned upside down and inside out when, in June 1645, thirteen leading Independent divines — such men as Goodwin, Owen, Nye, Burroughs, formerly friends and allies of Hooker and Davenport, men who might easily have come to New England and helped extirpate heretics — wrote the General Court that the colony's law banishing Anabaptists was an embarrassment to the Independent cause in England. Opponents were declaring, said these worthies, "that persons of our way, principall and spirit cannot beare with Dissentors from them, but Doe correct, fine, imprison and banish them wherever they have power soe to Doe." There were indeed people in England who admired the severities of Massachusetts, but we assure you, said the Independents, these "are utterly your enemyes and Doe seeke your extirpation from the face of the earth: those who now in power are your friends are quite otherwise minded, and doe professe they are much offended with your proceedings." Thus early commenced that chronic weakness in the foreign policy of Americans, an inability to recognize who in truth constitute their best friends abroad.

We have lately accustomed ourselves to the fact that there does exist a mentality which will take advantage of the liberties allowed by society in order to conspire for the ultimate suppression of those same privileges. The government of Charles I and Archbishop Laud had not, where that danger was concerned, been liberal, but it had been conspicuously inefficient; hence, it did not liquidate the Puritans (although it made halfhearted efforts), nor did it herd them into prison camps. Instead, it generously, even lavishly, gave a group of them a charter to Massachusetts Bay, and obligingly left out the standard clause requiring that the document remain in London, that the grantees keep their office within reach of Whitehall. Winthrop's revolutionaries availed themselves of this liberty to get the charter overseas, and thus to set up a regime dedicated to the worship of God in the manner they desired — which meant allowing nobody else to worship any other way, especially adherents of Laud and King Charles. All this was perfectly logical and consistent. But what happened to the thought processes of their fellows in England made no sense whatsoever. Out of the New Model Army came the fantastic notion that a party struggling for power should proclaim that, once it captured the state, it would recognize the right of dissenters to disagree and to have their own worship, to hold their own opinions. Oliver Cromwell was so far gone in this idiocy as to become a dictator, in order to impose toleration by force! Amid this shambles, the errand of New England collapsed. There was nobody left at headquarters to whom reports could be sent.

Many a man has done a brave deed, been hailed as a public hero, had honors and ticker tape heaped upon him — and then had to live, day after day, in the ordinary routine, eating breakfast and brushing his teeth, in what seems protracted anticlimax. A couple may win their way to each other across insuperable obstacles, elope in a blaze of passion and glory — and then have to learn that life is a matter of buying the groceries and getting the laundry done. This sense of the meaning having gone out of life, that all adventures are over, that no great days and no heroism lie ahead, is particularly galling when it falls upon a son whose father once was the public hero or the great lover. He has to put up with the daily routine without ever having known at first hand the thrill of danger or the ecstasy of passion. True, he has his own hardships — clearing rocky pastures, hauling in the cod during a storm, fighting Indians in a swamp — but what are these compared with the magnificence of leading an exodus of saints to found a city on a hill, for the eyes of all the world to behold? He might wage a stout fight against the Indians, and one out of ten of his fellows might perish in the struggle, but the world was no longer interested. He would be reduced to writing accounts of himself and scheming to get a publisher in London, in a desperate effort to tell a heedless world, "Look, I exist!"

His greatest difficulty would be not the stones, storms, and Indians, but the problem of his identity. In something of this sort, I should like to suggest, consists the anxiety and torment that inform productions of the late seventeenth and early eighteenth centuries — and should I say, some thereafter? It appears most clearly in *Magnalia Christi Americana,* the work of that soul most tortured by the problem, Cotton Mather: "I write the Wonders of the Christian Religion, flying from the Depravations of Europe, to the American Strand." Thus he proudly begins, and at once trips over the acknowledgment that the founders had not simply fled from depraved Europe but had intended to redeem it. And so the book is full of lamentations over the declension of the children, who appear, page after page, in contrast to their mighty progenitors, about as profligate a lot as ever squandered a great inheritance.

And yet, the *Magnalia* is not an abject book; neither are the election sermons abject, nor is the inventory of sins offered by the synod of 1679. There is bewilderment, confusion, chagrin, but there is no surrender. A task has been assigned upon which the populace are in fact intensely engaged. But they are not sure any more for just whom they are working; they know they are moving, but they do not know where they are going. They seem still to be on an errand, but if they are no longer inferiors sent by the superior forces of the Reformation, to whom they should report, then their errand must be wholly of the second sort, something with a purpose and an intention sufficient unto itself. If so, what is it? If it be not the due form of government, civil and ecclesiastical, that they brought into being, how otherwise can it be described?

The literature of self-condemnation must be read for meanings far below the surface, for meanings of which, we may be so rash as to surmise, the authors were not fully conscious, but by which they were troubled and goaded. They looked in vain to history for an explanation of themselves; more and more it appeared that the meaning was not to be found in theology, even with the help of the covenantal dialectic. Thereupon, these citizens found that they had no other place to search but within themselves — even though, at first sight, that repository appeared to be nothing but a sink of iniquity. Their errand having failed in the first sense of the term, they were left with the second, and required to fill it with meaning by themselves and out of themselves. Having failed to rivet the eyes of the world upon their city on the hill, they were left alone with America.

CHAPTER II

THOMAS HOOKER AND THE DEMOCRACY
OF CONNECTICUT

[Seminars in the Department of History at Harvard University cherish a reputation for giving graduate students a strenuous introduction to the profession. This investigation came out of the colonial seminar of Samuel Eliot Morison, and was published in *The New England Quarterly* (1931, 4:663–712). I had not then completed *Orthodoxy in Massachusetts* and so, like any overzealous youth, tried to tell all I knew. One of the many excitements of Professor Morison's seminars was their imparting, along with the strictest discipline, the spirit of adventure.

When I wrote, Massachusetts had barely survived its tercentennial celebration, and those who had witnessed the horrors were apprehensive about what Connecticut might perpetrate in 1936. Quite apart, however, from the prospect of more parades and orations, the scholar contemplated the myth that three hundred years ago the Hartford settlement had been a "democratic" secession from "theocratic" Massachusetts. I was not as clear then as I fondly suppose I am now about just how New England carried out its errand into the wilderness, but I was working close to the sources, and so I leave this effort substantially as it first appeared.

By 1931, Vernon L. Parrington and James Truslow Adams had in effect conspired to present Thomas Hooker as a sort of John the Baptist to Thomas Jefferson. Adams, ten year before (in *The Founding of New England*), announced that Hooker led the way which the people of the United States were to follow, but that Winthrop strove to found a state "in a politically impossible form." Parrington, noble soul that he was, hailed Hooker (along with Roger Williams) as a contribution of "Independency" to American life. The state of scholarship was so demoralized that sincere students, of the stature of Parrington and Adams, could solemnly make irresponsible statements about the differences between Lutheranism and Calvinism, let alone about those between Separatists and Nonseparatists, which clearly betrayed that they did not comprehend such matters. I yielded then, as still today, to nobody in my admiration for the mighty Thomas Hooker, but my historical conscience was outraged. The years between have given me no reason for altering my judgment, though many details have been filled in.

Were I to attempt revising this text, I would most call in question the assumption that Separatist and Nonseparatist Congregationalism should appear so closely intertwined as I here imply. Various researches now under way will, I wager, give us more precise information about the hectic developments in English Puritanism during the early years of Elizabeth's reign. Meanwhile, I suspect that we must more strongly insist that the line of Jacob, Bradshaw, Baynes, and Ames is something quite apart from the dynasty of the Separatists — of Browne, Ainsworth, and Robinson. Unless the highly developed state of the theory, long before the migration, is understood, then the springs of both Winthrop's and Hooker's action remain mysterious.

Also, I am now fully persuaded that the purely personal rivalry between Hooker and Cotton was much more of a factor in this removal than I had naïvely supposed.

This piece has excited a curiously sullen reaction. To speak as frankly as these notices permit, I may say that my critics have many times not condescended to review the facts, but have doggedly insisted that Connecticut *was* different from — and therefore more "free" than — Massachusetts. Without offering evidence, and indeed without displaying any comprehension of Congregational philosophy (without which Hooker is indeed incomprehensible), they blandly assert that the truth lies somewhere in the "middle," between Parrington and me. On this matter there is no middle. Parrington simply did not know what he was talking about.

Obviously, after a century or more of living in the landscape, the population of the Connecticut Valley — meaning not only the colony of Connecticut but also the Massachusetts towns along the river — ultimately worked out a social pattern — a wilderness pattern, if you will — vastly different from that of "civilized" Boston and Salem. Out of it came Stoddard, Edward Taylor, Jonathan Edwards, and — as Thomas H. Johnson has beautifully demonstrated — Emily Dickinson. Whether this system was more "democratic" than the eastern way of life may be doubted, at least in view of the ecclesiastical dictatorship of Solomon Stoddard, the behavior of the "River Gods," or the domineering manners of Squire Dickinson. However, there can be no doubt, the Valley ran its errand in its own way. In terms of distance as then measured by communication, the Valley in 1740 was more remote from the seacoast than Omaha is today from New York. The drama of Jonathan Edwards acquires meaning only when seen against the backdrop of this "western" area. Nevertheless, comprehension of how this evolution came about will never be coherent unless the origins of the migration to Hartford are properly understood.

Even so — and assuming that I am correct in my reading of the sources — we must also realize, as this account did not sufficiently realize, that the removal of Hooker and his band was an early stage in that search for a greater "fruitfulness" than the Lord appeared to have granted the pioneers of Boston. In that sense, this secession of a company of dedicated saints, within six years of the Great (and theoretically the final) Migration, indeed commenced the unfolding of the still-hidden meaning of Europe's errand into the wilderness; in that sense, it is true that Winthrop was trying prematurely to stabilize a conception of which the essence was instability. It was Hooker, I should have pointed out, who issued the most scholastic, the most learnedly abstract, of all New England's treatises on the divinely instituted ecclesiastical discipline, with an apology (how sincere is anybody's guess) that it appeared in a homely dress and coarse habit because "it comes out of the wilderness."]

THOMAS HOOKER arrived in Massachusetts only in 1633, when the three-year-old colony had already established its church discipline. Like other leaders in the bay, he was a Puritan who had been, as he thought, persecuted by the Established Church. But his coming to America was not simply a flight from affliction; in New England had been erected the ecclesiastical order of which he had long been an advocate, for which he had already suffered humiliation and exile.

The Congregational idea had first been preached by men who reasoned that since churches were commanded of God to consist only of the elect, they should therefore be separated from the corrupt mixture of the Established Church and constituted after the authorized Biblical model. These Separatists had not intended to impugn the universal Christian belief that every nation should permit only one orthodox church within its limits. Robert Browne was no tolerationist except for his own views, and a good part of the misery of his followers was their inability to make that point clear to their persecutors. Although Separatists were never themselves numerically effective, they preached a polity which carried a human appeal, and the scriptural proofs they offered impressed intellectuals. Shortly after the accession of James I, there developed among the Puritan ranks a clearly defined party which we might call Nonseparating Congregationalist. These men, while advancing the usual Puritan plea against separating from the church, and while admitting the church to be a "true church" even though it needed reforming, were converted to ideas of polity substantially similar to those of the Separatists. That is, they too were advocating a Congregational rather than a Presbyterian reform. Ames, Parker, Bradshaw, and Baynes were the leaders; Henry Jacob even founded a church of such a character in London in 1616, which endured through various vicissitudes until it migrated to Massachusetts in 1634. And to this party before they came to America also belonged most of the New England divines, Hugh Peter, Cotton, Davenport, and Thomas Hooker.[1]

[1] For a fuller account of the interconnections of this group, see my *Orthodoxy in Massachusetts* and Raymond P. Stearns, *Congregationalism in the Dutch Netherlands* (Chicago, 1940).

Hooker was a man of mark long before he left England. According to Samuel Collins, vicar of Braintree and agent of Laud, it was high time in 1629 that something be done about him:

I have lived in Essex to see many changes, and have seene the people idolizing many new ministers and lecturers; but this man surpasses them all for learning, and some other considerable parts, and . . . gains more and far greater followers than all before him.

When the authorities threatened him, his case created more "noise" in Essex than "the great question of tonnage and poundage," according to Collins (June 3, 1629), who was sure (May 20, 1629) that even if he were silenced, his "genius" would still "haunt all the pulpits" in the country, where any of his scholars might be admitted to preach.[2] Such a man had little reason to expect mercy from the High Commission, and Hooker chose the better part of valor when he forfeited his bond and fled to Holland. In Amsterdam he found John Paget in charge of a congregation of exiled Puritans, forming a church of the Presbyterian type, incorporated into the Dutch classis. Hooker applied to it for admission, but his Congregational leanings were already too conspicuous. The Dutch presbyters refused him,[3] and Paget continued to harass him when later he succeeded Hugh Peter as assistant in the English church of Forbes at Delft.

One of the distinguishing marks of Puritans of Hooker's stripe was their encouragement of a certain amount of intercourse with the Separatists, even while disclaiming Separation themselves. In 1633, Paget demanded that Hooker account for this, and Hooker revealed his full comprehension of the Congregational idea when he replied that though Separation was a sin, Separatist conventicles might lawfully be visited, or a former Separatist might be received into the church without being required to renounce his Separation,

vnless we will say that such a man (being in his iudgment and life otherwise altogether vnblameable) in Iudicious Charitie is not a visible Christian, which is a more rigid Censure then the wisest of the separation would giue waie vnto.[4]

On the strength of these statements Paget opposed Hooker, just as he opposed "Mr. Davenport, of later times; and also Mr. Parker, Dr. Ames, Mr. Forbes, Mr. Peters, etc."[5] All these men, he charged, professed to abhor schism, but indicated by their actions they did not "abhor" schismatics:

[2] *Calendar of State Papers: Domestic, 1628–1629*, CXLII, 554, no. 113; and CXLIV, 567, no. 36; quoted in John Waddington, *Congregational History* (London, 1869), II, 292.

[3] *Calendar of State Papers: Domestic, 1633–1634*, CCXXXVII, no. 48; Benjamin Hanbury, *Historical Memorials Relating to the Independents and Congregationalists* (London), 1839–1844), I, 532.

[4] Champlin Burrage, *Early English Dissenters* (London, 1912), II, 276.

[5] Hanbury, *Independents and Congregationalists*, II, 531.

Not Mr. Hooker; while he maintained that such of the Brownists as persisted in the Schism or Separation from the Church of England might lawfully be received of us for Members of our Church: while he would not disallow such of our church as went to hear the Brownists in their schismatical Assembly; while he maintained that Private men might preach and expound the Scriptures at set times and places where members of sundry families met together, and this without allowance of the church: while he maintained that churches combined together in the Classis, might choose a Minister either without or against the consent of the Classis under which they stood.[6]

Hooker, nevertheless, remained unshaken by such criticism. He was confident that he and his followers had attested their antipathy to Separation "by our Constant renouncing of their Course of the one side, and by our free and open profession of our intents, on the other side." [7] He blandly insisted that a particular congregation could give a complete call to a minister, "without any derived power from a Classis," and even "without, or against the approbation of the Classis, if they saw good reason." [8]

From Delft, Hooker moved to Rotterdam, where he was associated with Peter and with Ames, and where he wrote the preface for Ames's *Fresh Suit Against Human Ceremonies*. Meantime some of his English hearers had gone to New England, known there already as "Mr. Hooker's company." They invited Samuel Stone to be Hooker's associate; the two met in England and crossed on the same ship with Cotton. During the voyage Cotton's son was born, and all three ministers signified their thoroughgoing Congregationalism when they refrained from baptizing him, "1, because they had no settled congregation there; 2, because a minister hath no power to give seals but in his own congregation." [9]

In view of later developments, there are some significant aspects in this Congregationalism to which Hooker had so earnestly devoted himself. Those who maintained it were able to document every feature of the system with what seemed to them an appropriate Biblical text. "They hold and maintain, that the word of God . . . is of absolute perfection, given by Christ the head of the Church, to bee unto the same, the sole Canon and rule of matters of Religion"; therefore, "all Ecclesiastical actions invented and devised by man, are utterly to be excluded out of, the exercise of Religion." [10] And as their precarious position in the twilight zone between Nonconformity and Separatism required constant defense, they searched the Scripture with a vengeance. Their basic assumption was that for every single act of church government a specific chapter and verse must be cited:

[6] Hanbury, *Independents and Congregationalists*, II, 540–41.
[7] Burrage, *Dissenters*, II, 275.
[8] John Davenport, *An Apologeticall Reply* (Rotterdam, 1636), 248.
[9] J. K. Hosmer, ed., *Winthrop's Journal* (New York, 1908), 107.
[10] William Bradshaw, *English Puritanisme* (London, 1640), 3. The first edition appeared in 1605.

There are many indifferent Civill Matters. But of the parts of Divine Service and Church vse, ther is nothing at all Indifferent. All such things are heere simply commanded or forbidden.[11]

No church officer, therefore, could ever presume to act merely at his own discretion, for he was bound at all times by certain fundamental constitutions, and was always answerable for the authorization of his deed:

Ecclesiasticall officers laying to the charge of any man any errour . . . do stand bound themselves, first to prove that hee holdeth such an errour or Herisie, and secondly to prove directly unto him that it is an errour by the word of God, and that it deserveth such a Censure, before they do proceed against him.[12]

Whatever his political philosophy may then have been, Hooker no doubt was already familiar with the notions of a fundamental law and of the limitation of governors by a basic constitution.

The cornerstone of a Congregational church was a covenant. The scattered elect could not otherwise be gathered together and organized as a society; only thus, in fact, could any institution come into being,

by a free mutuall consent of Believers Joyning and covenanting to live as Members of a holy Society togeather in all religious and vertuous duties as Christ and his Apostles did institute and practise in the Gospell. By such a free mutuall consent also all Civill perfect corporations did first beginne.[13]

One result of such a conception was to strengthen what might be called the legalistic character of the government; not only was the officer subject to the fundamental scriptural rules, but also to the corporate will of the organization which selected him. The people had gathered and covenanted to devote themselves to Christ, and in the final analysis it was always the people who were to decide whether any act was in harmony with the avowed purposes of the covenant. Church officers can not make laws, but are to apply "the rules of order and comeliness taken from the Scripture and common sense"; but "neither the church, nor the meanest member thereof is further bound unto these determinations, than they appear to agree with order, and comeliness." Ministers are not in anything "to be obeyed for the authority of the commander, but for the reason of the commandment, which the ministers are also bound in duty to manifest, and approve unto the consciences of them over whom they are set." [14] There-

---

[11] Henry Jacob, in Burrage, *Dissenters*, II, 159.

[12] Bradshaw, *English Puritanisme*, 25.

[13] Jacob, in Burrage, *Dissenters*, II, 157.

[14] Robert Ashton, ed., *John Robinson's Works* (Boston, 1851), III, 61. Although Robinson was a Separatist, he was in contact with the members of the Nonseparating school of Congregationalism, was strongly influenced by them, and agreed with them on the main principles of discipline; his more profound philosophical grasp of the system justifies his being quoted as illustrating the character of Congregationalism before it was transported to New England.

fore, if the congregation approved not of the minister's conduct, it could "reject and reprobate" him, for "they that set up may pull down." [15]

Of course, this philosophy involved a progress in the direction of what today we call democracy. This implication was not overlooked by its foes: Congregationalists, whether Separatists or Nonseparatists, exerted themselves to ward off the insidious aspersion of a leveling tendency. The people, they had to admit, were the source of an officer's commission, but the process of government was decidedly not democratic:

> Wise men, having written of this subject, have approved as good and lawful, three kinds of polities, — monarchical, where supreme authority is in the hands of one; aristocratical, when it is in the hands of some few select persons; and democratical, in the whole body or multitude. And all these three forms have their places in the Church of Christ. In respect of Him, the Head, it is a monarchy; in respect of the eldership, an aristocracy; in respect of the body, a popular state.[16]

However, radical though the Separatists were in ecclesiastical polity, they were not unconventional in their social thinking. "So then for *popular government*," declared Henry Ainsworth, "we hold it not, we approue it not, for if the multitude gouern, then who shalbe gouerned?" [17] Congregationalism by no means gave carte blanche to the fraternity to rule as they wished; they were bound by the absolute and arbitrary laws of Christ the head, and in daily practice were supervised by the elders, the students and interpreters of the law. Robinson's exposition of the officers' function makes it fully evident that the fundamental democratic theory might be extensively counteracted in practice by the tutelary guidance of the elders:

> Now lest any should take occasion to conceive, that we either exercise amongst ourselves, or would thrust upon others, any popular, or democratical church government; may it please the Christian reader to make estimate of both our judgment and practise. . . . First, we believe, that the external church government under Christ . . . is plainly aristocratical, and to be administered by some choice men, although the state, which many unskilfully confound with the government, be after a sort popular and democratical. By this it appertains to the people freely to vote in elections and judgments of the church; in respect of the other, we make account it behooves the elders to govern the people, even in their voting, in just liberty, given by Christ whatsoever. Let the elders publicly propound, and order all things in the church . . . let the people of faith give their assent to their elders' holy and lawful administration.[18]

Nonseparating theorists were, as far as what we may call the purely political aspects of the program are concerned, even more conservative. According to Jacob, the church, once it was organized, was "to be informed, directed, and guided by the Pastor chiefly, and also by the grave

[15] Robinson, *Works*, II, 225.

[16] Robinson, *Works*, II, 140.

[17] Henry Ainsworth, *Counterpoyson* (London, 1642), 103. The first edition was published in 1608.

[18] Robinson, *Works*, III, 42–43.

assistant Elders"; [19] he intended that the members should be the source of elections and censures, but in their ordinary carriage were to avoid acting upon their own initiative, striving rather "freely to consent to their Guides preparing and directing every matter." [20] If the congregations followed such teaching literally, there would certainly not be much room in which a "democracy" could operate!

Finally, Congregationalism assured the maintenance of orthodoxy by a double safeguard: the consociation of churches and the supervision of the magistracy. True, the preachers opposed coercive synods of the Presbyterian variety, authorizing only persuasive or consultative gatherings, but these synods were expected to pronounce an erring church heretical and refuse it "the right hand of fellowship." Thereupon, it became the duty of a Christian magistrate to reduce the heretic to order, or to punish his transgression.

Thus it can be seen that Congregationalism, as it was brought to America by Hooker and Cotton, was a complex affair to which hardly any of the political adjectives in current use can clearly and simply apply. There certainly were in it democratic stirrings; there were undoubtedly in it provisions that could effectively stifle those impulses. It was largely a question of where the emphasis was to be put; if upon the eldership, the result would be an aristocracy, an oligarchy, a theocracy; if upon the congregation, the result would be more democratic. But there were various degrees between, and to theorists of the time the two elements were not irreconcilable.

So then, Hooker reached Massachusetts in the fall of 1633, and in the approved Congregational fashion the expectant parishioners of Newtown chose and ordained him pastor. He had been settled there hardly more than a half year before his people grew restive; they complained they did not have enough land and petitioned the General Court for permission to remove. Liberty was readily granted them to find a new site somewhere within the patent, but even so large an opportunity did not satisfy. In June 1634, six of the town went in the *Blessing* "to discover Connecticut River," [21] and in September the citizens asked the Court for leave to settle there. They told of the scarcity of their land, Hooker alleging "as a fundamental error, that towns were set so near to each other"; they instanced the fruitfulness of Connecticut and the danger of having it possessed by others; and finally they declared "the strong bent of their spirits to remove thither." To these arguments, Winthrop tells us "it was said" that such a removal outside the patent would be a breach of covenant, they "being knit to us in one body and bound by oath to seek the welfare of this commonwealth," that furthermore it was politically unwise, for it would

[19] Henry Jacob, *The Devine Beginning and Institution of Christs true Visible or Ministeriall Church* (Leyden, 1610), A3 verso.

[20] Burrage, *Dissenters*, II, 160.

[21] Winthrop, *Journal*, I, 128.

weaken the state — "the departure of Mr. Hooker would not only draw
many from us, but also divert other friends that would come to us" — and
would expose the settlers to the Dutch and Indians. Again, Newtown was
offered a place within the patent, or else an enlargement of its bounds.
When the matter came to a vote, the deputies and the assistants found
themselves divided, the majority of the magistrates opposing the motion.
They thereupon claimed the power of an upper legislative house to a negative vote, and with the aid of a sermon by Cotton carried their point. Newtown was assigned thirty acres out of Watertown and a sizable area on the
banks of Muddy River.[22] But during the winter the crowded feeling became contagious. The next May, in 1635, Watertown and Roxbury, com-
plaining that all towns were "much straitened by their own nearness to one
another," were allowed to remove "whither they pleased, so as they continued under this government," [23] and in the summer men of Watertown
and Dorchester, apparently without formal permission, found their way
into Connecticut and settled there, the Dorchester group trespassing upon
the territory of a Plymouth trading post.[24] Other parties followed during
the year, one of them from Newtown,[25] whose citizens were apparently
resolved, for in October they sold their houses to the recently arrived congregation of Thomas Shepard.[26] In May 1636, Winthrop noted briefly,
"Mr. Hooker, pastor of the Church at Newtown, and the most of his
congregation went to Connecticut." [27]

Such, in bare outline, are the facts of the removal of the settlers from
Massachusetts to the towns upon the river. About this story has gathered a
haze of mystery and conjecture, and the attempt to dispel it has exercised
the ingenuity and sometimes the prejudices of historians. Was it, after all,
merely a matter of more land? Why could not some place be found within
the patent commodious enough to suit the disgruntled townsmen? Or was
there some other motive, some deeper dissatisfaction, that inspired the strong
bent of the spirits of Hooker's congregation to remove beyond the reach of
the Massachusetts government? Can we find in the history of the colonies
or in their respective policies any hints of a genuine cleavage?

As Johnson told the story in 1651, he seemed aware only of the economic motives and spoke contemptuously of those whose lack of faith allowed considerations of that sort to influence them.[28] In 1635 a citizen of

[22] Winthrop, *Journal*, I, 132–34; *Records of Massachusetts* (Boston, 1853), I,
129–30.
[23] Winthrop, *Journal*, I, 151.
[24] Winthrop, *Journal*, I, 157, 175; William T. Davis, ed., *Bradford's History of
Plymouth Plantation* (New York, 1908), 323–27.
[25] William DeLoss Love, *The Colonial History of Hartford* (Hartford, 1914), 5.
[26] Alexander Young, *Chronicles of . . . the Colony of Massachusetts Bay* (Boston,
1846), 545.
[27] Winthrop, *Journal*, I, 180.
[28] Edward Johnson, *Wonder-Working Providence*, ed. W. F. Poole (Andover,
1867), 75.

Newtown, one John Pratt, was disciplined by the Court for having written a letter of complaint into England, and his apology, countersigned by Hooker, indicates that his objections concerned only the paucity and poverty of the soil.[29] But the historian William Hubbard, writing about 1680, and possibly in the possession of some authentic tradition, several times implies a rivalry and even an enmity between Hooker and Cotton, and between Hooker's wealthy and ambitious friend, John Haynes, and the great John Winthrop.

What evidence is there of any such untoward state of affairs in the Puritan Canaan? We know that Hooker's congregation had approached Cotton and asked him to fill the position that later devolved upon Stone, and that Cotton had declined. It is possible that Hooker, much the more celebrated figure in Europe, found it galling that honors should be heaped upon Cotton and that the former rector of St. Botolph's should so soon become the mouthpiece of the ruling powers. It may be significant that when the two branches of the Court were divided in 1634, Cotton preached the sermon which brought the deputies into line, after Hooker's "instant excuse of his unfitness for that occasion." We may also reflect there could hardly be so much smoke without some fire when we find Winthrop hastening to assure Sir Simonds D'Ewes in 1635 that though Hooker was like to go to Connecticut next year, it was,

not for any difference between Mr. Cotton and him (soe reporte) for they doe hould a most sweet and brotherly communion together (thoughe their judgments doe somewhat differ about the lawfullnesse of the Crosse in the ensigne) but that the people and cattle are so increased as the place will not suffice them.[30]

The whole question is beclouded because Hooker evidently became implicated in other men's quarrels, though just what part he took can not be determined. Shortly after his arrival, he found himself siding with Dudley — who then lived at Newtown — against Winthrop. Newtown had a grievance in the matter of public defenses. We should note that Dudley's letter, "full of bitterness," was carried to Winthrop by Haynes and Hooker, and that when Winthrop tried to placate Dudley with the gift of a hog, "he made Mr. Haynes and Mr. Hooker (who both sojourned in his house) partakers with him." [31] This looks more like a sectional than a political difference, but Dudley, serving as governor in 1634, supported the Newtown proposal to emigrate although he did not intend to go himself. Haynes was still on the side of Dudley in March 1636, when a conference of ministers was called to judge between the two men, and Haynes agreed with Dudley that Winthrop's rule had been too lenient.

That some personal animus lay behind the situation may also be indicated from the early relations between Massachusetts Bay and Connecticut. These

[29] *Records of Massachusetts*, I, 358–60; Winthrop, *Journal*, I, 165.

[30] *Publications*, Colonial Society of Mass., VII, 73.

[31] Winthrop, *Journal*, I, 113–14.

were embittered by a dispute about their respective jurisdictions over Springfield, but even before that argument broke out, Connecticut showed a marked disinclination to give the Bay authorities any voice in her affairs: "the ground of all was their shyness of coming under our government, which, though we never intended to make them subordinate to us, yet they were very jealous." [32] About the same time Hooker referred in a public sermon to what he deemed very unneighborly doings in the bay:

If anything could have hindered, either by truth or falsehood, to keep men from coming to these parts hitherto, it had been done; but yet, notwithstanding, men's minds informed, their consciences convicted, their hearts persuaded to come and to plant.[33]

He returned directly to this charge in his famous letter to Winthrop in 1638, and insinuated that the Governor himself was responsible:

I suppose you are not a stranger only in Israel, nor yet usually ignorant of these things, being they are not done in a corner, but in the open streets, and not by some frantic, forlorn creatures, or madmen, who know not nor care what they say; but, before the ships can come to anchor, whole boats are presently posted out to salute persons, ordinarily, with such relations.[34]

Winthrop replied, belittling the slanders; "if you could shewe us the men that reproached you, we should teache them better manners." But he excused whatever of them existed as being repayment in kind for Connecticut's attempt "to drawe Mr. Shepard and his wholl church from us. *Sic fama est.*" [35] In 1670 Roger Williams told Mason that about this time,

that heavenly man, Mr. Haynes, Governor of Connecticut, though he pronounced the sentence of my long banishment against me, . . . yet said unto me, in his own house at Hartford, being then in some difference with the Bay: "I think, Mr. Williams, I must now confess to you, that the most wise God hath provided and cut out this part of his world for a refuge and receptacle for all sorts of consciences. I am now under a cloud, and my brother Hooker, with the Bay, as you have been; we have removed from them thus far, and yet they are not satisfied." [36]

These evidences are fragmentary and tantalizing, but they do give color to the imputation that the Connecticut groups found themselves at odds with the vested interests in Massachusetts. In themselves they do not warrant the assertion that Hooker, because he was a liberal and a democrat, was therefore hostile to Winthrop. Some difference over fundamental principle may have lurked in the background, but the personal element, or the element of local jealousies, was not absent. However, whatever the character of the rift, a few years seemed to restore the leaders to amity. Fear of the

[32] Winthrop, *Journal*, I, 287.
[33] G. L. Walker, *Thomas Hooker* (New York, 1891), 102.
[34] *Collections*, Connecticut Historical Society, I, 5.
[35] Robert C. Winthrop, *Life and Letters of John Winthrop* (Boston, 1869), II, 421.
[36] *Publications*, Narragansett Club, VI, 344.

Dutch at length produced in Connecticut a greater inclination to meet Massachusetts halfway, and Hooker's letter to Winthrop in 1643 sounds the unmistakable note of reconciliation:

My heart would not suffer me but as vnfeynedly to acknowledge the Lords goodness, so affectionately to remember your candid and cordiall cariage in a matter of so great consequence. . . . To be the repayrer of the breach, was of old counted matter of highest prayse and acceptance with God, and man. . . . My ayme is nakedly this; to be in the number, and have my voyce with those, that whyle your self and your faythfull Assistants . . . be laying the first stone of the foundation of this combynation of peace, I may crye grace, grace to your indeavors.[37]

On the other side, Winthrop's comment upon Hooker's death seems to have forgotten whatever differences had ever been between them:

who, for piety, prudence, wisdom, zeal, learning, and what else might make him serviceable in the place and time he lived in, might be compared with men of greatest note; and he shall need no other praise: the fruits of his labors in both Englands shall preserve an honorable and happy remembrance of him forever.[38]

And John Cotton contributed to the foreword of the *Survey* a lucubration which has at least the virtue of an apparent sincerity:

> To see three things was holy Austins wish:
> Rome in her Flower, Christ Jesus in the Flesh,
> And Paul i'th Pulpit; Lately men might see
> Two first, and more, in Hookers Ministry.

In the usual account of the migration, the episode of the magistrates' blocking the removal in 1634 figures prominently, the implication being that the Connecticut settlers objected to the negative voice. Hooker's refusal to preach the sermon and Cotton's unhesitating support of the magistracy seem to most writers proof that Hooker tacitly disapproved. Stoughton's remark, that he knew no one that had read the patent who believed in the veto "excepting Magistrates," and his alleging he wrote against it chiefly at the instigation of the Reverend Mr. Warham,[39] who soon after settled at Windsor, may reveal a popular sentiment in which Hooker and his congregation shared. The *Fundamental Orders* provided that if the governor or magistrates refused to call a court, the freemen had the right to summon one, choose a moderator, and perform any act which any other General Court might do; in the normal course of voting the *Orders* merely required questions to be put to the house, and the governor was to vote only in case of tie. These seem to be provisions against the evolution of an upper house, but if Connecticut started out with such a unicameral intention, by 1644 the colony had changed its mind, for it then ordered that

[37] 4 *Collections*, Mass. Hist. Soc., VI, 389–90.
[38] Winthrop, *Journal*, I, 326.
[39] *Proceedings*, Mass. Hist. Soc., LVIII, 451, 456.

no act shall passe or stand for a law, which is not confirmed both by the major part of the said Magistrats, and by the major parte of the deputyes there present in Court, both Magistrats and deputyes being alowed, eyther of them, a negatiue voate.[40]

Certainly we can not list this feature as proof of a greater degree of democratic sentiment among Hooker's followers, and it is not improbable that the first gestures were dictated by a grudge against the specific conduct of the Massachusetts magistrates. In this connection it may be noticed that Winthrop's conflict with the town of Hingham in 1646 centered about the magistrates' power to confirm the local election of militia officers. Shortly after that affair a Connecticut statute ordered

that the souldears shall only make choyse of their millitary officers and present them to the particuler Court, but such only shalbe deemed Officers as the Court shall confirme.[41]

Evidently this was designed to forestall a similar dispute in Connecticut, and it would seem to indicate that by this date the river magistrates had come to fill a position hardly different from that of the assistants in the bay.

Parrington surmised that Hooker's great exposition of the Congregational polity, *A Survey of the Summe of Church Discipline*, was democratic, and could be contrasted with Cotton's numerous treatises. It is probably true that Hooker was less concerned with the technicalities of polity; his surviving works bespeak a preoccupation with what might be termed the evangelical element. Cotton Mather confirms this view: "the very spirit of his ministry lay in the points of the most practical religion, and the grand concerns of a sinner's preparation for, implantation in, and salvation by, the glorious Lord Jesus Christ." [42] Cotton Mather further tells us that Hooker was eager to keep public censures in his church as few as possible, so that in his ministry but one person was admonished and one excommunicated, and that he criticized exorbitant use of censure in other congregations.[43] He revealed a decided aversion to strife, a disposition to listen to the other side, in his preface to the *Survey*:

He that will estrange his affection, because of the difference of apprehension in things difficult he must be a stranger to himself one time or other. If men would be tender and careful to keep off offensive expressions, they might keep some distance in opinion, in some things, without hazard to truth or love.[44]

However, we must distinguish between a trait of character and a doctrine. If Hooker inclined to peace and mutual forbearance in things difficult,

[40] J. Hammond Trumbull, ed., *The Public Records of the Colony of Connecticut* (Hartford, 1850), I, 119.

[41] Trumbull, *The Public Records of the Colony of Connecticut*, I, 151.

[42] *Magnalia Christi Americana* (Hartford, 1853), I, 346.

[43] *Magnalia*, I, 349.

[44] *Survey* (London, 1648), A4 recto.

it does not follow that he broke with the philosophy of his more short-tempered brethren in many things obvious. On the contrary, if we compare him with Roger Williams, it is quite clear that his basic principles synchronize with those of the orthodoxy. He coöperated with it in all the major crises: he was appointed to dispute with Williams in the attempt to bring the latter to reason; he was associated with Bulkley as moderator of the synod which condemned Anne Hutchinson, and he not only registered no dissent from the judgment of that assembly, but urged the good work forward. When the trouble first broke out, he wrote to Winthrop that he rejoiced from the bottom of his heart that the Lord

hath gratiously kept you from any taynt of these new-coyned conceits. The Lord strengthen and establish you in every holy word and work. In a good cause He hath given you gratious abilityes to do Him much service, and I am perswaded He will blesse you in such indeavors. You know my playnnesse; you can not keepe your comfort, nor an honorable respect in Christ in the hearts of His, more then in keeping closse to the truth. You shall have what interest I have in heaven to help you in that work.[45]

Later he asserted that for Mistress Anne "to be cast out as unsavory salt" would be "for ever marvellous in the eyes of all the saints." [46] Hooker was joint moderator with Cotton at the synod of 1643, which condemned Presbyterianism; and although he was unable to attend the synod of 1646, his church sent Stone and Deacon Stebbins and accepted the codification of the Congregational way which that gathering ultimately produced. When, in 1645, New England saw Presbyterianism likely to triumph in England and at the same time perceived a growing sentiment there for that awful heresy, "liberty of conscience," on the part of the sects and even of their fellow Congregationalists, several ministers were commissioned to send over defenses of the New England position. Hooker thus wrote his *Survey*, and his work was dispatched, along with with treatises by Davenport and Cotton, as a manifesto for all New England. It is strange to find Parrington assuming the book expresses views at variance with Massachusetts when Hooker himself took care to state:

In all these I have leave to professe the joint judgement of all the Elders upon the river: of New Haven, Guilford, Milford, Stratford, Fairfield: and of most of the Elders of the Churches in the Bay, to whom I did send in particular, and did receive approbation from them under their hands: of the rest (to whom I could not send) I cannot so affirm; but this I can say, That at a common meeting, I was desired by them all, to publish what now I do.[47]

There is no reason to question this statement. There was but one important respect in which Hooker ever quarreled with the disciplinary philoso-

---

[45] 4 *Collections*, Mass. Hist. Soc., VI, 388.
[46] Thomas Hutchinson, *The History of the Colony of Massachusetts-Bay* (Boston, 1764), I, 71.
[47] *Survey*, B2, recto.

phy of Cotton, Davenport, or Mather, and that difference can easily be overemphasized. However much Congregational theorists had attempted to counteract the polity's democratic tendencies, they had seen no logical way to take the ultimate control of excommunication from the hands of the brotherhood. The whole membership of a corporate society must, in the final analysis, both admit newcomers and expel undesirables. Although early thinkers had declared that the congregation should be guided in these matters by the elders, they had not had the effrontery to deny the power of the congregation to excommunicate not only individual ministers, but, if necessary, the whole eldership, pastor, teacher, and lay elder. The Massachusetts clergy, however, perceived in this reservation a lurking threat to their control, and Cotton finally decided, in his *Keyes of the Kingdome of Heaven*, that though a transgressing elder could be excommunicated, still all the elders of a church could not be expelled at once, because the concurrence of at least one of them was necessary to give a sentence validity. Hooker was more thoroughly imbued with the pristine theory, and to him Cotton's emendation seemed a gratuitous violation of the covenant idea. Persons who have not understood the workings of New England Congregationalism have seen in this difference a greater issue than actually existed. Daniel Cawdrey, an English Presbyterian, declared in 1651 that Hooker's position made the "power of officers a meer complement or cypher," and he remarked to Cotton, "It is strange that all this while you should agree no better." [48]

The truth of the matter is that Cawdrey, like most observers removed in space or time from early New England, did not quite appreciate the delicate position which the elders had come to occupy in the New England "Way," a position which Hooker warns us is "to be understood with a grain of salt, and requires a wise and wary explanation." [49] Even if the congregation possessed a theoretical right to excommunicate at once all its officers who were bad, such officers as could not be shown to deserve censure remained anything but "cyphers." For the divines had made a nice distinction between election to office and the power of office itself. They still admitted that an elder owed the assumption of his ministry to the congregation's summons, but they had called attention to the fact that the office was not the creation of the people. Instead, it was the immediate institution of Christ; its powers derived directly from Him and not from the people. These simply designated upon *whom* the office should be bestowed, not *what* the powers of the office should be. As Thomas Shepard put it, though a minister's outward call came through the church, it was none the less a call "from Christ," and election by the church no more made him "the servant of the church than a Captain (by leave of the Generall) chosen by

---

[48] *The Inconsistencie of the Independent way, With Scripture, and It Self* (London, 1651), 160, 23.

[49] *Survey*, part I, 187.

a Band of Souldiers is the servant of his Band." [50] With this philosophy Hooker was in perfect accord. The voluntary subjection of the people, he held, invested the ministers "with rule and right to govern," but the congregation did not prescribe how the right should be exercised. Christ alone, "out of his supreme and regal power, . . . appoints the work, laies out the compasse thereof, the manner of dispensing, and the order and bounds of their dispensation." The church controlled the gateway to the office, not the office, and its submission merely permitted persons "to put forth their abilities and Ministerial authority over such a people." Thus congregations could ordain pastors, although the powers of a pastor never passed through their hands; they might "give a call and power to such and such to be Pastors, and yet themselves not Pastors." [51]

Since the elected elders ruled by a sort of divine right, since a definite and immutable power was given them, so to speak, over the heads of their flocks, the only grounds upon which they could be impeached would be for going clearly "beyond their place and power." [52] A congregation which undertook to excommunicate an elder had to prove to the satisfaction of the authorities that he had obviously abused his "place," and if it expelled him, it had no choice but to elect another elder and submit once more to the authority instituted by Christ. There would, therefore, be no vital distinction if the congregation expelled three erring elders simultaneously instead of one at a time. Cotton himself made just that point when he said that his difference with Hooker lay "rather in Difference of *Logicall Notion,* than in *Doctrine of Divinity,* or Church Practice." [53] Cotton had introduced a qualification into the system which had no real excuse for being; the more logical Hooker objected to distorting the original theory, but his aim was simply historical consistency. He did not advocate the traditional view because he thought Cotton's innovation autocratical or because he wanted to keep the churches safe for democracy.

In only one other respect does there seem to exist a distinction between Hooker and the polity of the Bay. Early Congregationalism, by restricting church membership to the proved elect, had had the courage of its predestinarian convictions; it had embodied the exalted ideal of identifying the visible and the invisible church. But when the discipline no longer served as a protest against the formalism of an established church, when it became a vested interest, the emphasis upon this high spirituality was visibly lessened. As Cotton Mather confessed, the "prodigious and astonishing scandal given by the extraordinary miscarriages of some that have made a more than ordinary profession of religion" [54] gave rise to the suspicion that something

[50] Thomas Shepard and John Allin, *A Defence of the Answer Made unto the Nine Questions* (London, 1648), 130.

[51] *Survey,* part I, 191.

[52] *Survey,* part II, 74.

[53] *A Defence of Mr. John Cotton From the imputation of Selfe Contradiction* (Oxford, 1658), 40.

[54] *Magnalia,* II, 493.

might be lacking in even the best technique for examining candidates. If there were those being admitted who turned out to be hypocrites, there were probably others who were actually elected but were unable to give satisfactory evidence. Furthermore, many baptized children of members were coming of age without experiencing the emotional conversion which the polity had originally held was prerequisite to full membership. But the Massachusetts divines were now intent upon perfecting an established order. They deplored these dislocations but shrugged their shoulders. Many of the "hypocrites" were substantial citizens whose support the clergy appreciated, and naturally the churches wanted to keep the children and grandchildren of the responsible classes within the fold. Hooker, as his sermons attest, was vitally interested in the problem of conversion, and he saw the incongruity of excluding large numbers upon the basis of their spiritual inadequacy when it was quite apparent that many were getting in under the ropes on false pretenses. His first reaction was an impulse to lower the standards for admission, so that even if more hypocrites were accepted, still fewer of the regenerate would be held out. His position was evidently well known, for one R. Stansby wrote to the Reverend John Wilson in 1643, saying there were various rumors afloat in England that

there is great diuision of judgment in matter of religion amongst good ministers and people, which moued Mr. Hoker to remoue. . . . That you are so strict in admission of members to your church, that more then one halfe are out of your church in all your congregations, and that Mr. Hoker before he went away preached against yt (as one reports who heard him).[55]

Hooker confronted the problem directly in the *Survey* and frankly recognized that the imperfect technique of examination was probably excluding from the churches many who were in reality better Christians than some it admitted. There were times when he wished "that such persons (many whereof we hope are godly) might enjoy all such privileges, which might be useful and helpfull to them and theirs," but his protracted meditation had convinced him that it was impossible, "and the main pillar principle which fortifies the judgment against all approaching assaults, is the nature and truth of Church-covenant." So he came regretfully to the same conclusion which Cotton reached more abruptly and callously, that those "who by God are excluded from his Covenant . . . as unfit, they are not fit to have Communion with the Church." [56] Hooker was incited to this protest not by any conscious democratic sympathies, but simply by an exceptionally keen concern with the realities of spiritual life, realities which he knew were being sacrificed to more worldly considerations. Once again we have to recognize that he had perhaps a greater feeling for the inner meaning of the Congregational tradition, but that he, like Cotton, was caught in the

---

[55] 4 *Collections*, Mass. Hist. Soc., VII, 10–11.
[56] *Survey*, part III, 12.

toils of the system. He certainly invoked no larger democratic principles to extricate himself.

Otherwise, Hooker never even suggested differences with the theory of Cotton and of Massachusetts. He reiterated the conventional claim that Congregationalism is derived out of the Word, he denounced Separation as a sin. He shared with Cotton his conceptions of the functions of elders, the role of synods, and the duties of the magistrate — features which the Massachusetts leaders had continued to emphasize to the suppression of the democratic and the exaltation of the aristocratic principle of Congregationalism, the features which provided the basis for the now much censured theocracy. The elders, sole interpreters of the law by which they ruled, acquired an almost irresistible social force, in which Hooker conspicuously shared. Elements of discord, says Hubbard, never discovered themselves in Hartford "during the time of Mr. Hooker's life, and if there had any such thing appeared, his interest and authority would easily have suppressed it." [57] Hooker's defense of all these "theoretical" practices is thorough and conclusive. The elders, he declares, should consult on all business before it is submitted to the church; they should investigate rumors against individuals, discuss their cases in private, and, if necessary, lead the action and pronounce sentence "legally and judicially . . . according to the rules and orders provided for that end." [58] He holds that the decisions of Congregational synods are in all probability "no other then *Gods Commands*," and smack of "a Divine Authority which is now by them discovered, and in His *Name applied* to the particulars under hand." [59] He repudiates any notion of toleration; he is not "yet perswaded that the Chief Magistrate should stand Neuter and tolerate all Religions." [60] Neither does he question that magistrates should call synods and enforce by the sword what doctrine and practices they, in brotherly consultation, decide to be orthodox:

> That a right opinion and worship of God should be openly professed within the territories and jurisdiction of a State, appertains to them, as that which comes within the verge and object of the state and policy to attend. . . . Hence the supream Magistrate hath liberty and power both to inquire and judge of professions and Religions, which is true, and ought to be maintained, [and] which is false, and ought to be rejected.[61]

The civil power "may compell Ecclesiastical persons to do, what they ought in their offices," [62] and a particular church is always

> subject unto, and under the supreme power politicke in the place where it is; so that the Magistrate hath a coactive power to compel the Church to execute the

---

[57] 2 *Collections*, Mass. Hist. Soc., VI, 315.

[58] *Survey*, part II, 15–34.

[59] *Survey*, part IV, 3.

[60] *Survey*, part I, 13.

[61] *Survey*, part III, 75.

[62] *Survey*, part I, 13.

ordinances of Christ, according to the orders and rules of Christ . . . and in case she swerve from her rule, be a strong hand to constraine her to keepe it.[63]

Finally, Hooker asserts that the magistrate must compel universal attendance at meeting, with, of course, the usual provision that only those whom the church approves may become formal members.

There may in practice have been a greater leniency in Connecticut. One gets an impression from the records that the Bible Commonwealth notion was not quite so insistent as in Massachusetts. But the Connecticut records are meager, and to some extent the difference may have resulted from the character of the population. It was a smaller, more intimate and homogeneous group. Furthermore, New England's battles against heresy were fought in the Bay, and the banished heretics did not come to Connecticut. But if the practice was less stringent, the theory was still the same. There were numerous cases adjudged by the Court simply upon the Mosaic code: "vncleane practices," "wanton dallience and selfe pollution," "excess in apparell," "loathsome and beastly demenour," and, of course, fornication, attempted or accomplished. It was not much safer in Connecticut than in Massachusetts to cast aspersions upon the elect:

The Courte adiudgeth Peter Bussaker, for his fillthy and prophane expressions (viz. that hee hoped to meete some of the members of the Church in hell ere long, and hee did not question but hee should) to bee committed to prison, there to bee kept in safe custody till the sermon, and then to stand in the time thereof in the pillory, and after sermon to bee seuerely whipt.[64]

When the state had to deal with moral issues, the elders were consulted — as in the bay:

Mr. Webster and Mr. Phelps are desiered to consult with the Elders of boath Plantations to prepare instructions against the next Court for the punisheing of the sin of lying which begins to be practised by many persons in this Commonwelth.[65]

The capital laws were codified in 1642, and all of them except political treason were authorized by two or more Biblical citations: thus:

If any man after legall conuiction shall haue or worship any other God but the Lord God, he shall be put to death. Deu. 13.6, and 17.2: Ex: 22.20.[66]

Death was the penalty for witchcraft, blasphemy, murder, bestiality, sodomy, adultery, rape, kidnapping, false witness with intent to deprive of life, and attempting "inuasion, insureection or rebellion against the Commonwealth"; in 1650 the list included also children of sixteen or over

---

[63] *Survey*, part II, 80.
[64] *Connecticut Records*, I, 168.
[65] *Connecticut Records*, I, 62.
[66] *Connecticut Records*, I, 77–78.

who curse or smite their parent, and stubborn and rebellious sons.[67] Convictions for scandalous offenses after 1646 deprived one of his vote both in town and commonwealth "vntil the Court shall manifest their satisfaction." [68] These laws sufficiently attest that in Connecticut the idea of a Bible Commonwealth lay at the basis of the body politic. In fact, it was distinctly stated in the preamble to the *Fundamental Orders,* which purposed not only to preserve the civil government, but "to mayntayn and presearue the liberty and purity of the gospell of our Lord Jesus which we now professe, as also the disciplyne of the Churches, which according to the truth of the said gospell is practiced amongst vs." [69] Magistrates were to administer justice according to "the Lawes here established, and for want thereof according to the rule of the word of God." [70] Upon recommendation of the United Colonies, Connecticut accepted without demur in 1644 the proposal that taxation for church maintenance be levied upon all, members or nonmembers,

and if any man refuse to pay a meet proportion, that then he be rated by authority in some iust and equall way; and if after this any man withhould or delay due payment the civill power to be exercised as in other iust debts.[71]

Finally, in the codification of 1650 the religious ideal was again affirmed:

Forasmuch as the open contempt of Gods word, and messengers thereof, is the desolating sinne of Ciuill States and Church, and that the preaching of the Word by those whome God doth send is the chiefe ordinary meanes ordained by God for the converting, edefying and sauing of the soules of the elect . . . and according to the respect or contempt of the same and of those whome God hath set aparte for his owne worke and imployment, the weale or woe of all Christian States is much furthered and promoted,

it was provided that persons should be punished if they spoke contemptuously of the doctrine preached by the ministers, that nonattendance at church should be fined, and that,

forasmuch as the peace and prosperity of Churches and members thereof, as well as Ciuill rights and Libberties are carefully to bee maintained, — It is ordered by this Courte and decreed, that the Ciuill Authority heere established hath power and liberty to see the peace, ordinances and rules of Christe bee obserued in euery Church according to his word.[72]

In Hooker's ecclesiastical theory and Connecticut's practice there does not appear any substantial departure from the basic theory and practice

[67] *Connecticut Records,* I, 515.

[68] *Connecticut Records,* II, 138.

[69] *Connecticut Records,* I, 20.

[70] *Connecticut Records,* I, 21.

[71] *Connecticut Records,* I, 112, *note,* cited from the minutes of a meeting of the Commissioners for the United Colonies at Hartford, September 5, 1644. *Plymouth Colony Records,* IX, 20.

[72] *Connecticut Records,* I, 523–25.

of Massachusetts; assuredly there can be no comparison with the theories of Roger Williams and the practices of Rhode Island. Yet Mr. Adams brackets these two commonwealths as fortunate because "in them, at least at their beginning, the influence of the clergy was wholly upon the side of freedom." [73] However, Mr. Adams, of course, was here thinking of the political realm. There undoubtedly were features in Connecticut politics which were the reverse of certain Massachusetts regulations. The electorate was not limited to church members; the *Fundamental Orders* provided that deputies should be chosen by admitted inhabitants of the towns, and magistrates and governors by admitted freemen. The governor was not eligible for more than one term in two years. Finally, there exist the notes of an election sermon delivered by Hooker in 1638 which seem so emphatically to express a philosophy of democracy that, ever since their discovery in the mid-nineteenth century, they have constituted the basis for the usual encomiums of the Connecticut regime.

The essence of Hooker's sermon is its three "doctrines" or principal contentions:

I. The choice of public magistrates belongs unto the people by God's own allowance.

II. The privilege of election, which belongs to the people, therefore must not be exercised according to their humours, but according to the blessed will and law of God.

III. They who have power to appoint officers and magistrates, it is in their power, also, to set the bounds and limitations of the power and place unto which they call them. [74]

These statements obviously support the case for Hooker's political democracy. But they have usually been allowed to appear detached from their context; there are other factors which should receive consideration before it can be confidently maintained that the famous election sermon preaches a political philosophy at odds with the Massachusetts practice and tradition.

The church-membership qualification on the Massachusetts electorate was enacted, so the records say, "to the end the body of commons may be preserved of honest and good men." [75] This statement may well be interpreted as an oblique declaration from the oligarchy that they intended to remain in power. But even so, it was a pertinent rationalization, for there were diverse human elements within the Bay, and the magistrates were not necessarily dishonest in feeling that only responsible persons, sympathetic with the Bible Commonwealth ideal, should share the government. This feeling was comparatively absent in Connecticut, for there the populace was more compact and homogeneous; the people moved in large groups, and there was less cause to fear a vulgar upheaval. Furthermore, the

[73] *The Founding of New England*, 195.

[74] Walker, *Thomas Hooker*, 125.

[75] *Records of Massachusetts*, I, 87.

Fundamental Orders did not quite break down the religious qualification. Even if the church members were a very small minority — which is doubtful — the towns would not have bestowed the status of "inhabitant" upon someone of whom the godly strongly disapproved. The governor was required to be a member "of some approved congregation, and formerly of the Magistracy within this Jurisdiction." [76] After 1646, as we have seen, conviction for a scandalous offense deprived one of his vote, and in the same year a certificate of good behavior from one's town and the consent of three magistrates was required to become a registered voter. This was quite sufficient to keep the government from running into too "democratic" a channel, and to give the magistracy a certain supervision over the make-up of the electorate.

As for the *Fundamental Orders* themselves, we should observe that they were not evoked *in vacuo*, but only after the colony had been in existence almost three years; they were not dictated by an a priori philosophy, but were rather the legalizing of existing practice. Massachusetts Bay was endowed at its birth with a charter, a legitimate government of which the main lines were predetermined. When the Connecticut settlers prepared to move into new lands, without a specific organization, they had to create a government of their own. To tide over the formative period a provisional arrangement was devised, which was simple and well adapted to the facts. It so happened that the Earl of Warwick had in 1632 granted to Lords Say and Seale, Brook, and to others, the territory upon which the colonists proposed to build. John Winthrop, Jr., was the authorized agent for the patentees. After some negotiations he agreed that the settlers could erect their own government if they would recognize the validity of the Warwick Grant, thus giving the river towns something better than mere squatters' rights.[77] As four distinct settlements were established, the simplest procedure was to select two representatives from each of them and empower them as magistrates. This selection was ratified in the Massachusetts Court by an act entitled a "Commission graunted to severall Persons to governe the People att Connecticott," but which actually was only a confirmation of the arrangement.[78] Thus the first government in the Connecticut Valley inevitably took the form of geographical representation, and representatives chosen in this manner naturally stood for a whole town. Under this commission the government functioned for the first year. The towns, meantime, were not incorporated and elected no officers; their affairs were ordered simply in meetings of the proprietors; under the conditions of frontier settlement, all proprietors who had

[76] *Connecticut Records*, I, 22.

[77] Love, *Hartford*, 18–21.

[78] The Court, as a third party, simply acted "on the behalfe of our said members, and John Winthrop, Junior Esq., Gouernor, appoyncted by certaine noble personages and men of quallitie interesed [*sic*] in the said ryver, which are yet in England" (*Records of Massachusetts*, I, 170).

assumed a share of the risk assumed also a share in the direction.[79] When the year ran out, the commissioners called for another election; seven of the same magistrates were returned, the only change being the substitution of Thomas Welles, a south-side Hartford man, for one of the two north-side men. This change seems to have been a recognition of the principle of geographical representation upon which the commission was built.[80] The difficulties of calling the citizens of the four towns into a General Court were obvious; hence by May 1, 1637, the settlements were each represented by "committees."[81]

Consequently, when in 1639 the colony was ready to establish a more formal government, the "democratic" principles of the *Fundamental Orders* — regional constituencies, suffrage unqualified by religious membership, and a representative Court — these had already materialized. The *Orders* merely codified what already existed. When Hooker delivered his election sermon, the people of Connecticut had already held one election on the assumption that the choice of public magistrates belongs to the people, and by that time his first "doctrine" at least was not news to them.

When the citizens, under these circumstances, determined to bestow a formal status upon their government, they had no immediate political precedent; but they were not without a theory to guide them. The social covenant had been completely recognized as a theoretical basis for society by Buchanan in Scotland and by Richard Hooker in England; but as we have already seen, the social covenant idea was a peculiar tenet of Congregationalism, and the theorists had inevitably posited it in the state as well as in the church. For ecclesiastical governors to assume their calling, Browne had said, there must be an agreement of the church; so "for ciuil Magistrates, there must be an agreement of the people or Common welth."[82] Penry had held that "it is the crown and honour of princes . . . to be in covenant with their subjects,"[83] and the Separatists aboard the *Mayflower* found a covenant the obvious answer to their first problem of political organization. Henry Jacob had pointed out that the covenant was basic to the existence of a church, and had added, "By such a free mutuall consent also all Civil perfect Corporations did first beginne."[84] Even before the migration reached America, Winthrop declared that the immigrants had entered into a compact not only with each other but with God:

For the worke wee haue in hand, it is by a mutuall consent through a speciall overruleing providence, . . . to seeke out a place of Cohabitation and Consorte-

[79] Love, *Hartford*, 48.

[80] Love, *Hartford*, 69.

[81] Love, *Hartford*, 70–71; *Connecticut Records*, I, 9.

[82] Williston Walker, *Creeds and Platforms of Congregationalism* (New York, 1893), 25.

[83] Robert William Dale, *History of English Congregationalism* (London, 1907), 158.

[84] Burrage, *Dissenters*, II, 157.

shipp vnder a due forme of Government both ciuill and ecclesiasticall. In such cases as this the care of the publique must oversway all private respects. . . . Wee are entered into Covenant with him for this worke. . . . We haue professed to enterprise these Accions vpon these and these ends. . . . For this end, wee must be knitt together in this worke as one man.[85]

The actual creation of the Massachusets state by the deliberate assemblage of the people dramatized the theory, and it became a fixed idea in the New England sociology. Hooker was thoroughly familiar with it:

Mutuall covenanting and confoederation of the Saints in the fellowship of the faith according to the order of the Gospel is that which gives constitution and being to a visible Church.[86]

Inevitably he finds analogies outside the ecclesiastical realm; the covenant can be justified by

that resemblance which this polity hath with all other bodies politick. . . . Each whole or intire body, is made up of his members, as, by mutuall reference and dependence they are ioyned each to the other. Thus Corporations in towns and cities, as they have their charter granted from the King or State, which gives them warrant and allowance . . . so their mutual ingagement each to other, to attend such terms, to walk in such orders, which shall be sutable to such a condition, gives being to such a body. Its that sement which soders them all, that soul as it were, that acts all the parts and particular persons so interested in such a way, for . . . he that will enter, must also willingly binde and ingage himselfe to each member of that society to promote the good of the whole, or else a member actually he is not.[87]

Like Winthrop he regarded participation in the enterprise as an equivalent to the taking of a compact; when William Pynchon withdrew Springfield from the Connecticut Confederacy, before the *Fundamental Orders* had been framed, Hooker accused him of breach of covenant:

If Mr. Pynchon can devise ways to make his oath bind him when he will, and loosen him when he list; if he can tell how, in faithfulness, to engage himself in a civil covenant and combination (for that he did, by his committees, in their act,) and yet can cast it away at his pleasure, before he give in sufficient warrant, more than his own word and will, he must find a law in Agaam for it; for it is written in no law nor gospel that ever I read.[88]

Therefore when it seemed necessary that the implicit political compact should become explicit, the example of the church covenant was naturally

[85] *Winthrop Papers*, Mass. Hist. Soc., II (1931), 283–94.

[86] *Survey*, part I, 47.

[87] *Survey*, part I, 50.

[88] *Collections*, Conn. Hist. Soc., I, 14. Without conscious irony, Hooker is here assuming precisely the same position Cotton and the Massachusetts magistrates took up against him when in 1634 they answered the strong bent of the spirits of the would-be emigrants with the argument that by departing they would break their covenant.

followed. Just as those who had been called into the religious communion by God signalized their fellowship by an act of formal dedication, so those for whom God had so disposed that they were "cohabiting and dwelling in and vppon the River of Conectecotte" gave being to their civil society by a mutual engagement:

And well knowing where a people are gathered togather the word of God requires that to mayntayne the peace and vnion of such a people there should be an orderly and decent Gouernment established according to God, to order and dispose of the affayres of the people at all seasons as occation shall require; doe therefore assotiate and conioyne our selues to be as one Publike State or Commonwelth; and doe, for our selues and our Successors and such as shall be adioyned to vs att any tyme hereafter, enter into Combination and Confederation togather.[89]

And because God had so disposed of all the people in the settlement, regardless of their church membership, there was no occasion that any of them should be excluded from the open declaration. Which is precisely the point William Hubbard made when writing his *History of New England* in 1680:

They entered into a combination among themselves, and so became a body politick by mutual consent, and framed such laws and constitutions as were necessary for the foundation of a civil government . . . which possibly was the occasion, that those of that colony took a larger compass, as to their freemen, than the Massachusetts had done before them; not restraining the freedom of their civil government to the membership of their churches; for where a government is founded on the consent of the people, it will be necessitated to extend the favour of a civil freedom to many, who otherwise might be looked upon, not so capable, at least not so worthy thereof.[90]

The *Fundamental Orders,* therefore, were not only a summary of Connecticut's experience, they were a version of that experience presented in the familiar form of a covenant attested by all the members of the society upon whom they were to bind. The Massachusetts Company, confronting the task of adapting a joint-stock corporation to the purposes of a state constitution, had, like Connecticut, instinctively regarded an individual's participation in the enterprise as his swearing to a social compact. But the leaders, fearing that the purposes of agreement were too abstruse or too exalted for the easy comprehension of the vulgar, and that if they themselves lost the direction, the adventure would come to a bad end, inevitably put the emphasis upon the more aristocratical principle of Congregationalism and exalted the function of the magistrates as they did that of the elders. Thereby those who best knew the purposes of the covenant should interpret it and direct the multitude accordingly. Connecticut, evolving more naturally, nurtured by a provisional government that had already taken the form of regional representation, also applied the analogy of the

[89] *Connecticut Records,* I, 20–21.
[90] 2 *Collections,* Mass. Hist. Soc., V, 309.

church to the state, but took over the principle that the whole body of participants in a political covenant should declare that covenant's purpose. Once committed to its policy, the Massachusetts orthodoxy had to persist; Connecticut, much less threatened with internal dissension, required only such milder safeguards as Hooker's second doctrine to ensure law and order in the state and conformity in the church. Yet both policies grew out of the original body of Congregational thought, the general features of the two systems were alike; it was simply that in each case the emphasis lay at a different point, and the discrepancies did not yet indicate an antagonism of fundamental points of view.

In the course of the colonies' several deductions from their common premises, one circumstance in the actual situation created a genuine issue between them. The Massachusetts rulers looked upon their charter as the symbol of their covenant; all those who joined the colony were assumed to join the compact which the original members had formally created when they organized the company. But the charter was totally inadequate for what was demanded of it. The magistrates had tried to set it aside in the first years in order to assure the control they felt was essential. The freemen, in 1634, demanded a view of the charter and in the next General Court overturned the usurpation of the magistrates and asserted their constitutional rights. But even after the government had been bound to the original provisions of the charter, the freemen discovered large fields for which there was not sufficient rule in that document. They had nothing by which they could hold the magistrates accountable. For many years they agitated for a codification of the laws, "having conceived great dangers to our state, in regard that our magistrates, for want of positive laws, in many cases might proceed according to their discretions." [91] The magistrates staved off this demand, and meantime developed the theory of political covenant in such a fashion as to give themselves precisely the discretionary powers against which the deputies protested. Winthrop, as usual, was the spokesman, and he attacked the issue most directly in his controversy with Henry Vane in 1637. During the Hutchinson affair the Court ordered that no town or person should offer hospitality to a stranger unless two of the magistrates approved of him. Vane called this tyranny. Winthrop came to the defense.[92] The first consideration, he said, is that of what constitutes the essence of a government, "which I conceive to be this, — the consent of a certaine company of people, to cohabite together, under one government for their mutual safety and welfare." Otherwise no organized society could exist:

It is clearly agreed, by all, that the care of safety and welfare was the original cause or occasion of common weales and of many familyes subjecting themselves to rulers and laws; for no man hath lawfull power over another, but by birth or

[91] Winthrop, *Journal*, I, 151.
[92] The documents of this controversy are in Thomas Hutchinson, *The Hutchinson Papers* (Prince Society, 1865), I, 79–107.

consent, so likewise, by the law of proprietye, no man can have just interest in that which belongeth to another, without his consent.

Now if Massachusetts is such a corporate society, she has a right to admit whomsoever she pleases, and, conversely, "may we lawfully refuse to receive such whose dispositions suite not with ours." No one denies this privilege to churches; "why then should the common weale be denied the like liberty?"

Vane, in the name of a full-fledged constitutionalism, took issue with Winthrop on his fundamental position. Massachusetts, he said, does not rest solely upon a compact; it is, in the first place, a commonwealth founded upon the Bible, and in the second place is "dependant upon the grant also of our Soveraigne." Therefore Winthrop's reasons, "taken from the nature of a common-wealth, not founded upon Christ, nor by his Majestyes charters," do not apply here, and "must needs fall to the ground." The issue was not whether the government could exclude undesirables, but whether it could proceed otherwise than had been specifically authorized by God or king, and entrust the matter to "such unlimited and unsafe a rule, as the will and discretion of men." If men were to be sent away, it should be by virtue of a concrete law, not by "the illimited consent or dissent of magistrates." The argument from the churches Vane dismissed by noting that the churches do have a fundamental law; they do not "receive or reject at their discretions . . . but at the discretion of Christ." As the elders continually affirmed, their power was merely "ministerial" or "stewardly." The state should copy them, using its charter for a guide just as they used Scripture. Otherwise, to give the magistrates power on the basis of some vague social theory "setts down no rule" for them, and is a tyranny, quite of a piece with the unauthorized taxation of a Stuart monarch.

Winthrop had the last word, and thereby gave the most complete exposition of the theory of the Massachusetts magistracy that has come down to us. Vane's approach he declared to be limited; his own description had been given in general, philosophic terms which Vane did not appreciate. "The definition or description of the genus may be applyed to all the species, reserving the specificall differences." Among these latter are both the charter and the religion; the patent is only an accidental circumstance, not the basis, for the state; the society came into being not so much when the charter was granted as when,

to cohabit in the Massachusetts and under the government set up among us by his Majesty's patent or grant for our mutual safety and wellfare, we agreed to walke according to the rules of the gospell. And thus you have both a christian common weale and the same founded upon the patent, and both included within my description.

The commonwealth itself is thus the reality; both its charter and its Christianity are only the language in which this particular compact was enunciated. As for Christ and not men determining in the churches, how else could the voice of God be expressed but through the men composing the congregation?

> Did he never heare, that our practise is, that none are propounded to the congregation, except they be first allowed by the elders, and is not this to admitt or reject by discretion?

If the state, therefore, is an organic entity, the magistrates, representing in their offices the will of the whole, have the powers granted them by this law, or any law, and Vane's distinction between their will and the will of the whole is "frivilous discourse." Winthrop, the English Puritan, had been, and still was, heart and soul in the campaign against royal absolutism; Winthrop, the Massachusetts governor, looked upon the appeal to fundamental law on the part of the citizens as a stalking-horse to the indulgence of their corrupt desires. The magistrates were sufficiently limited as it was; they were church members and freemen, and they had taken the magistrates' oath; they were tied up with the corporate society, and their actions gave expression to the will of the state — and hence to the will of God. "Whatsoever sentence the magistrate give, according to these limitations, the judgement is the Lords, though he do it not by any rule particularly prescribed by civil authority."

Obviously Winthrop was striving, with all the ingenuity of a man trained in the logic of the schoolmen, to reconcile the constitutional limitations which the Bible and the charter had placed upon the government with that discretionary exercise of executive power which he felt was essential to a respectable state. But so long as he argued upon purely political grounds, he could not make much headway. The men who settled New England had contended against the king's refusal to accept constitutional limitation — they believed, indeed, that their migration had been precipitated by precisely that refusal. The colonies could never afford publicly to disown the imperishable principle for which the brethren were still striving and suffering in England. Puritans had learned their lesson thoroughly, and even the mouthpiece of the Massachusetts theocracy, John Cotton himself, preached that it was altogether unwholesome to give officers in church and state more power than was good for them:

> It is necessary, therefore, that all power that is on earth be limited, Church power or other. . . . It is counted a matter of danger to the State to limit Prerogatives, but it is a further danger not to have them limited. . . . It is therfore fit for every man to be studious of the bounds which the Lord hath set: and for the People, in whom fundamentally all power lyes, to give as much power as God in his word gives to men: And it is meet that Magistrates in the Commonwealth, and so officers in the Churches, should desire to know the utmost bounds of their own power.

"If you tether a Beast at night," he said, with a grimness that carries us back to Pym and Hampden, "he knows the length of his tether before morning." [93] It had been in this frame of mind that the deputies in 1634 demanded a look at the charter, and asserted their rights in such a fashion as the magistrates did not immediately forget.

A few months before this revolution, it will be remembered, Hooker reached Massachusetts. The coincidence has been noted before: "After Mr. Hooker's coming," says Hubbard, "it was observed that many of the freemen grew to be very jealous of their liberties." [94] But there is nothing more positive than this insinuation to connect him with that episode. Yet it is apparent that the Connecticut settlers had some sympathy with the deputies' action; the Connecticut statement of the powers of its General Court is almost a verbatim reiteration of the passage which the Massachusetts freemen caused to be inscribed upon the records of the Bay. The significant fact about Hooker's famous election sermon is not the first doctrine, which was Congregational commonplace, nor the second, which Congregationalists had always advanced as the safeguard against popularity. The significant fact is the stress put at that moment upon the third doctrine, that they who appoint officers have also the power to set bounds and limitations to them. The content of the paragraph was no more novel than that of the other two, but Hooker flaunted the idea in deliberate contradiction to Winthrop's disposition to keep that element of the theory in the background. It is at this point that we are at last able to see where, if at all, the views of Hooker diverged from those of the Massachusetts theocracy, and to show some basis for the "democracy" of Connecticut.

Hooker's letter to Winthrop in 1638 is clear and definite on the people's power to set bounds to their rulers:

And here, I fully assent to those staple principles which you set down; to wit, that the people should choose some from amongst them — that they should refer matter of counsel to their counsellors, matter of judicature to their judges; only, the question here grows — what rule the judge must have to judge by; secondly, who those counsellors must be.

He repudiates the reasoning Winthrop had invoked against Vane:

That in the matter which is referred to the judge, the sentence should lie in his breast, or be left to his discretion, according to which he should go, I am afraid it is a course which wants both safety and warrant. I must confess, I ever looked at it as a way which leads directly to tyranny, and so to confusion, and must plainly profess, if it was in my liberty, I should choose neither to live nor leave my posterity under such a government.

By carrying Congregationalism into politics Hooker could conclude that as the people constitute the society, they are to determine to what ends they shall be governed, and are therefore to determine what laws their officers shall observe:

[93] Cotton, *Exposition on the 13th Chapter of the Revelation* (London, 1656), 72, 77.
[94] 2 *Collections*, Mass. Hist. Soc., V, 165.

Reserving smaller matters, which fall in occasionally in common course, to a lower counsel, in matters of greater consequence, which concern the common good, a general counsel, chosen by all, to transact businesses which concern all, I conceive, under favour, most suitable to rule and most safe for relief of the whole.[95]

Connecticut well learned its lesson from Hooker. In October 1639, a committee was appointed to codify all the laws then in force and to have them published in the towns; thus, in the first year of rule under the *Orders*, there was achieved what the deputies were still contending for in the Bay. When other laws accumulated, another codification was ordered — in 1650. The colony was aware that in this respect she differed from Massachusetts, and when commissions were issued to Haynes and Hopkins in 1643 to represent her in the Confederation, they were told they were to act, "researueing the priuiledges we haue in fundamentall lawes."

But that the difference, important as it was, was one of degree rather than of kind, seems to be indicated by Pynchon's stand when the General Court of Connecticut, upon the pronouncement of Hooker, censured him for unfaithful dealing in providing a corn supply. The Court evidently took Hooker's word that Pynchon's conduct was immoral, and acted without investigating the case any further or citing a specific statute. Pynchon was thus able to hurl into Hooker's teeth the very charge Hooker had flung at Winthrop:

I must expect to see this charge demonstrated by positive proofe such as may stand with the iust censure of a Court of equity, for certaine punishment must be grounded vppon certaine proofe, and not vppon surmises or preiudice or the like mistaken groundes.

The issue was largely a question of whose ox was being gored. The Court held that in this emergency Pynchon should, even without a warrant, have impressed a canoe from a fellow townsman, although he knew the loss of the boat would seriously injure the owner's welfare. This position implied nothing less than that the magistrate should act at his own discretion, regarding not the fundamental law, but *salus populi*, and Pynchon at once perceived the point:

If magistrates in N. E. should *ex officio* practise such a power ouer mens proprieties, how long would Tyrany be kept out of our habitations; Truly the king might as legaly exact a loan *Ex officio* of his subjects by a distresse on mens proprieties (because he pleades as great necessity) as to presse a Cano without a legall order. The lawes of England count it a tender thing to touch another mans propriety and therefore many have rather chosen to suffer as in a good cause then to yeeld their goods to the king *ex officio*: and to lose the liberty of an English subject in N. E. would bring woefull slaviry to our posterity: But while governments are ordered by the lawlesse law of discretion, that [which] is transient in particular mens heades may be of dangerous consequence quickly.[96]

---

[95] *Collections*, Conn. Hist. Soc., I, 11–12.
[96] *Proceedings*, Mass. Hist. Soc., XLVIII, 47–48.

When Hooker's colony faced a famine, they could forget their great constitutional principle and copy the methods of Winthrop.

In relatively recent times a few persons, inspired by the argument that Hooker was the pioneer democrat, have been moved to read his publications. In him they have discovered, as they should, a magnificent stylist, whereupon they become content to leave Cotton unread. They pounce upon this or that passage to prove that Hooker's exposition of the theology carries a democratic implication antipathetic to Cotton's.

For example, Hooker says that the poorest, the most "humbled" sinner, though of the meanest capacity, can apprehend more of a spiritual truth than the most erudite:

> In a word, take the meanest Saint that ever breathed on the earth, and the greatest scholar for outward part, and learning, and reach and policie, the meanest ignorant soule, that is almost a naturall foole, that soule knowes and understands more of grace and mercy in Christ, than all the wisest and learnedst in the world, than all the greatest schollers.[97]

We, I suppose, can hardly read this without feeling a slight clutch at the throat: here, if anywhere, is stated the democracy implicit in the Puritan inheritance.

Yet, in his less dramatic fashion, John Cotton (indeed, every one of the founding ministers) says the same thing. Maybe the less striking fashion is just what we are talking about; maybe Hooker's vividness is the beginning of a real difference between the Valley and the Bay. Nevertheless, as for the idea itself, Cotton is as explicit as Hooker. By study and learning, he asserts, men may come to a knowledge of divinity — they may even master enough to overcome an opponent — yet all the time have no genuine understanding of the doctrines they defend:

> A man that wants this Unction may say, he understands these, and believes them, but hee cannot say he knows them by any sensible work of God on his own soul.[98]

Thus, though there is a difference in the quality of the language, there is here no issue of democrat versus aristocrat. Both Cotton and Hooker were expounding that preëminence of spiritual insight over mere intellectual formulation which they learned from their English preceptors. John Preston, for example, had already shown them how to embellish this lesson with tropes authorized by the plain style. There are illuminations, Preston had written, which no theologian can impart: "As a man may looke on a Trade, and never see the mystery of it, he may look on artificial things, pictures or any thing else, and yet not see the Art by which they are made." So there are things in divinity "that an unsound-hearted man can never know." [99]

[97] Hooker, *The Soules Vocation* (London, 1638), 108.
[98] Cotton, *A Practical Commentary . . . upon the First Epistle Generall of John* (London, 1656), 171.
[99] Preston, *The New Covenant* (London, 1629), 275.

All of which is to say, once more, that there was an irrepressibly democratic dynamic in Protestant theology, though all good Protestants strove to stifle it. As a principle of piety, the English Puritans learned it from the great reformers, as they in their day had learned it from Augustine. If the saint must believe in order to understand, rather than the other way around, then there was always a real possibility that the common man, if he believed, might understand better and more than the scholar, no matter how massive the latter's erudition. Some of the more extravagant claims that have been advanced for Hooker's democracy come from secularists no longer capable of grasping this Protestant paradox. And then, it is true that by translating this position into an organized polity, Congregationalists inadvertently opened a bit wider — wider than they ever intended — a door for the democratic propulsion. But in this historical process, Cotton and Hooker were so closely in step that they are not to be distinguished, one against the other, into such opposing camps as are presumed in the modern usage of theocrat and democrat.

If, therefore, we speak accurately about early Connecticut, we must say that the towns settled along the river naturally responded to their situation by drafting the *Fundamental Orders*, but their response was dictated by concepts equally regnant in Massachusetts Bay. The three towns organized a government simply by following the obvious analogy of the church covenant. By thus beginning with a fundamental law adapted to their circumstances, the towns were able to carry over completely into practice that emphasis which the Congregational system had placed upon the responsibility of officers to their constituents. They were able to insist that their rulers should be amenable to the fundamental laws of the society and the express will of the whole group. Massachusetts, however, had placed the emphasis upon another principle of Congregationalism, which was present in the Connecticut government, but not so strongly — the principle that the wise, the able, and the good knew the purposes of the covenant better than most of those who entered it and should be allowed freedom to interpret it at their discretion. To what extent this difference in opinion caused the migration in 1636 is difficult to say. No doubt all honor is due Connecticut for having stood, if not always consistently, for a great political idea. But that honor becomes fulsome praise if we forget that Connecticut theory was a product of its age, an evolution from its background and circumstances, that there were inconsistencies and limitations in its practice, and finally that while it represented another development from the same premises upon which the Massachusetts theocracy was erected, it was in no sense a breaking away from that philosophy.

CHAPTER III

THE MARROW OF PURITAN DIVINITY

[It was not I who first broached the argument that the founders of New England were adherents of the "federalist" redaction of Calvinist theology. The tenets of this peculiar school, and its position in the development of Protestant thought during the seventeenth century, were set forth, for instance, by George Park Fisher in *The History of Christian Doctrine* (1896) and by Arthur Cushman McGiffert in *Protestant Thought Before Kant* (1919). Also, the inherent connection between the idea of the church covenant and that of the cosmic covenant had been at least adumbrated by Champlain Burrage in *Early English Dissenters in the Light of Recent Research* (1912).

Unfortunately, these theological gentlemen wrote in a manner so pontifical, out of a concern which I may venture to call so purely taxonomic, that their works never penetrated the awareness of historians of American civilization. All I did was to gather up these disquisitions, along with a few scattered intimations, and devote myself to reading the sources. Out of my explorations came, as a first and preliminary survey, this excited report, printed in *The Publications of the Colonial Society of Massachusetts* for February 1935.

Preliminary and excited the piece was, and so it remains. I have reworked the thesis into less aggressive formulations in *The New England Mind*, but students tell me that this initial statement is still the more arresting.

The history of the reception of this paper is, on a minor level, an instructive lesson in the vagaries of American scholarship. At first ignored (since not many persons outside the Colonial Society pant for its *Publications*), it rather suddenly enlisted an almost universal, not to say embarrassing, acceptance, as though everybody had learned about it from George Park Fisher. Then the annoying consequence inevitably followed: friends of the delicate proposition so freely embraced it that they presented it to a world not generally skilled in theological discrimination as a solid block of historical fact. They published the happy tidings, in my name, that the Puritans were not and never had been Calvinists. Consequently, what was intended to be an investigation into the subtleties of human development has been vulgarized into a platitude obstructive both to living appreciation and to further analysis.

There is a pronounced disposition in modern America to resent the suggestion that the colonial leaders (for that matter, also the architects of the

American Constitution) were intellectuals. In the vicinity of Boston one can encounter an aversion that amounts to settled hostility against any account implying that the founders of New England were primarily occupied with religious ideas, and even more against the supposition that they gave their days and nights to abstract speculation. In the most learned society of the Puritan capital I have heard antiquarians quote the words of the fishermen of Marblehead, that they came here not to save their souls but to fish, as an exoneration of the whole migration. Great, therefore, was my chagrin, and shameful it remains, when several commentators, having sketchily apprehended my presentation of the covenant theology, rushed to the joyous conclusion that New England had never preached what the world calls "Calvinism." Innate depravity and original sin, these popularizers proclaimed, need not be taken by modern New Englanders as serious propositions, since these ideas had never been seriously entertained in the first place.

I strove (as on pp. 93–97) to warn against this misconstruction, but I did not warn hard enough. The difficulty is that the modern mind has so little appreciation for such nuances as the federal theology contains that it can think only in terms of black or white. Let me, therefore, try to put the issue as bluntly as possible, the more as I am convinced that in expounding the federal marrow of Puritan theology I am calling attention to a constellation of ideas basic to any comprehension of the American mind.

It was never my intention to deny that in the large sweep of history there is an essential continuity between the New England theology and that of the Reformed, or as they are called, the Calvinistic churches. The New Englanders were correct in claiming that they were not followers of John Calvin, because they honestly believed that they were reading the Bible with their own eyes. Yet in the historical perspective, their way of interpreting the Bible must be called Calvinist. The federal theology was not a distinct or antipathetic system: it was simply an idiom in which these Protestants sought to make a bit more plausible the mysteries of the Protestant creed. That the idiom many times took such mastery over the creed as in effect to pervert it is one of the ironic dramas of the human intellect; but this happenstance must not blind us to the fact that fundamentally the Puritan conception of the predicament of man was that which all the Reformed groups maintained. Were I to rework this piece today — as I dare not — I should more strongly emphasize the underlying connection; though even so, I should retract nothing from the fascinating peculiarity of the federal phraseology.

One note more: the last sentence of the article is a total miscomprehension. Jonathan Edwards was willing (as the founders were not) to call himself a Calvinist, at least as against those he supposed his "Arminian" opponents. But actually, in his substitution of the revolutionary psychology of John Locke for the medieval scheme of the faculties (which John Calvin automatically assumed), and by his replacing of the medieval physics with the new science of Sir Isaac Newton, Edwards was unable — even had he so desired — to retrieve the original positions of John Calvin. What I meant to say, and miserably spoiled in the saying, is only that Edwards brushed aside the (by his day) rusty mechanism of the covenant to forge a fresh statement of the central Protestant definition of man's plight in a universe which God created.]

I

W E think of the original settlers of New England as "Calvinists." So indeed they were, if we mean that in general terms they conceived of man and the universe much as did John Calvin. But when we call them Calvinists, we are apt to imply that they were so close in time and temperament to the author of the *Institutes* that they carried to America his thought and system inviolate, and to suppose that their intellectual life consisted only in reiterating this volume. Yet students of technical theology have long since realized that Calvinism was in the process of modification by the year 1630. There had come to be numerous departures from or developments within the pristine creed, and "Calvinism" in the seventeenth century covered almost as many shades of opinion as does "socialism" in the twentieth. The New England leaders did not stem directly from Calvin; [1] they learned the Calvinist theology only after it had been improved, embellished, and in many respects transformed by a host of hard-thinking expounders and critics. The system had been thoroughly gone over by Dutchmen and Scotsmen, and nothing ever left the hands of those shrewd peoples precisely as it came to them; furthermore, for seventy years or more English theologians had been mulling it over, tinkering and remodeling, rearranging emphases, and, in the course of adapting it to Anglo-Saxon requirements, generally blurring its Gallic clarity and incisiveness.

Much of this adaptation was necessitated because, to a later and more critical generation, there were many conundrums which Calvin, and all the first reformers for that matter, had not answered in sufficient detail. He had left too many loopholes, too many openings for Papist disputants to thrust in embarrassing questions. His object had been to compose a sublime synthesis of theology; he sketched out the main design, the architectural framework, in broad and free strokes. He did not fill in details, he did

---

[1] They did not even consider him the fountainhead of their thought, but regarded him as one among many "juicious" divines. To an English correspondent who asked if Calvin had not definitely settled a certain point, Thomas Shepard replied: "I have forgot what he hath wrote and myself have read long since out of him" (*Works*, John Albro, ed., Boston, 1853, I, 326). Thomas Hooker did not hesitate to point out in a sermon that Calvin "casts a different construction" upon some words of Scripture, and to insist upon his own interpretation (*A Comment Upon Christs Last Prayer in the Seventeenth of John*, London, 1656, 157).

not pretend to solve the metaphysical riddles inherent in the doctrine. He wrote in the heyday of Protestant faith and crusading zeal, and it is not too much to say that he was so carried along by the ecstasy of belief that an assertion of the true doctrine was for him sufficient in and for itself. There was no need then for elaborate props and buttresses, for cautious logic and finespun argumentation.

Hence the history of Reformed thought in the late sixteenth and early seventeeth centuries reveals the poignant inability of Calvin's disciples to bear up under the exaction he had laid upon them. He demanded that they contemplate, with steady, unblinking resolution, the absolute, incomprehensible, and transcendent sovereignty of God; he required men to stare fixedly and without relief into the very center of the blazing sun of glory. God is not to be understood but to be adored. This supreme and awful essence can never be delineated in such a way that He seems even momentarily to take on any shape, contour, or feature recognizable in the terms of human discourse, nor may His activities be subjected to the laws of human reason or natural plausibility. He is simply the sum of all perfections, that being who is at one and the same the embodiment of perfect goodness and justice, perfect power and mercy, absolute righteousness and knowledge. Of course, man will never understand how these qualities in unmitigated fullness exist side by side in one being without conflict or inconsistency; though man were to speculate and argue to the end of time, he can never conceivably reconcile plenary forgiveness with implacable righteousness. Calvin said that it is not man's function to attempt such speculation. Man has only to discover the specific laws, the positive injunctions which God has laid down in His written word, to take God's statements as recorded, and to accept them through faith. "To desire any other knowledge of predestination than what is unfolded in the word of God, indicates as great folly, as a wish to walk through unpassable roads, or to see in the dark." [2] There does not have to be any necessary or discernible reason for these decrees, they do not have to form any comprehensive and consistent system; Calvin may with titanic effort marshal them in the form of a coherent logical pattern, but each individual item rests, in the final analysis, not upon the logic of its place in the system, but upon the specific and arbitrary enactment of God. The object of our faith, as far as His personal character is concerned, is an utter blank to human comprehension; He is a realm of mystery, in whom we are sure that all dilemmas and contradictions are ultimately resolved, though just how, we shall never in this world even remotely fathom.

It is of the essence of this theology that God, the force, the power, the life of the universe, remains to men hidden, unknowable, unpredictable. He is the ultimate secret, the awful mystery. God's nature "is capable properly of no definition," so that all that one can say is that "God is an

---

[2] *Institutes*, III, xxi, 2.

incomprehensible, first, and absolute Being." [3] He cannot be approached directly; man cannot stand face to face with Him, "for in doing so, what do we else but draw neere to God, as the stubble or the waxe should draw neer to the fire? . . . He is a consuming fire to the sonnes of men, if they come to him immediately." [4] The English Puritans may be called Calvinists primarily because they held this central conception, though the thought is older in Christian history than Calvin, and they did not necessarily come to it only under Calvin's own tuition. "Now, sayth the Lord, my thoughts go beyond your thought as much as the distance is betweene heaven and earth." [5] William Ames, whose *Medulla Sacrae Theologiae* was the standard textbook of theology in New England, lays it down at the very beginning that "what God is, none can perfectly define, but that hath the Logicke of God himselfe," [6] and argues that therefore our observance of His will can never be based upon God's "secret will," but only upon His explicitly revealed command.[7] William Perkins, from whom Ames and English Puritans in general drew a great share of their inspiration, asserted squarely once and for all that even the virtues of reasonableness or justice, as human beings conceive them, could not be predicated of God, for God's will "it selfe is an absolute rule both of iustice and reason"; and that nothing could therefore be reasonable and just intrinsically, "but it is first of all willed by God, and thereupon becomes reasonable and just." [8] The glory of God no man or angel shall know, preached Thomas Shepard; "their cockle shell can never comprehend this sea"; we can only apprehend Him by knowing that we cannot comprehend Him at all, "as we admire the luster of the sun the more in that it is so great we can not behold it." [9]

This system of thought rests, in the final analysis, upon something that cannot really be systematized at all, upon an unchained force, an incalculable essence. For the period of Protestant beginnings, for the years of pure faith and battle with Babylon, this doctrine, as Calvin expressed it, was entirely adequate. It took the mind off speculation, economized energies that might have been dissipated in fruitless questionings, simplified the intellectual life, and concentrated attention on action. The warriors of the Lord were certain that in the innermost being of God all the cosmic enigmas which the Scholastics had argued and debated to the point of exhaustion were settled, that they need not bother with ultimate truth in the metaphysical sense, because in faith and revelation they had clear and explicit truth once and for all. But by the beginning of the seventeenth cen-

[3] John Preston, *Life Eternall, or, A Treatise of the Knowledge of the Divine Essence and Attributes* (London, 1631), 94.

[4] Preston, *The New Covenant, or the Saints Portion* (London, 1629), 503.

[5] Preston, *New Covenant*, 111.

[6] *Medulla Sacrae Theologiae* (The Marrow of Sacred Divinity) (London, 1643), 11.

[7] *Medulla*, 191.

[8] *Works* (Cambridge, 1626), 278.

[9] *Works*, I, 14.

tury Protestant schools and lectureships had been established; the warfare with Rome had become a matter of debate as well as of arms, and logic had become as important a weapon as the sword. Calvinism could no longer remain the relatively simple dogmatism of its founder. It needed amplification, it required concise explication, syllogistic proof, intellectual as well as spiritual focus. It needed, in short, the one thing which, at bottom, it could not admit — a rationale. The difference between Calvin and the so-called Calvinists of the early seventeenth century cannot be more vividly illustrated than by a comparison of the *Institutes* with such a representative book as Ames's *Medulla* (1623). Where the *Institutes* has the majestic sweep of untrammeled confidence, the *Medulla*, though no less confident, is meticulously made up of heads and subheads, objections and answers, arguments and demonstration. The preface admits that some readers may condemn the author's care for "Method, and Logicall form" as being "curious and troublesome," but such persons would "remove the art of understanding, judgement, and memory from those things, which doe almost onely deserve to bee understood, known, and committed to memory." [10] Even if the specific doctrines of Calvinism were unchanged at the time of the migration to New England, they were already removed from pure Calvinism by the difference of tone and of method. It was no longer a question of blocking in the outlines; it was a question of filling in chinks and gaps, of intellectualizing the faith, of exonerating it from the charge of despotic dogmatism, of adding demonstration to assertion — of making it capable of being "understood, known, and committed to memory."

II

The history of theology in this period indicates that the process of development was accomplished in many guises. Learned doctors wrote gigantic tomes on the Trinity of the Incarnation, and soon were creating for Protestantism a literature of apologetics that rivaled the Scholastic, not only in bulk, but in subtlety, ingenuity, and logic-chopping. For our purposes it is possible to distinguish three important issues which particularly occupied the attention of Dutch and English Calvinists. These are not the only points of controversy or development, but they may be said to be the major preoccupations in the theology of early New England. Calvinism had already by 1630 been subjected to attack for what seemed to Catholic, Lutheran, and Anglican critics its tendency toward self-righteousness at the expense of morality; in spite of Calvin's insistence that the elect person must strive to subject himself to the moral law — "Away, then," he cried, "with such corrupt and sacrilegious perversions of the whole order of election" [11] — there was always the danger that the doctrine

[10] *Medulla*, A3 verso.
[11] *Institutes*, III, xxiii, 12.

of predestination would lead in practice to the attitude: "If I am elected, I am elected, there is nothing I can do about it." If man must wait upon God for grace, and grace is irrespective of works, simple folk might very well ask, why worry about works at all? Calvinist preachers were often able to answer this question only with a mere assertion. Calvin simply brushed aside all objection and roundly declared: "Man, being taught that he has nothing good left in his possession, and being surrounded on every side with the most miserable necessity, should, nevertheless, be instructed to aspire to the good of which he is destitute." [12] Perkins taught that the will of man before it receives grace is impotent and in the reception is purely passive: "by it selfe it can neither beginne that conuersion, or any other inward and sound obedience due to Gods law"; [13] he distinctly said that God's predestination is regardless of any quality or merit in the individual, and that man can achieve any sort of obedience only after being elected. Ames restated this doctrine; yet at whatever cost to consistency, he had to assert that though without faith man can do nothing acceptable to God, he still has to perform certain duties because the duties "are in themselves good." [14] The divines were acutely conscious that this was demanding what their own theory had made impossible, and they were struggling to find some possible grounds for proving the necessity of "works" without curtailing the absolute freedom of God to choose and reject regardless of man's achievement.

Along with this problem came another which Calvin had not completely resolved, that of individual assurance, of when and how a man might reach some working conviction that he was of the regenerate. The decrees of election and reprobation were, according to Calvin, inscrutable secrets locked deep in the fastness of the transcendent Will:

> Let them remember that when they inquire into predestination, they penetrate the inmost recesses of Divine wisdom, where the careless and confident intruder will obtain no satisfaction to his curiosity, but will enter a labyrinth from which he will find no way to depart. For it is unreasonable that man should scrutinize with impunity those things which the Lord has determined to be hidden in himself; and investigate, even from eternity, that sublimity of wisdom which God would have us to adore and not comprehend, to promote our admiration of his glory.[15]

This was sufficient for men of 1550, but men of 1600 wished to ascertain something more definite about their own predicament. The curve of religious intensity was beginning to droop, and preachers knew that a more precise form of stimulation had to be invoked to arrest the decline; men wished to know what there was in it for them, they could not forever be incited to faith or persuaded to obey if some tangible reward could not be

---

[12] *Institutes*, II, ii, 1.
[13] *Works*, 21.
[14] *Medulla*, 198.
[15] *Institutes*, III, xxi, 1.

placed before them. Yet to say roundly that all the elect would be immediately satisfied by God of their promotion was to say that God was bound to satisfy human curiosity. The theologians could only rest in another inconsistency that was becoming exceedingly glaring in the light of a more minute analysis. Assurance is sealed to all believers, said Ames, yet the perceiving of it "is not always present to all";[16] this uncertainty, he was forced to admit, is a detriment to "that consolation and peace which Christ hath left to believers." [17]

In both these discussions the attempt to arrive at bases for certainty led directly to the fundamental problem: no grounds for moral obligation or individual assurance could be devised so long as God was held to act in ways that utterly disregarded human necessities or human logic. In order to know that God will unquestionably save him under such and such circumstances, man must know that God is in reality the sort of being who would, or even who will have to, abide by these conditions, and none other. He must ascertain the whys and wherefores of the divine activity. In some fashion the transcendent God had to be chained, made less inscrutable, less mysterious, less unpredictable — He had to be made, again, understandable in human terms. If the sway of the moral law over men were to be maintained, men must know what part it played in their gaining assurance of salvation; if men were to know the conditions upon which they could found an assurance, they must be convinced that God would be bound by those conditions, that He would not at any moment ride roughshod over them, act suddenly from an abrupt whimsy or from caprice, that salvation was not the irrational bestowal of favor according to the passing mood of a lawless tyrant.

The endeavor to give laws for God's behavior was attended with apparently insuperable obstacles, for it was clear that such principles as men might formulate would be derived from reason or from nature, and Calvin had made short work of all rational and natural knowledge in the opening chapters of the *Institutes*. Not only does God transcend reason and nature, but the corruption of the universe which followed the sin of Adam has vitiated whatever of value once existed in them. Reason was originally endowed with an inherent knowledge of God, which is now hopelessly extinguished by ignorance and wickedness; the knowledge of God may be conspicuous in the formation of the world, but we cannot see it or profit by it. We may still have the light of nature and the light of reason, but we have them in vain. "Some sparks, indeed, are kindled, but smothered before they have emitted any great degree of light." [18] Ames went as far as he dared toward bringing order into God's character by saying that since God is obviously perfect, He must be perfectly rational; that in His mind must preëxist a plan of the world as the plan of a house preëxists in the mind of

[16] *Medulla*, 131.
[17] *Medulla*, 118.
[18] *Institutes*, I, iii–vi.

an architect; that God does not work rashly, "but with greatest perfection of reason." [19] But we can never in our discourse attain to that reason. The principles of other arts may be polished and perfected "by sense, observation, experience, and induction," but the principles of theology must be revealed to us, and "how ever they may be brought to perfection by study and industry, yet they are not in us from Nature." [20] Divinity may utilize "Intelligence, Science, Sapience, Art or Prudence," but it cannot be the product of these natural faculties, but only of "divine revelation and institution." [21] Knowledge and rational conviction may be prized by the theologian, and may be preached by him as much as doctrine, but in the final analysis he must declare that reason is not faith, that it is not necessary to justification, and that in itself it cannot produce the effects of grace.[22] He may also study nature and natural philosophy, but his knowledge will always be vain and useless; his faculties are too corrupted to observe correctly; nature is under God's providence, and God's ways are past finding out; and, finally, the works of nature "are all subject to corruption." [23]

Here, then, was the task which seventeenth-century Calvinists faced: the task of bringing God to time and to reason, of justifying His ways to man in conceptions meaningful to the intellect, of caging and confining the transcendent Force, the inexpressible and unfathomable Being, by the laws of ethics, and of doing this somehow without losing the sense of the hidden God, without reducing the Divinity to a mechanism, without depriving Him of unpredictability, absolute power, fearfulness, and mystery. In the final analysis this task came down to ascertaining the reliability of human reason and the trustworthiness of human experience as measurements of the divine character — in short, to the problem of human comprehension of this mysterious thing which we today call the universe.

III

The Arminian movement in Holland (and the "Arminian" theology in the Church of England) represented one Calvinist attempt to supply a reasonable explanation of the relation of God to man. But Arminians went too far; they jeopardized the foundations of Calvinism, and were stigmatized as heretics at the Synod of Dort. In the seventeenth century Arminianism stood as a ghastly warning to all Calvinists. It was an admonition to stay well inside the structure of the creed, whatever redecorations they undertook. The orthodox soon perceived that the basic error in Arminianism was not any one of its "five points" formulated at Dort, but its exaltation of the human reason and consequently its reconstruction of God

[19] *Medulla,* 24.
[20] *Medulla,* 2.
[21] *Medulla,* 1.
[22] *Medulla,* 117.
[23] Preston, *New Covenant,* 556.

after the human image. William Ames said that grace as conceived by the Arminians "may be the effect of a good dinner sometimes"; [24] and Thomas Shepard pointed out that by their putting into the unregenerate will and the natural reason an ability to undertake moral duties and to work out assurance without the impetus of grace, they became no better than heathen philosophers and Roman stoics.

I heard an Arminian once say, If faith will not work it, then set reason a-work, and we know how men have been kings and lords over their own passions by improving reason, and from some experience of the power of nature men have come to write large volumes in defence of it; and . . . the Arminians, though they ascribe somewhat to grace, . . . yet, indeed, they lay the main stress of the work upon a man's own will, and the royalty and sovereignty of that liberty.[25]

The Arminians yielded too far to the pressure for constructing theology in a more rational fashion and so succumbed to the temptation of smuggling too much human freedom into the ethics of predestination. A more promising, if less spectacular, mode of satisfying these importunities without falling into heresy was suggested in the work of the great Cambridge theologian, William Perkins, fellow of Christ College, who died in 1602. Anyone who reads the writings of early New Englanders learns that Perkins was indeed a towering figure in Puritan eyes. Nor were English and American divines alone in their veneration for him. His works were translated into many languages and circulated in all Reformed communities; he was one of the outstanding pulpit orators of the day, and the seventeenth century, Catholic as well as Protestant, ranked him with Calvin. He was one of the first to smell out the Arminian heresy [26] — "a new devised doctrine of Predestination," he called it — and his works were assailed by Arminius as being the very citadel of the doctrine he opposed. As I read Perkins today, it seems to me that the secret of his fame is primarily the fact that he was a superb popularizer. His books were eminently practical in character. He was typically English in that he was bored by too intricate speculation on a purely theoretical plane, and that he wanted results. Thomas Fuller hit him off with his customary facility when he said that Perkins "brought the schools into the pulpit, and, unshelling their controversies out of their hard school-terms, made thereof plain and wholesome meat for his people." [27] I cannot find that in making wholesome meat out of controversy Perkins added any new doctrines to theology; he is in every respect a meticulously sound and orthodox Calvinist. What he did contribute was an energetic evangelical emphasis; he set out to arouse and inflame his hearers. Consequently, one of his constant refrains was that the minutest, most microscopic element of faith in the soul is sufficient to be accounted the work of God's spirit. Man can start the labor of regeneration as soon as he

[24] Shepard, *Works*, I, 329.
[25] Shepard, *Works*, II, 283.
[26] *Works*, 107–12.
[27] *The Holy State*, book II, chap. x.

begins to feel the merest desire to be saved. Instead of conceiving of grace as some cataclysmic, soul-transforming experience, he whittles it down almost, but not quite, to the vanishing point; he says that it is a tiny seed planted in the soul, that it is up to the soul to water and cultivate it, to nourish it into growth.[28]

This idea was palliative; it lessened the area of human inability and gave the preacher a prod for use on those already, though not too obviously, regenerate. In Perkins' works appear also the rudiments of another idea, which he did not stress particularly, but which in the hands of his students was to be enormously extended. He occasionally speaks of the relationship between God and man as resting on "the Covenant of Grace," and defines this as God's "contract with man, concerning the obtaining of life eternall, upon a certaine condition." [29] He uses the covenant to reinforce his doctrine of the duty that man owes to God of cultivating the slightest seed of grace that he may receive.

The most eminent of Perkins' many disciples was Dr. William Ames, who in 1610 was so prominent a Puritan that he found it advisable to flee to Holland, where he became professor of theology at the University of Franeker. He was the friend and often the master of many of the New England divines, and I have elsewhere claimed for him that he, more than any other one individual, is the father of the New England church polity.[30] Like Perkins, Ames was an orthodox Calvinist. His was a more logical and disciplined mind that that of his teacher, and his great works, the *Medulla Sacrae Theologiae* (1623) and *De Conscientia* (1630), became important textbooks on the Continent, in England, and in New England because of their compact systematization of theology. There is very little difference between his thought and Perkins', except that he accords much more space to the covenant. He sets forth its nature more elaborately, sharply distinguishes the covenants of works and of grace, and provides an outline of the history of the covenant of grace from the time, not of Christ, but of Abraham.[31]

In 1622, John Preston became Master of Emmanuel College, Cambridge. Preston was the statesman, the politician among Puritan divines. He was that Puritan upon whom the Duke of Buckingham showered his favor while fondly endeavoring to delude the Puritans into rallying about his very un-Puritanical banner. Preston had been converted in 1611 by a sermon of John Cotton, and was a close friend of Cotton, Davenport, and Hooker; his works, like those of Perkins, were a mainstay of New England libraries. Like Perkins, he was a magnificent preacher, but he was so active

---

[28] Cf. "A Graine of Mustard Seed," *Works*, 637ff; "A Treatise Tending unto a Declaration Whether a man be in the estate of damantion," 356ff; "A Case of Conscience," 423ff.

[29] *Works*, 32.

[30] *Orthodoxy in Massachusetts* (Cambridge, 1933), chap. VI.

[31] *Medulla*, 101–03.

a man that he published little before his death in 1628. His works were issued posthumously, one of the editors being John Davenport. Thomas Goodwin, later the great Independent leader, was another editor, and in the preface to one volume says that Preston spent his living thoughts and breath "in unfolding and applying, the most proper and peculiar Characters of Grace, which is Gods Image; whereby Beleevers came to be assured, that God is their God, and they in covenant with him." [32] This passage reveals the great contribution of Preston to the development of Calvinist thought, for in the elaborate exegesis which Preston devoted to unfolding and expounding the philosophy of the covenant, which he held to be "one of the main points in Divinitie," [33] he contrived the seeming solution of the problems which then beset his colleagues. His greatest work on this subject (though all his many books deal with it to some extent) was entitled *The New Covenant, or The Saints Portion* (London, 1629). This work is prerequisite to any understanding of thought and theology in seventeenth-century New England.

Another friend of Preston, probably his closest, was Richard Sibbes, preacher at Gray's Inn from 1617 until his death in 1635, and Master of St. Catherine's Hall, Cambridge, from 1626. He, too, was an editor of Preston's work; it was to a sermon of his that John Cotton owed his own conversion, and Davenport and Goodwin edited many volumes of Sibbes's writings after 1635. Throughout these writings the covenant is expounded and all the theology reshaped in the light of this doctrine. One of the fascinating aspects of the history of this idea is the intimate connection that seems to exist among most of its exponents; they form a group bound together by personal ties, and the completed theology is the work of all rather than of any one man. Sibbes was associated with Gouge in the "feofees" scheme; he was the friend and correspondent of Bishop Ussher. He edited a work of John Ball, and one of his students at St. Catherine's was William Strong, who died in 1654, and whose treatise *Of the Covenant* was prepared for the press by Sibbes's friend Lady Elizabeth Rich in 1678. In the work of all these authors the covenant plays a conspicuous part. Furthermore, this group seems to coincide frequently with the coherent group who formulated the peculiar philosophy of Nonseparating Congregationalism.[34] They were students or friends of Ames, whose works they quote frequently. Sibbes owed his conversion to a sermon of Paul Baynes, and he edited Baynes's *Exposition of Ephesians*. There are many ascertainable relations of almost all the school with one or more of the New England divines; their works were read in New England, and Perkins, Ames, Preston, and Sibbes are clearly the most quoted, most respected, and most influential of contemporary authors in the writings and sermons of early Massachusetts. Sibbes revealed his awareness of the Great

[32] *Life Eternall*, A6 recto.
[33] *New Covenant*, 317.
[34] *Orthodoxy in Massachusetts*, 73–102.

Migration in the year 1630 when he said in *The Bruised Reed*: "The gospel's course hath hitherto been as that of the sun, from east to west, and so in God's time may proceed yet further west." [35] Both in the works of all these men, including Cotton, Hooker, Shepard, and Bulkley, and in their lives, there is evidence for asserting that they constituted a particular school, that they worked out a special and peculiar version of theology which has a marked individuality and which differentiates them considerably from the followers of unadulterated Calvinism. And the central conception in their thought is the elaborated doctrine of the covenant.[36]

IV

The word "covenant" as it appears in the Bible presents for the modern scholar a variety of meanings. Possibly suspecting or intuitively sensing these confusions, Luther and Calvin made hardly any mention of the covenant, and the great confessions of sixteenth-century Protestantism avoided it entirely. But with Preston and his friends the word seemed to suggest one simple connotation: a bargain, a contract, a mutual agreement, a document binding upon both signatories, drawn up in the presence of witnesses and sealed by a notary public. Taking "covenant" to mean only this sort of commitment under oath, Preston proceeded, with an audacity which must have caused John Calvin to turn in his grave, to make it the foundation for the whole history and structure of Christian theology. He says:

we will labour to open to you now more clearely, and distinctly, this Couenant; though a difficult thing it is, to deliuer to you cleerely what it is, and those that belong to it; yet you must know it, for it is the ground of all you hope for, it is that that euery man is built vpon, you haue no other ground but this, God hath made a Couenant with you, and you are in Couenant with him.[37]

For all the members of this school, the doctrine of the covenant becomes the scaffolding and the framework for the whole edifice of theology; it is the essence of the program of salvation. As Peter Bulkley phrases it, "Whatsoever salvation and deliverance God gives unto his people, his setting them free from this misery, he doth it by vertue of, and according to his Covenant." [38]

The theology of the covenant of grace, invested with such importance by these authors, proceeds upon a theory of history. It holds that man has not only been in relation to God as creature to creator, subject to lord, but

[35] *Works*, Alexander B. Grossart, ed. (Edinburgh, 1862), I, 100. For interconnections of the group, see Grossart's introduction, I, *passim*.

[36] For the range of the literature of the covenant, and a bibliography of the major titles, see my *The New England Mind: The Seventeenth Century* (Cambridge, 1954), Appendix B, "The Federal School of Theology."

[37] *New Covenant*, 351.

[38] *The Gospel-Covenant, or the Covenant of Grace Opened* (2nd ed., London, 1651), 27.

more definitely through a succession of explicit agreements or contracts, as between two partners in a business enterprise. God entered into such a bond with man as soon as He created him. He stipulated that if Adam performed certain things He would pledge Himself to reward Adam and Adam's posterity with eternal life. In order that man might know what was required of him, Adam was given specific injunctions in the form of the moral law. In addition, the law was implanted in his heart, built into his very being, so that he might perform his duties naturally and instinctively. The original covenant of works, therefore, is the law of nature, that which uncorrupted man would naturally know and by which he would naturally regulate his life. Of course, Adam failed to keep this covenant, and by breaking the bond incurred the just penalties. But God did not rest there. Beginning with Abraham, He made a new covenant, and the seventeenth chapter of Genesis, which describes the new bargain, becomes thereby the basic text for the school. The new covenant is just as much an agreement as its predecessor, stipulating terms on both sides to which the contracting parties are bound:

these words containe the *Covenant* on both sides, sayth the *Lord*, this is the *Covenant* that I will make on my part, *I will be thy God* . . . you shall haue all things in me that your hearts can desire: The *Covenant* againe, that I require on your part, is, that you be *perfect with me*, that you be *upright*, that you be without *hypocrisie*.[39]

The idea of a mutual obligation, of both sides bound and committed by the terms of the document, is fundamental to the whole thought.

It has pleased the great God to enter into a treaty and covenant of agreement with us his poor creatures, the articles of which agreement are here comprised. God, for his part, undertakes to convey all that concerns our happiness, upon our receiving of them, by believing on him. Every one in particular that recites these articles from a spirit of faith makes good this condition.[40]

Furthermore, in form at least, a bargain between two persons with duties on both sides is an arrangement between equals:

he takes *Abraham* as a friend for ever, and *Abraham* takes God as his friend for ever; and this league of friendship implyes not only preservation of affection, but it requires a kinde of secret communication one to another, and a doing one for another.[41]

In the covenant of grace, God, observing the form, contracts with man as with a peer. But since the Fall man is actually unable to fulfil the law or

---

[39] *New Covenant*, 38. The innovation of this theology upon the theology of Calvin becomes apparent when its interpretation of Biblical texts is compared with his. Calvin, for instance, finds no such proposal of terms in Genesis, XVII, but only a statement of the permanence of God's promises (*Institutes*, II, viii, 21; x, 9) or the institution of the sacraments of circumcision and baptism (IV, xvi, 3; xvii, 21–22).

[40] Sibbes, *Works*, I, civ.

[41] John Cotton, *Christ the Fountaine of Life* (London, 1651), 35.

to *do* anything on his own initiative. Therefore God demands of him now not a deed but a belief, a simple faith in Christ the mediator. And on His own side, God voluntarily undertakes, not only to save those who believe, but to supply the power of belief, to provide the grace that will make possible man's fulfilling the terms of this new and easier covenant. "In the Covenant of works a man is left to himselfe, to stand by his own strength; But in the Covenant of grace, God undertakes for us, to keep us through faith." [42] Man has only to pledge that, when it is given him, he will avail himself of the assistance which makes belief possible. If he can believe, he has fulfilled the compact; God then must redeem him and glorify him.

The covenant which God made with Abraham is the covenant of grace, the same in which we are now bound. The only difference is that Abraham was required to believe that Christ would come to be mediator for the covenant and compensate God for the failure of Adam; since Christ we have merely to believe that He has come and that He is the "surety" for the new covenant. But from Abraham to Peter Bulkley the covenant between God and man is one and the same. "We are the children of *Abraham;* and therefore we are under *Abrahams* covenant." [43] This arrangement between the two is not simply a promise on God's part, it is a definite commitment. These authors, in fact, practically do away with the conception of God as merely promising, and substitute a legal theory of God's delivering to man a signed and sealed bond. "It is impertinent to put a difference betweene the promise and the Covenant . . . The promise of God and his Covenant . . . are ordinarily put one for another." [44] The covenant, therefore, is the only method by which God deals with man at all. Salvation is not conveyed by simple election, influence, promise, or choice; it comes only through the covenant and only to those who are in the covenant with God.

> God conveys his salvation by way of covenant, and he doth it to those onely that are in covenant with him . . . this covenant must every soule enter into, every particular soul must enter into a particular covenant with God; out of this way there is no life.[45]

This legalized version of Biblical history may at first sight seem to offer nothing toward a solution of the problems of Calvinism. It may even appear an unnecessarily complicated posing of the same issues, for the grace which gives salvation even in the covenant comes only from God and is at His disposing. But in the hands of these expert dialecticians the account leads to gratifying conclusions. In their view it succeeded in reconciling all con-

---

[42] Bulkley, *Gospel-Covenant*, 86.

[43] Bulkley, *Gospel-Covenant*, 133 (cf. 38, 112–13, 120); Preston, *New Covenant*, 352–53, 357; Hooker, *The Saintes Dignitie* (London, 1651), 104; Cotton, *The Grounds and Ends of the Baptisme of the Children of the Faithfull* (London, 1647), 38; Shepard, *Works*, III, 521.

[44] Cotton, *Grounds and Ends*, 32.

[45] Bulkley, *Gospel-Covenant*, 47; cf. 28.

tradictions, smoothing out all inconsistencies, securing a basis for moral obligation and for assurance of salvation while yet not subtracting from God's absolute power or imposing upon Him any limitations prescribed by merely human requirements.

v

Because a definition of the divine nature must be preliminary to deductions concerning assurance and morality, the problems enumerated may be considered in reverse order. The first effect of the doctrine was to remove the practical difficulty of conceiving of the Deity as a definite character. He might still remain in essence anything or everything, incomprehensible and transcendent. That no longer need concern mankind, for in His contacts with man He has, voluntarily, of His own sovereign will and choice, consented to be bound and delimited by a specific program. He has promised to abide by certain procedures comprehensible to the human intellect. He has not, it is true, sacrificed His sovereignty by so doing; He has not been compelled by any force of reason or necessity. He has merely consented willingly to conform in certain respects to stated methods. For all ordinary purposes He has transformed Himself in the covenant into a God vastly different from the inscrutable Divinity of pure Calvinism. He has become a God chained — by His own consent, it is true, but nevertheless a God restricted and circumscribed — a God who can be counted upon, a God who can be lived with. Man can always know where God is and what He intends. Thus Preston represents the Almighty speaking as He lays down the terms of the covenant:

I will not onely tell thee what I am able to doe, I will not onely expresse to thee in generall, that I will deale well with thee, that I haue a willingnesse and ability to recompence thee, if thou walke before mee and serue me, and bee perfect; but I am willing to enter into Couenant with thee, that is, I will ginde my selfe, I will ingage my selfe, I will enter into bond, as it were, I will not bee at liberty any more, but I am willing euen to make a Couenant, a compact and agreement with thee.[46]

If God speaks to us thus, we then have His own authorization for ceasing to be concerned about His hidden character, His essence, and instead are warranted in assuming that in our experience we will find Him abiding by definite regulations. He will no longer do all the unimaginable things that He can do, but He "will do all things which he hath promised to doe," [47] because the covenant is a mutual bond, and by consenting to it God has committed Himself — "by which God binds us to himselfe, as well as he binds himselfe to us." [48] He is no longer an unpredictable fury that strikes

[46] *New Covenant*, 316.
[47] Bulkley, *Gospel-Covenant*, 276.
[48] Bulkley, *Gospel-Covenant*, 314.

like the lightning without warning or reason — at any rate not in the business of salvation. John Cotton said, professing that he spoke with all reverence, that since the establishment of the covenant, God has become "muffled" as though with a cloak, so that "he cannot strike as he would, . . . he is so compassed about with his nature and property, and Covenant, that he hath no liberty to strike." [49]

As soon as the theologians of this school had explained what a covenant involved, they realized that they had come upon an invaluable opportunity to present the hitherto stern Deity in a new light. The very fact that God allows Himself to become committed to His creature must be in itself some indication of His essential disposition. Hence, if God condescends to treat with fallen man as with an equal, God must be a kindly and solicitous being:

how great a mercie it is, that the glorious God of Heauen and Earth should be willing to enter into *Couenant*, that he should be willing to indent with vs, as it were, that he should be willing to make himselfe a debtor to vs. If we consider it, it is an exceeding great mercie, when wee thinke thus with our selues, he is in heauen, and wee are on earth; hee the glorious God, we dust and ashes; he the Creator, and we but creatures; and yet he is wiling to enter into Couenant, which implyes a kinde of equality betweene vs.[50]

We need no longer torture ourselves trying to imagine a being made up at once of both justice and mercy, because in stooping to the covenant the Lord has shown that His mercy takes command of His justice. He is bearing in mind the frailties and desires of man; He is endeavoring to bind His will and His requirements to suit man's abilities. He tried the covenant of works with Adam, and it failed; He knew, says Preston, that it would fail if He tried it again. "There was no other way to make mankinde partaker of the Couenant of Grace, but onely by faith." [51] He is not aiming directly at His own glory, regardless of man's suffering, but is exerting Himself to secure man's happiness at the same time; His commandments to men "are for their good, and not for his profit." [52] "He stoops to all conditions of men," says Sibbes. "It is a most sweet sign of God's great love, that he will stoop so low as to make a covenant with us." [53] In the same terms the New England ministers expatiated upon God's mercy and condescension as proved by the existence of the covenant. He might easily have dealt with men "without binding himselfe in the bond of Covenant," said Thomas Shepard, "but the Lords heart is so full of love . . . that it cannot

---

[49] *The Way of Life* (London, 1641), 415. Cf. Hooker, *The Application of Redemption* (London, 1659): "Its Gods usual way so to deal not that he is tyed . . . to this manner of dealing upon necessity, but that he hath expressed it to be his good pleasure so to dispense himself" (337).

[50] Preston, *New Covenant*, 330–31.

[51] Preston, *New Covenant*, 364.

[52] Preston, *New Covenant*, 105.

[53] *Works*, VI, 6.

be contained so long within the bounds of secrecy." [54] Therefore Shepard rhapsodized upon the covenant thus:

> Oh the depth of Gods grace herein . . . that when he [man] deserves nothing else but separation from God, and to be driven up and downe the world, as a Vagabond, or as dryed leaves, fallen from our God, that yet the Almighty God cannot be content with it, but must make himselfe to us, and us to himselfe more sure and neer then ever before! [55]

Naturally the burden of these reflections was that man should respond in kind: seeing God no longer harsh and cruel, but full of compassion, man's heart "melts toward the Lord, it relents, it comes to be a soft heart, that is easie and tractable." [56]

Certainly the implacable mystery celebrated in the *Institutes* has been materially transformed by the time He appears as the God of the covenant. He may still be essentially unknowable, but He has told enough about Himself, and betrayed enough of His character, so that He is not an utter blank. His eternal purposes are still "sealed secrets," but in the covenant He has given us more than a glimpse of their direction. "In Gods Covenant and promise we see with open face Gods secret purpose for time past. Gods purposes toward his people being as it were nothing else but promises concealed, & Gods promises in the Covenant being nothing else but his purposes revealed." [57]

Some of the deductions which followed these premises carry us still further from the conventional notion of the Puritan Jehovah. For one thing, the terms of the contract are decidely reasonable. God has not only limited Himself to specific propositions, but to propositions that approve themselves to the intellect. "All the Commandments of God, are grounded upon cleare reason, if we were able to finde it out." [58] By propounding the covenant He has enabled us to find out the clear reason for salvation or reprobation. We do not have to do with "a confused God," Cotton says, one "that vanisheth away in a general imagination, but God distinctly considered," and it is as such that "the Lord giveth himself to Abraham and

---

[54] Preface to Bulkley, *Gospel-Covenant*, B1 recto. Bulkley, in the text of this volume, finds God committed by His covenant not only to mercy, but to ensuring both the success of the Massachusetts Commonwealth — "The Lords end in taking us into covenant with himself, is to make us a happy and blessed people" (194) — and the material prosperity of individuals within the covenant: "for any one to say, I feare I am none of Gods people, because I prosper in the world, is all one as if he should say, I feare the Lord intends me no good, because he makes good unto me the blessings which he hath promised in his Covenant" (299). Cf. John Ball, *A Treatise of Faith* (London, 1632), 63–64, 351, 363; Thomas Cobbett, *A Just Vindication of the Covenant* (London, 1648), 40.

[55] Preface to Bulkley, *Gospel-Covenant*, B1 recto.

[56] Preston, *New Covenant*, 321.

[57] Shepard, Preface to Bulkley, *Gospel-Covenant*, B2 verso.

[58] Preston, *New Covenant*, 32.

his seed." [59] Upon this basis these theologians thought that they could avoid the inconveniences of resting reason and justice upon the fiat of His arbitrary will. An eloquent section in Shepard's *Theses Sabbaticae* is devoted to proving that the particular laws which God has established are also the very laws of reason. Though by virtue of His absolute sovereignty God might have promulgated any laws He chose, those which He has voluntarily invested with moral signficance are exactly the same laws which reason finds ethical, precisely as the terms to which He has voluntarily consented in the covenant are humanly understandable ones. "It is his will and good pleasure to make all laws that are moral to be first good in themselves for all men, before he will impose them upon all men." Goodness is consequently discoverable by right reason; the goodness of a moral law "is nothing else but that comely suitableness and meetness in the thing commanded unto human nature as rational, or unto man as rational, and consequently unto every man." [60] Theoretically God is above and beyond all morality as we formulate it; yet by committing Himself to the covenant God has sanctioned as His law not just any absurdity, but things which are in their own nature suitable, good, and fitting. The difficulty of reconciling God's will with reason vanishes in this interpretation; reasonable justice and His sovereign power of enactment "may kiss each other, and are not to be opposed one to another." [61]

A God who conforms thus cheerfully to reasonable terms must obviously be all-excellent, "and therefore reasonable, he must have the most excellent faculties," [62] and would therefore be such a one as would endeavor also to abide by reason in the ordering and governing of nature. Probably no other tenet reveals so clearly how earnestly these writers were striving to bring Calvinism into harmony with the temper of the seventeenth century. They made their gesture of obedience to the unconfined deity of Calvinism. They prefaced their remarks with the statement that He always *could* interrupt the normal course of nature if He wished to, but they said that a God who voluntarily consented to a covenant would generally, as a matter of choice, prefer to work through the prevailing rules. The realm of natural law, the field of scientific study, and the conception of mathematical principle presented few terrors to this variety of Calvanist.[63] Preston declares: "*God* alters no Law of nature"; nature is not to be feared, it is "to be observed and regarded." [64] One and all, they insisted that God's

---

[59] *A Treatise of the Covenant of Grace* (3rd ed., London, 1671), 6.

[60] Shepard, *Works*, III, 31–37. It should be noted that by "reason" (as Shepard carefully points out) he does not mean reason as it is corrupted by sin, but "right" reason. However, he can pronounce with perfect certainty the rules of right reason by which to test the rationality and so the validity of a moral law (37–41).

[61] Shepard, *Works*, III, 42.

[62] Hooker, *Christs Last Prayer*, 422.

[63] Consequently the federal theologians of Holland were among the earliest adherents of Descartes.

[64] *New Covenant*, 46.

dignity as ruler of the material universe is not curtailed if He be held to operate whenever possible through secondary causes rather than through miracles. He will appear even more admirable if He accomplishes His will by conspiring with nature, governing not the events themselves but the causes of events, without interrupting or jarring the normal process. "We must know, God's manner of guiding things is without prejudice to the proper working of the things themselves. He guideth them sweetly according to the instincts he hath put into them." [65] He may come to the aid of His people by direct interposition in moments of crisis, as in the passing of the Red Sea; more often He will contrive that assistance come by guiding the natural causes,[66] and when He has arranged "a course of means, we must not expect that God should alter his ordinary course of providence for us." [67]

Dr. Ames defined the law of nature as "that order in naturall things . . . common to all things of the very nature of things." [68] Preston stressed still more the inviolability of this order, and on such matters could quote Aristotle as easily as could Thomas Aquinas: "Nature, it cannot be altered againe, for that is the property of Nature, it still stickes by us, and will not be changed, but, as Aristotle observes, throw a stone up a thousand times, it will returne againe, because it is the nature of it to returne." [69] Ames was willing to carry his veneration for law almost to the point of relinquishing miracles. He replies to the "atheist" theory of pure mechanism, not by stressing Biblical marvels, but by insisting that there is more religious inspiration in the daily operations of Providence than in special acts, and that God's power is better demonstrated by His controlling nature without going contrary to it than in turning its course: "The things that are ordinary amongst us, wherein there is no such swarving, but they are constant in their course, doth not *God* guide them and dispose of them as he pleaseth?" [70] So in the government of man, God does not boot him about like a football, but leads him by persuasion and demonstration: "As God hath made man a free agent, so he guides him, and preserves that free manner of working which is agreeable to man's nature." [71] Even in dispensing grace, God does not thrust it abruptly or rudely into the soul. He does not act upon man with unnatural violence, but conveys grace along the ordi-

---

[65] Sibbes, *Works*, I, 204–05.

[66] Cotton, *Christ the Fountaine*, 33. On another occasion Cotton paraphrases "the Philosopher" to this effect: "Miracula sine necessitate sunt multiplicanda" (*Way of the Congregational Churches Cleared*, London, 1648, part I, 42); though the Providence of God is not always predictable, yet "there is a settled order and constancy in that instability, as there is in the motions of the Heavens and heavenly bodies" (*Briefe Exposition upon the Whole Book of Ecclesiastes*, London, 1654, 66).

[67] Sibbes, *Works*, I, 225.

[68] *Medulla*, 40–41.

[69] *The New Creature* (London, 1633), 97.

[70] *Life Eternall*, 33.

[71] Sibbes, *Works*, I, 197.

nary channels; He contrives that it come to man in the regular course of events:

for he doth in the worke of grace, as he doth in the worke of nature. . . . *God* carries all things to their end, by giving them a nature suitable to that end. An Archer makes an impression vpon an Arrow, but it is a violent impression; *God* carrier every thing to that end, to which he hath appointed it; but with this difference, that he makes not a violent impression, . . . & therefore he doth it not by an onely immediate hand of his owne, as we doe, but he causeth the Creature to goe on of it selfe, to this or to that purpose, to this or that end. And so he doth in the worke of grace; he doth not carry a man on to the wayes of righteousnesse, leaving him in the state of nature, taking him as he is, but he takes away that heart of his, and imprints the habits of grace in it, & he changeth a mans heart, so that he is carried willingly to the wayes of *God*, as the Creature is carried by a naturall instinct to its own place, or to the thing it desires.[72]

Normally the instruments by which He engenders faith in an individual are the sermons of ministers and the sacraments of the church. These ordinances, it should be noted, are not in themselves the causes of faith, they are simply the "means." Though God is at perfect liberty to summon a man by a direct call, in the vast majority of cases He will work upon him through these secondary causes. When the sound of the preacher's voice comes to the ear, and the sense of his words to the mind, then by that means the Spirit comes into the soul, "either to convert thee, or to confound thee." [73] The physical impressions are not to be confused with grace itself. Nevertheless they are almost always the indispensable vehicles of grace: "they are meanes to convey grace, mercy and comfort from Christ to our Soules. Though they are not meat, yet they are as dishes that bring the meat. . . . These are the conduits to convey this water of life." [74] Therefore Cotton expressed the theory of sermonizing in New England when he said: "While we are thus speaking to you, God many times conveys such a spirit of grace into us, as gives us power to receive Christ. . . . The word that we speake conveyes spirit and life vnto . . . [you]." [75] The grace of God is still theoretically free as the wind to blow where it listeth, but in most instances it is channelized in a sequence of causes that are understandable on a natural — we might almost say, in the jargon of today — "behavioristic" plane.

VI

The historical theory of the covenant of grace, its progressive unfolding from Abraham to the Christian era, permitted these theologians to add the final touches to their portrait of the divine character. God did not

[72] Preston, *New Covenant*, 118.
[73] Hooker, *The Soules Exaltation* (London, 1638), 27–28.
[74] Hooker, *The Soules Humiliation* (London, 1638), 59–60.
[75] *Christ the Fountaine*, 174.

simply present the covenant point-blank to fallen man, but introduced it
by degrees, unfolding it gradually as men could be educated up to it. The
beginnings of this conception are to be found in Ames, and it was probably
his chief contribution to the system. He said that though from the time of
Abraham there has been one and the same covenant, "yet the manner . . .
of administring this new Covenant, hath not alwayes beene one and the
same, but divers according to the ages in which the Church hath been
gathered." [76] While other writers in the school sometimes drew up charts
of the stages different from Ames's,[77] all agreed that God has allowed the
covenant to grow with time. He first administered it through conscience,
then through the prophets and ceremonies, now through Christ, preaching of the Word, and the sacraments. He has done this, the writers agreed,
out of solicitous consideration for man's limitations; had the whole thing
been enunciated to Abraham, it would have put too great a strain upon his
faith, already overburdened as it was in the effort to believe that Sarah
would conceive. " Dr. *Ames* saith well," Bulkley wrote, "the Church was
then considered . . . Partly as an heire, and partly as an infant" [78] By
the long period of tuition in the covenant in its Old Testament form, the
church was educated up to grasping it clearly and distinctly:

the nature of man is so exceeding opposite to the doctrine of Christ and the
Gospel, that if it had not been long framed by the tutoring of many hundred
yeers by the Law, it had never been convinced of the necessitie of salvation of
Christ, and the Gospel.[79]

The effect of this theory was to introduce an element of historical relativ-
ity into the absolute dogmatism of original Calvinism. God is seen deliberately refraining from putting His decisions fully into effect until man can
cope with them and profit by them. He is not so much a mail-clad seigneur
as a skillful teacher, and He contrives on every hand that men may be
brought to truth, not by compulsion, but by conviction. For these reasons
theologians of this complexion were eagerly disposed to prize knowledge,
logic, metaphysics, and history. They were prepared to go as far as their
age could go in the study of Biblical history and commentary, for truth to
them resided in the history as well as in the doctrine. Preston confesses that
intellectual persuasion and historical research are not in themselves sufficient for absolute faith in the Scriptures unless God also "infuseth an inward light by his Spirit to worke this faith." Yet even so he holds that sufficient testimonies exist in the Scriptures "to give evidence of themselves." [80]
Knowledge is not to be despised because faith also is necessary: "Wisedome

[76] *Medulla*, 170. Probably as a result of his teaching, Cocceius particularly stressed
the evolutionary theory, and in Holland more energies were devoted to this aspect of
the doctrine than in New England.

[77] *Medulla*, 38–42, 170ff; cf. Sibbes, *Works*, VI, 4.

[78] *Gospel-Covenant*, 118.

[79] Hooker, *Saintes Dignitie*, 105.

[80] *Life Eternall*, 57.

is the best of all vaine things under the Sunne." [81] Knowledge and faith must go hand in hand:

I deny not but a man may haue much knowledge, and want Grace; but, on the other side, looke how much Grace a man hath, so much knowledge he must haue of necessity. . . . You cannot haue more Grace than you haue knowledge.[82]

It is a significant indication of the bent of his mind that Preston argues for the reliability of Scripture because heathen histories corroborate Old Testament chronology.[83]

To describe this theology as "rationalism" would be very much to overstate the case; before the triumph of Newtonian science reason did not have the rigid connotation it was later to carry. Preston drew back from out-and-out mechanism, and he never doubted that even where God was steering events by the rudder of causation, He was charting the course according to His own pleasure. But in this way of thought appears an entering wedge of what must be called, if not rationalism, then reasonableness. It is a philosophy that put a high valuation upon intellect. Its tendency is invariably in the direction of harmonizing theology with natural, comprehensible process. The authors were prepared to welcome the scientific advance of the century with open arms, until some of their successors in the next century were to realize too late that they had let the wooden horse of rationalism into the Trojan citadel of theology. But thus early there were few misgivings; the Puritans were so secure in their faith that they could with perfect serenity make it as understandable as possible. It we today insist upon supposing that their philosophy was an absolute authoritarianism, we ought to be very much disconcerted by their continual appeals to experience and reason, appeals which, from our point of view, imply assumptions altogether at variance with those of the creed. John Winthrop, in his manuscript debate with Vane in 1637, took it as axiomatic that man is a reasonable creature, and his statement of political theory in these papers owes more to logic than to the Word of God.[84] Thomas Hooker constantly reinforced a dogma by such statements as that it "hath reason and common sense to put it beyond gainsaying," or that to deny it "is to go against the experience of all ages, the common sense of all men"; and Samuel Stone eulogized his colleague because "He made truth appear by light of reason," [85] Professor Morison has found that

[81] *New Covenant*, 155.

[82] *New Covenant*, 446.

[83] *Life Eternall*, 55. He instances Alexander Polyhistor, Josephus, Cyril, "Chaldee Historians," Diodorus Siculus, Strabo, Xenophon, "The Tables of Ptolemy, lately found." Cf. George Phillips, *A Reply to a Confutation* (London, 1645): "The Argument from humane authority is as easily rejected as propounded, though otherwise much good use may be made of their writing" (119).

[84] Thomas Hutchinson, *A Collection of Original Papers Relative to the History of the Massachusetts Bay* (Prince Society Publications), I, 79ff.

[85] *A Survey of the Summe of Church Discipline* (London, 1648), part I, 50, 79, C3 recto.

Elnathan Chauncy, while an undergraduate at Harvard in the 1660's, copied into his commonplace book the remark, "Truth and the rational soule are twins." According to the conventional notions of New England Calvinism this would seem to be somewhat startling. In view, however, of the disposition of the covenant theology, this truism was as appropriate to young Chauncy's background as some admonition concerning the integration of complexes might be to the undergraduate of today. Such passages make it increasingly clear that our notions of the Puritan philosophy, derived in the main from a casual acquaintance with "Calvinism," are in need of drastic reconsideration.

VII

Setting forth from the nature of God as defined by the covenant, these theologians enjoyed clear sailing to the haven of assurance. The covenant of grace defines the conditions by which Heaven is obtained, and he who fulfills the conditions has an incontestable title to glorification, exactly as he who pays the advertised price owns his freehold. God may continue to choose the elect in the impenetrable fastness of His will, but according to the covenant He has agreed to give the individual descernible grounds for His decision; He is bound to bestow salvation only upon those who achieve the qualifications, and, conversely, those who acquire the qualifications are absolutely certain of their salvation:

if thou beleeue, it is certaine then, thou art within the Couenant. . . . If thou canst finde this now, that thou art able to take *Iesus Christ*, to take him as a Lord and *Sauiour*, thou art able to beleeue all the Couenant of Grace, thou art by that put into the Couenant.[86]

And to be really in the covenant is to be through with all doubts and misgivings: "If ever thou are in covenant with *God*, and hast this seale in thy soule, that there is a change wrought in thee by the covenant, then thy election is sure." [87] The union with God is not torturing uncertainty, it is not a ravishing of the surprised soul by irresistible grace, unexpected and undeserved; it is a definite legal status, based on a *quid pro quo*, an "if I believe" necessitating a "you have to save me." God's will is originally free to pick and choose in any fashion, but once the covenant is drawn up, He no longer acts without a reason, He does not appear to man as a brutal or capricious tyrant. He is bound by certain commitments; He is compelled to play the game of salvation according to ascertained rules.

God comes and sayes; For my owne sake will I do thus and thus unto you in an absolute promise; here is a ground for the faith of adherence to cleave unto. . . . There be also conditionall promises, (*He that believeth shall be saved*) by meanes

[86] Preston, *New Covenant*, 390.
[87] Preston, *Life Eternall*, part II, 84.

of which (we having the experience and feeling of such grace in our selves) we grow to an assurance that we are of those that he will shew that free grace upon.[88]

The contract between God and man, once entered into, signed by both parties and sealed, as it were, in the presence of witnesses, is ever afterwards binding. This exceedingly legal basis furnishes the guarantee, not only for the assurance of the saints, but even for their perseverance. In the covenant, says Hooker, the soul "is inseparably knit to Christ"; [89] though you falter in action and fall short of holiness, if you have once become a member of the covenant, the covenant "doth remain sure and firm," said John Cotton. "If we be hemm'd in within this Covenant, we cannot break out." [90]

Thus bound by His own commitment, God must live up to His word. If you do your part, He must, willy-nilly, do His. As Bulkley says, "He hath passed over those things by covenant, and he cannot be a covenant breaker"; hence, "we might have the more strong consolation, assuring ourselves of the fulfilling of his gracious promise towards us." [91] Pursuing this logic, these men broached one of their most daring ideas: if a man can prove that he has faith, he has then done his part and can hold God to account, hale Him into court and force Him to give what has become the man's just and legal due: "You may sue him of his own bond written and sealed, and he cannot deny it." [92]

when faith hath once gotten a promise, be sure that thou keepe thy hold, pleade hard with the *Lord*, and tell him it is a part of his Couenant, and it is impossible that he should deny thee . . . when thou art on a sure ground, take no denyall, though the *Lord* may defer long, yet he will doe it, he cannot chuse; for it is a part of his Couenant.[93]

We do not surrender ourselves to God without getting something in return: "we require this back againe of God, that as we give up our selves a sacrifice to him, so that the Lord Jesus Christ might be imputed unto us." [94] If we are in the covenant, "we are then out of danger, wee need not to fear." [95] Considering what the background of Protestant thought had been, what ruthless determination had been postulated behind the predestinating Divinity, one might well feel that Preston comments upon this conception of salvation with an understatement that is almost comic: "This is a very comfortable doctrine, if it be well considered." [96]

[88] Bulkley, *Gospel-Covenant*, 323–24.
[89] *Soules Exaltation*, 8.
[90] *The Covenant of Gods Free Grace* (London, 1645), 18.
[91] *Gospel-Covenant*, 321.
[92] Preston, *New Creature*, 23.
[93] Preston, *New Covenant*, 477.
[94] Cotton, *Christ the Fountaine*, 32.
[95] Cotton, *The Covenant of Gods Free Grace*, 18.
[96] *New Creature*, 23.

The covenant theory admitted into the official theology many ideas that bade fair to undermine it entirely, and this idea, that man can by fulfilling terms extort salvation from God, might well seem the most incongruous. But at the moment the authors were confident that they had skillfully incorporated the new device into the old orthodoxy. Their account does not deny that God and God alone elects or rejects according to His mere pleasure; the grace which enables us to fulfill the covenant still comes from above, and only God knows whether we have it or not. But in practical life the dogmatic rigors of absolute predestination are materially softened. A juridical relationship is slyly substituted for the divine decree. Men cannot trace the private thought of God, but since God has agreed to manifest what He thinks concerning certain persons in an explicit bond, the individual has a way of knowing that much of the divine determination: "Now we can never know the things which are given unto us of God, but by knowing of the covenant which conveys all the blessings which God doth impart unto his people." [97] Stating the theory of predestination within this frame shifts the point of view from that maintained by Calvin. We no longer contemplate the decrees in the abstract, as though they were relentlessly grinding cosmic forces, crushing or exalting souls without regard for virtue or excellence; instead we are free to concentrate our attention upon what immediately concerns us. We do not have to ask whether God be ours; we need ask only whether we be God's. Sibbes presented this reversal in emphasis most clearly, though it can be found consciously recognized in the works of all the covenant theologians. A man has no grounds, he says, to trouble himself about God's election as it exists in God's own mind. "It is not my duty to look to God's secret counsel, but to his open offer, invitation, and command, and thereupon to adventure my soul." [98] To commence from the unfathomable election in the mind of God and endeavor then to discover if it pertains to oneself is the wrong procedure; one should begin with oneself, one's own response to God's proffered covenant, and argue from the degree of one's success in fulfilling it the fact of one's being chosen.

Some are much troubled, because they proceed by a false method and order in judging their estates. They will begin with election, which is the highest step of the ladder; whereas they should begin from a work of grace wrought within their hearts. . . . Otherwise it is as great folly as in removing of a pile of wood, to begin at the lowest first, and so, besides the needless trouble, to be in danger to have the rest to fall upon our heads.[99]

In fact, Sibbes carried this argument so far that he can actually tell men to reach out for the covenant, to promise to abide by it, to take it upon themselves, before they have had any recognizable experience of regeneration. If they can succeed, they can very probably secure faith, not only by prayer

---

[97] Bulkley, *Gospel-Covenant*, 182.
[98] *Works*, I, 266.
[99] *Works*, I, 137.

and fasting, but by demanding that God reward them according to His bond.

The way, therefore, will be to put this into the condition of your promise now, and prayer after. Lord, I have promised this; but thou knowest I cannot perform the promise I have made, and the condition thou requirest, of myself. But in the covenant of grace, thou hast said that thou wilt make good the condition . . . If we come with sincere hearts, and with resolution to please God, we may look for all the promises of God. All that he hath promised he is ready to perform, if we in faith can allege the promise.[100]

The covenant made it possible to argue that while God elects whom He pleases, He is pleased to elect those who catch Him in His plighted word, and that it is up to fallen man to do so. The subtle casuistry of this dialectic is altogether obvious. Yet the spectacle of these men struggling in the coils of their doctrine, desperately striving on the one hand to maintain the subordination of humanity to God without unduly abasing human values, and on the other hand to vaunt the powers of the human intellect without losing the sense of divine transcendence, vividly recreates what might be called the central problem of the seventeenth century as it was confronted by the Puritan mind.

VIII

These considerations as to the grounds of assurance paved the way for the supreme triumph of the school — the establishment of a code of ethics and of moral obligation. In two respects they could achieve this end: first, by partial rehabilitation of natural man, and second, by incorporating moral effort into the terms of the covenant. For in this theory man as well as God is no longer left in precisely the state decreed by original Calvinism. God is seen condescending to behave by reason because in man there exists at least a potential rationality. Calvin himself had admitted that in depraved man lingered some remnants of the divine image in which Adam had been created, but, as we have seen, he held them too feeble to be of any use. The federal theologians also held that these remains, in the form of natural reason or "the light of nature," were exceedingly unreliable, but they rescued them from the rubbish heap where Calvin had cast them. Perkins remained fairly close to Calvin on this question, but in Ames there are signs of the development. While repeating the usual dictum upon the deterioration of human nature, he points out that in all men some knowledge of truth is written in the heart, that a rudimentary inclination to goodness is found in the will, so that men pursue at least "shadowes" of virtue, and that we can learn enough from contemplating the natural universe to conclude, without the aid of revelation, that God exists and is to be worshipped.[101] In the work of Preston the importance of these

[100] *Works*, VI, 24–25.
[101] *Medulla*, 56–57, 60–61, 63, 219.

"remains" is considerably accentuated. This achievement was greeted with hosannas by some of his contemporaries, one of his editors boasting that while his *Life Eternall* emblazons the glory of the Divine Essence, at the same time it delineates "the most noble dispositions of the Divine Nature in us, which are the prints and imitations of those his attributes." [102] Preston's sermons frequently remind his hearers that the soul, though fallen, "is the Image of the Essence of God," that it possesses both understanding (which in these discussions is used synonymously with "reason") and will, so that man "understands all things, and wils whatsoever he pleaseth." [103] The speculative faculty he defines as "that by which we know and judge aright concerning God and morall vertues," and its decisions are corroborated by the natural conscience and an innate inclination in the will:

There is in naturall men not onely a light to know that this is good, or not good, and a Conscience to dictate; this you must doe, or not doe, but there is even an Inclination in the will and affections, whereby men are provoked to doe good, and to oppose the Evill. And therefore the proposition is true, that naturall men have some truths, because they have this Inclination remaining, even in the worst of them.[104]

As a matter of fact, Preston comes startlingly close to agreeing at times with Lord Herbert of Cherbury; all that the *De Veritate* says man may know by the unassisted use of reason, the Puritan author would admit; he differs from the father of English deism only in feeling that these conclusions are not quite enough in themselves for a religious man to live by:

when such a man knowes there is an almighty power, by his naturall wit, hee is able to deduce, if there be a God, I must behave my selfe well towards him, I must feare him as God, I must be affected to him as God, I must worship him with all reverence as God; but the most ignorant man confesses there is a God, no Nation denyes it.[105]

[102] *Life Eternall*, A7 recto.
[103] *Life Eternall*, 15.
[104] *The Saints Qualification* (London, 1633), 129.
[105] *The Saints Qualification*, 222. How far the covenant thought had strayed from pristine Calvinism is nowhere better illustrated than in the contrast between Preston and Calvin on this very question of the "remains." What Preston says every man can know by nature Calvin says has at best been barely guessed by only the wisest of philosophers, and even their glimmerings are of no value, because they are overwhelmed in a mountain of falsehoods. "Human reason, then, neither approaches, nor teaches, nor directs its views toward this truth, to understand who is the true God, or in what character he will manifest himself to us" (*Institutes*, II, ii, 18). Calvin does grant that in secular realms — civil polity, domestic economy, mechanical arts, and liberal sciences — reason is capable of discovering good principles. But his explanation for this ability indicates the immense gulf between his thought and Preston's: the achievements of reason in any of these respects result from the talents possessed by occasional individuals, and these are temporary gifts bestowed here and there by God, not instances of an inherent ability still remaining in the soul (*Institutes*, II, ii, 12–17). Calvin is arguing for the utter incapacity of nature, relieved by occasional grants of power bestowed at the mere pleasure of an arbitrary sovereign. Preston is arguing

Even when he insists that something more is necessary to man than the deductions of natural wit, Preston does not view them as antagonistic to faith. Imperfect as they are, they do not run contrary to supernatural illumination. Within the sphere of demonstration, for instance, the evidence of the senses is sound, Calvin to the contrary notwithstanding:

> Of all demonstrations of reason that we have to prove things, nothing is so firme as that which is taken from sense: to prove the fire is hot, we feele it hot, or honey to be sweet, when we taste it to be sweet: There is no reason in the world makes it so firme as sense: As it is true in these cases, so it is an undoubted truth in Divinity, that in all matters of sense, sense is a competent judge.[106]

Faith may be above reason, but since reason comes as directly from God as does revelation, there can be no conflict between them:

> But, you will say, faith is beyond sense and reason, it is true, it is beyond both, but it is not contrary to both; faith teacheth nothing contrary to reason, for sense and reason are Gods workes as well as grace, now one worke of God doth not destroy another.[107]

Seen in this light, the imperfections of the human mind are not so much a vitiation resulting from sin, as simply the limitations under which a finite being inevitably labors. Confined in time and space, we cannot conceivably "see all the wheeles, that are in every businesse," or if we do see them, we are "not able to turne euery wheele." [108] In these purely physical terms Preston occasionally interprets original sin, and ideas of this sort can be matched in all the writings upon the covenant. Sibbes declares that "the soul of man, being an understanding essence, will not be satisfied and settled without sound reason"; [109] and Thomas Hooker defines man as "a living creature indued with a reasonable soul." [110] Thomas Shepard interpreted the law of nature as "all that which is agreeable and suitable to natural reason, and

---

for an innate and universal capacity in nature to achieve some good things in and by itself, even though the capacity is imperfect and can not reach to the attainment of salvation. Cf. Hooker, *Application of Redemption* (142): "The Lord hath left in thee the remainder of many natural abilities, hath lent thee the help of many common Gifts and Graces, which by Art and Education have grown to some ripeness." Hooker goes as fas as to assert that in the human will, considering it "merely as it ariseth from the power of those natural principles whereof its made," there exist certain principles "which were at the first imprinted upon it," and which naturally incline it "to close with God" (*Application of Redemption*, 369).

[106] *The Cuppe of Blessing* (London, 1633), 10. Cf. Calvin: "Are all our industry, perspicacity, understanding and care so depraved, that we cannot conceive or meditate anything that is right in the sight of God? . . . In the estimation of the Holy Spirit . . . such a representation is consistent with the strictest truth" (*Institutes*, II, ii, 25).

[107] *Cuppe of Blessing*, 12–13.

[108] Preston, *New Covenant*, 565.

[109] *Works*, I, 409.

[110] *Survey*, part I, 44.

that from a natural innate equity in the thing," and taught that it is made known "either by divine instruction or human wisdom." [111] If rightly managed, the results of research, logic, and demonstration will therefore coincide with the teaching of Scripture, and should be held in almost as great esteem by Christians.

If traces of the image of God are still to be found in the soul, they should even more clearly be manifested in the material universe, where all can decipher them if they will. "The heavens are the worke of his hands, and they declare it, and every man understands their language." [112] "When a man lookes on the great volume of the world, there those things which God will have known, are written in capital letters." [113] Quite apart from faith, therefore, there are two important sources of truth to which man has immediate access: himself and his experience of the world. Hence, secular knowledge — science, history, eloquence, wisdom (purely natural wisdom) — is doubly important for these Puritans; for knowledge is not only useful, it is a part of theology. Of course, the writers are always careful to stipulate, we must have Scripture to supplement the discovery of God in nature and Providence, but having made that concession, they go on valiantly to exonerate the study of nature from the charge of obscuring the religious goal, and confidently press it into the service of theology. They insist that we can reach God through science as well as through revelation:

For, though I said before, that Divinity was revealed by the *Holy Ghost*, yet there is this difference in the points of *Theologie*: Some truths are wholly revealed, and have no foot-steps in the creatures, no prints in the creation, or in the works of *God*, to discerne them by, and such are all the mysteries of the *Gospell*, and of the *Trinitie*: other truths there are, that have some *vestigia*, some characters stamped upon the creature, whereby wee may discerne them, and such is this which we now have in hand, that, *There is a God*.[114]

"The workes of Nature are not in vaine," [115] and it behooves us to study them with as much care and precision as the Bible:

Can we, when we behold the stately theater of heaven and earth, conclude other but that the finger, arms, and wisdom of God hath been here, although we see him not that is invisible, and although we know not the time when he began to build? Every creature in heaven and earth is a loud preacher of this truth. Who set those candles, those torches of heaven, on the table? Who hung out those lan-

---

[111] *Works*, III, 177. Cf. Cotton, *A Practical Commentary upon the First Epistle Generall of John* (London, 1656): "Though the Law of Nature was more dimly and darkly known, *Moses* Law was but a new draught of the Law of Nature in innocency. Heathen law givers, Philosophers, and Poets have expressed the effect of all the commandements save the tenth" (234).
[112] Preston, *Saints Qualification*, 130
[113] Preston, *Saints Qualification*, 182.
[114] Preston, *Life Eternall*, 4–5.
[115] Preston, *Life Eternall*, 15.

terns in heaven to enlighten a dark world? . . . Who taught the birds to build their nests, and the bees to set up and order their commonwealth? [116]

Shepard pronounced a flat condemnation upon those who would cast the law of nature from the domain of theology merely because it is not so perfect today as at the creation; these, he said, "do unwarily pull down one of the strongest bulwarks." [117]

The theologians were treading on dangerous ground at this point; they were perilously close to talking Arminianism. But in their own opinion they were still safe. They were carrying the frontiers of reason to the very boundaries of faith, yet they were not allowing them to encroach. They were careful to point out that regeneration cannot come by the intellect without the inspiration of grace, at the same time adding that the road to grace is also the highway of knowledge. They denied that faith imparts any new doctrines or enlarges the scope of the understanding; the doctrine, as such, can be grasped by anyone. "They may be enlightened to understand all the truths of God; there is no Truth we deliver to you, but an unregenerate man may understand it wholly, and distinctly, and may come to some measure of approbation." [118] Consequently, though by understanding alone no man may achieve salvation, any man does by nature learn so much of God's law that he cannot plead ignorance as an excuse for not obeying it. Here was indeed a triumph in the justifying of God's ways to man! Natural knowledge, such as all men can attain, cannot make a man holy, but it can at least render him inexcusable, and God is exculpated from the charge of injustice in His condemnations. An individual may not be able to deliver himself from the bondage of sin, but in the meantime he can be held personally responsible for doing what the light of nature teaches him is wrong.

It is true, a man hath not power to performe these, but yet withall, I say, he hath power to doe those things, upon the neglect of which, God denyes him ability to beleeve and repent: So that, it is true, though a man cannot beleeve and repent, and neverthelesse for this is condemned; yet withall take this with you, there be many precedent Acts, which a man hath in his liberty to doe, or not to doe, by which he tyes God, and deserves this Iustly, that God should leave him to himselfe, and deny him ability of beleeving and repenting. [119]

Because man still has reason, and reason is not utterly decayed, he has the power to recognize the good, to know when he sins, and to desire a better

[116] Shepard, *Works*, I, 10.

[117] Shepard, *Works*, III, 178.

[118] Preston, *Saints Qualification*, 152.

[119] Preston, *Saints Qualification*, 225. It should be noted that the idea of the law of nature being written in the heart sufficiently to render men inexcusable is good Calvinist doctrine (*Institutes*, II, ii, 22–25); but in Calvin natural knowledge of natural law serves *only* this use. It is of no validity for any further regulation of life, and it is incapable of formulating an ideal of righteousness; it merely exists to make men know they have fallen short of something which they can not even conceive.

life. By thus reasserting a distinct validity for the natural reason, the federal theologians took a long stride forward, entailing an obligation upon natural man to aspire toward moral perfection.

But when a reasonable creature lookes on a thing as *Eligible* or *non Eligible*, and not only so, but is able to reason on both sides, is able to see arguments for both, that makes it differ from Spontaneity, when there is no outer impediment, when you may take or refuse it, when you have Arguments to reason, and see the commodity and discommodity of it, your will is now free, so that I may truly affirme every man hath a free-will to doe that, for the not doing of which he is condemned.[120]

In accordance with their disposition to enlarge the sphere and opportunities of natural reason, the authors redefined, or rather redescribed, the nature of grace itself. They did not forget that grace is an influx from the supernatural, but they preferred to concentrate upon its practical operations in the individual, and to conceive of it, not as a flash of supernal light that blinded the recipient, but as a reinvigoration of slumbering capacities already existing in the unregenerate soul. As in the ruins of a palace, so runs one of their favorite metaphors, the materials still exist, but the "order" is taken away; grace reëstablishes the order by rebuilding with the same materials.[121] Or as another image has it, natural promptings, passions, and desires are like the wind; holiness is the rudder. "So Nature, the strength of nature, affections, or whatsoever they be, are like the wind to drive the ship, thou mayst retaine them, only godliness must sit at the Sterne." [122] Grace, once infused into the soul, becomes itself "natural," just as when a man has learned to play a lute, the instrument becomes second nature to him; "so is this, it is planted in the heart, as the senses are, it is infused into the Soule, and then we exercise the operations of it; so that it is another Nature, it is just as the thing that is naturall." [123] Hence the faith preached in early New England was not the violent convulsion of the camp meeting, but the exercise, under divine guidance, of reason and virtue. Thomas Hooker conceived that "the main principall cause of faith is rather an assisting power working upon, than any inward principall put into the soule to worke of its self." [124] In this description, faith emerges, not as prostration on the road to Damascus, but as reason elevated. It enables us to see existing truths exactly as a telescope reveals new stars:

and therefore they are said to be *revealed*, not because they were not before, as if the revealing of them gave a being unto them; but, even as a new light in the night discovers to us that which we did not see before, and as a prospective glasse

[120] Preston, *Saints Qualification*, 224–25.
[121] Preston, *New Covenant*, 62.
[122] Preston, *New Creature*, 129.
[123] Preston, *New Creature*, 95–96.
[124] *Soules Exaltation*, 29.

reveales to the eye, that which we could not see before, and by its own power, the eye could not reach unto.[125]

Faith does not require acquiescence in irrationalities, but empowers us to believe thoroughly in that which we can also accept intellectually. Faith is not intoxication, it is education.

Faith addeth to the eye of reason, and raiseth it higher; for the understanding is conversant, as about things of reason, so also about things of Faith; for they are propounded to the understanding, only they are above it, and must have faith to reveale them. . . . as one that hath dimme eyes, he can see better with the help of spectacles: even so doth the eye of reason, by a supernaturall faith infused. So that all the things which wee beleeve, have a credibilitie and entity in them, and they are the objects of the understanding; but we cannot finde them out, without some supernatural help.[126]

Consequently, once more, "faith teacheth nothing contrary to sense and reason." [127] Preston appears the most audacious of the school in this intellectualizing of grace, but his friends in New England were not far behind him. Shepard, for example, declared that God does not work upon believers as upon blocks, propelling them by an "immediate" act, because believers are rational creatures and therefore capable of acting as rational creatures. Grace is the renewal of God's image in them, "like to the same image which they had in the first creation, which gave man some liberty and power to act according to the will of Him that created him." [128] Hooker said that after grace has done its work and removed the obstructions of sin, "now Conscience is in commission and hath his scope, & the coast is now clear that reason may be heard." [129] According to this theology, the regenerate life is the life of reason.

This line of argument indicates a predisposition in the minds of early New England theologians to minimize the power of original sin, so that by pointing out the advantages which all men inherently possess, they could at least hold the unregenerate responsible for their own damnation. As far as we have followed them at this point, their conclusions concerning what remains of God's image in man since the Fall resulted simply from their strong bent toward making the most of what reasonable elements they could find in the original doctrine of Calvin, and thus far did not necessarily involve the covenant theory. But from the theory they were able to derive an ingenious support for their contentions, to construct a theoretical basis for maintaining that the image of God in man was not so hopelessly debauched as Calvin had imagined. For by conceiving the relationship between man and God as a contract, the sin of Adam appeared in a

[125] Preston, *Life Eternall*, 21.
[126] Preston, *Life Eternall*, 46–47.
[127] Preston, *Cuppe of Blessing*, 13.
[128] Shepard, *Works*, III, 96–97.
[129] Hooker, *Application of Redemption*, 556.

new light. Adam in his disobedience had broken a bond, had violated a lease. The punishment which he received as a consequence was not deterioration so much as it was the infliction of a judicial sentence; it was expulsion for nonpayment, it was not inherent pollution. It was just such a disability as a man would suffer who was under sentence for embezzlement or defalcation. Adam had stood as the agent, the representative of all men, the "federal" head of the race. When he, as the spokesman for man in the covenant, broke it and incurred the penalty for disobedience, it was imputed to his constituents as a legal reponsibility, not as an inherent disease. These writers did not openly deny that all men were by birth partners in Adam's guilt, as Augustine had said and Calvin [130] had repeated after him, but they were very much inclined to give lip service to this historic theory of transmission and then concentrate upon their own version of legal imputation. Both theories at once are outlined by Ames,[131] and amplified by Preston, who argues that men are corrupted first because they come from Adam's loins, but secondly and more importantly because they, as the heirs of Adam, have imputed to them the blame for breach of covenant.

There being a compact and covenant betweene God and him, that if Adam stood, all his seed should stand with him; but if he fell, then that all that were borne of him should by vertue of that covenant, compact, or agreement have his sinne imputed to them, and so should be corrupted, as hee was, and die the death.[132]

Hooker in turn preached the double doctrine that men inherit a fallen nature from Adam but also incur the legal penalty for his failure as their agent: "Adam in innocencie represented all mankind, he stood (as a Parliament man doth for the whole country) for all that should be born of him." [133] Shepard taught that this was justice itself, "it being just, that as if he standing, all had stood, by imputation of his righteousness, so he falling, all should fall, by the imputation of his sin." [134] Original sin in this version becomes something like the poverty and disgrace a young man might suffer if his father were executed for treason and the estate confiscated. Such an explanation for the persistence of original sin seemed to these lawyer-like theologians more intelligent, more in keeping with the manners of a God who dealt with men through legal covenants. Man is born owing God a debt; his creditor compounds with him, making a new agreement out of consideration for his bankrupt state. When man fulfills the new and easier terms, the debt is canceled. Though the debt is a serious hindrance to man's freedom of action, it is not an utterly crushing burden, and it does

[130] There is no suspicion of the legal imputation theory in Calvin (see *Institutes*, II, i, 7–8).

[131] *Medulla*, 67.

[132] Preston, *New Creature*, 19.

[133] *Saintes Dignitie*, 29.

[134] *Works*, I, 344.

not entirely obliterate the qualities of reason and intelligence he possessed before he acquired it. So something of these qualities remains in him, enough to make him inexcusable for a neglect of God's law, enough to leave him no defense if he fails in moral effort, particularly since God in the covenant has condescended to deal with him by appealing to precisely these qualities and ordering the scheme of salvation in just such a fashion as he can understand by virtue of them.[135]

IX

Thus the federal theory, freeing man from the absolute moral impotence of the strict doctrine, first made possible an enlargement of his innate capacities. Second, it provided a logical device for immediately enlisting these capacities in the service of morality, even before they had been further invigorated by divine grace. It had been with these considerations in mind that God framed the covenant precisely as He did, and thereby demonstrated His cleverness by devising a scheme to insure the continuation of moral obligation even in a covenant of forgiveness. He did not discard the covenant of works after Adam's fall; He included it within the covenant of grace. "For the Morall Law, the Law of the ten Commandments, we are dead also to the covenant of that law, though not to the command of it." [136] But in this arrangement it exists no longer as a command, the literal fulfillment of which is required of man, but as a description of the goal of conduct toward which the saint incessantly strives. The law, which no man can perfectly fulfill any more, exists as a "schoole-master"; it teaches us what we should do, whether we can or no, and as soon as we realize that we cannot, we flee to Christ for the assistance of grace. And since Christ has satisfied God by fulfilling the law, there is no necessity that we do it also. It is only necessary that we attempt it. God's agreement in the second covenant is that if a man will believe, he will receive the grace enabling him to approximate a holy life, but his failure to reach perfection will not be held against him. "We ought not to thinke. because we are not exact in keeping all the Commandements of *God* . . . that therefore *God* rejects us" [137] The regeneration of any man, as long as he is in the body, will be imperfect at best. It will manifest itself in a perpetual strug-

---

[135] The entire direction of this argument — the enlarging of natural abilities to provide a fulcrum for the lever of moral incitement — had been condemned by Calvin in so many words. He held that all the Fathers except Augustine committed precisely this error for the same reason. They attributed to the reasoning faculty more power toward the pursuit of virtue than was proper, because otherwise "they supposed it impossible to awaken our innate torpor" (*Institutes*, II, ii, 4). From the heights of spiritual intensity upon which Calvin dwelt, he could afford to spurn all such devices for the coddling of faith.

[136] Cotton, *Way of Life*, 229.

[137] Preston, *New Covenant*, 102.

gle to an unattainable end, and according to the covenant of grace God will accept the intention and the effort for the deed:

there will bee impuritie in the heart wherein there is faith, but yet where there is faith, there is a continuall purging out of impuritie, as it manifesteth it selfe You may conceive it by a similtude, if a pot be boyling upon the fire, there will a scum arise, but yet they are good house-wives, and cleanly, and neat, they watch it, and as the scum riseth up, they take it off and throw it away, happily more scum will arise, but still as it riseth they scum it off.[138]

The demand made upon benighted human nature in the covenant of grace is not exorbitant, and demonstrates again how solicitous God appears as He is pictured by this school. It is indeed a little surprising to the modern student to find how large a part of Puritan sermons was devoted to proving to people that they need not be weighed down with too great a sense of sin. The ministers seem to have been fully aware that the stark predestination of early Calvinism was too often driving sincere Christians to distraction, and that it needed to be softened, humanized. Hence they said again and again that there need be very little difference between the performances of a saint and the acts of a sinner; the difference will be in the aims and aspirations of the saint and in the sincerity of his effort. The proof of election will be in the trying, not the achieving. "God accepts at our hands a willing minde, and of childe-like indeavours; if we come with childe-like service, God will spare us; a father will accept the poor indeavours of his childe for the thing it selfe." [139]

Yet while our endeavors will be satisfactory though poor, they must still be real endeavors. Since the conception of grace in this theory is not so much that of rapture as of the reawakening of dormant powers, grace is by definition the beginning of a moral life. It is a strengthening of the remains of the law that still exist in the natural heart, in unregenerate reason, and in conscience. Saints are not able to do all they should, "yet this they doe . . . . they carry a constant purpose of heart to doe it. . . . They never come to give over striving to doe it." [140] The regenerate, by the very fact of being regenerate, exert themselves to become sanctified:

by the same faith whereby we receive Christ to dwell in us, we receive the holy Spirit also, to work from Christ and through Christ, all that power of godlinesse which a Christian life holds forth, and from that day forward.[141]

Conversely, it follows as night the day that sanctification is a very handy evidence of justification, and that we may even receive grace first in the form of a moral ability before we have any inward experience of re-

[138] Hooker, *Saintes Dignitie*, 4–5.

[139] Cotton, *Covenant of Gods Free Grace*, 12.

[140] Preston, *A Sermon Preached at A Generall Fast Before the Commons-House of Parliament* (London, 1633), 281.

[141] Cotton, *Way of Life*, 347–348.

generation.[142] God's predestination is of course absolute; He picks and chooses without regard to merit. But in the covenant He has consented to bestow His favor upon those who fulfill the conditions, and to guarantee to those who do so the assurance of their salvation. In this devious fashion the Puritans avoided the Arminian heresy of conditional election, but gained almost all that the Arminians sought by preaching a "conditional" covenant, which entailed the obligations of morality as thoroughly as did the erroneous doctrine, and yet did not bind the Lord to attend upon human performance.[143] "Though God's grace do all," said Sibbes, "yet we must give our consent," [144] and Thomas Shepard wrote:

> God hath so linked together the blessing of the Covenant (which is his to give) with the duty and way of it (which is ours to walk in) that we cannot with comfort expect the one, but it will work in us a carefull endeavour of the other.[145]

Peter Bulkley reveals what the New England divines thought this version had gained over that of primitive Calvinism when he explains that if God simply predestined without imposing conditions, morality would fall to the ground, nothing would be required of men one way or another; but in the

---

[142] Shepard, *Works*, III, 128. It was in the tangle of this argument that Mrs. Hutchinson tripped and fell, and consequently denounced the law and works and called upon the regenerate to live by grace alone. And it was by the doctrine of the covenant that she was found in error and excommunicated by the church of Boston: "If any therefore accuse the Doctrine of the Covenant of free grace, of Antinomianisme . . . and if they commit any sin, they plead they are not bound unto the Law . . . . The children of the Covenant of grace will onely tell you, that they are free from the Covenant of the Law, but not from the Commandment of it" (Cotton, *The New Covenant*, 134–35).

[143] How strained the reasoning became at this point to distinguish the conditional covenant from Arminianism is illustrated by the argument of Peter Bulkley:

"The grace of the Covenant is free notwithstanding the condition, because we doe not put any condition as antecedent to the Covenant on Gods part, whereby to induce and move the Lord to enter in Covenant with us, as if there were any thing supposed in us, which might invite and draw him to take us into Covenant with himselfe; but onely we suppose a condition antecedent to the promise of life, which condition we are to observe and walke in; and in the observation thereof to expect the blessing of life which the Covenant promiseth" (*Gospel-Covenant*, 383).

The difference between the federal theory and Arminianism, therefore, hinges upon the fact that in the covenant theory good works are not the cause, but the accompaniment of salvation. In the twentieth century, when theology has become a wearisome desert, this difference may seem to be a mere quibble over words, but to the first generation in New England it involved the fundamental problems of philosophy and of life: "Where we finde the promise of life made unto good workes, wee must not looke at them as workes of the Law, but as workes and fruits of Faith . . . . These kind of promises . . . are . . . not casuall, but declarative, making manifest who be those true believers . . . . In these promises workes are not set as the causes of our salvation, but as evidences and signes of those that do believe unto life" (*Gospel-Covenant*, 384).

[144] *Works*, VI, 8.

[145] Preface to Bulkley, *Gospel-Covenant*, A2 verso.

covenant our endeavors are made, not the cause, but the *sine qua non* of a heavenly future: "But hereby he would teach us, that when he makes with us a Covenant of Grace and mercy, he doth not then leave us at liberty to live as we list; but he binds us by Covenant to himself." [146] The legalistic tone of the thought is illustrated by Cotton's comparison of the conditions attached to the covenant to those of becoming "a free man of a Corporation," which are, he says, apprenticeship or purchase. Into the corporation of the godly there is no admission by purchase, and consequently all who hope for grace must serve an apprenticeship in learning the trade of godliness.

If we give our selves to be bound to this service, if we come to God, submit our selves to him in all things, to do with us as hee pleaseth, and as shall seem good in his sight, submitting our selves to be ruled and squared by him in all things, hee shall have our whole hearts to do with us what he will; here is the Covenant made up between God and a good Christian.[147]

Armed by this logic at every point, the theologians were prepared to concentrate their attack upon the question of passivity. They were equipped to counteract the danger of lassitude which threatened to result from the fatalistic doctrine of predestination. They could show that men are responsible for a great deal, even though God alone bestows grace, and in more ways than one they could prove that a sinner brings reprobation upon himself. All those who live within the hearing of Christian doctrine — particularly of covenant doctrine — are offered the opportunity of taking up the covenant, because to them its terms are made clear. An offer of the covenant from God includes also an offer of enabling grace, because God is under obligation to supply grace when He presents the contract to men. Therefore, when the covenant is presented, through the sermon of a minister, to a particular individual, and the individual does not then and there embrace it, or attempt to embrace it, then he must be resisting it. Though faith comes from God, yet because it is not forced upon any, but is presented through reasonable inducements, and is conveyed by "means," by sermons, and by sacraments, men have of themselves the power to turn their backs upon it, to refuse to be convinced by the most unanswerable demonstrations, to sneer at the minister, and to pay no attention to the sermon. Thereafter the onus is entirely on their own shoulders:

Take heede of refusing the acceptable time . . . Beloued, there is a certaine acceptable time, when God offers Grace, and after that hee offers it no more . . . there are certaine secret times, that *God* reserues to himselfe, that none knowes but himselfe, and when that time is past ouer, he offers it no more.[148]

Consequently, men must be constantly in readiness to take up the cove-

[146] Bulkley, *Gospel-Covenant*, 315.
[147] Cotton, *Covenant of Gods Free Grace*, 19–20.
[148] Preston, *New Covenant*, 434–35.

nant, so that they will not fail to respond when the acceptable time comes to them individually.

The covenant theory, then, was an extremely strategic device for the arousing of human activity: it permitted divine grace to be conceived as an opportunity to strike a bargain, a chance to make an important move, an occasion that comes at a specific moment in time through the agency of the ministry. If an individual does not close the deal when he has the chance, he certainly cannot blame God because it gets away from him. "The Lord is a suitor to many a man," said Shepard, "that never gives himself to him." [149] The heathen, indeed, might have some grounds for complaint, but not those who live under a ministry, because to them the preaching of the Word is *ipso facto* the presentation of the covenant:

> they that live under such means, that are ever learning, and never come to the knowledge of the Truth, and so have brought a sottishnesse on themselves, they are inexcusable, because themselves are the cause of their not profiting, as a man that is drunke, though he is not able to understand the commands of his Master, yet because he was the first author of the drunkennesse, (which caused such sottishnesse), he is inexcuseable. . . . So . . . God requires no more of any man, than either he doth know, or might have knowne.[150]

Of course, God must give the faith; but by these agencies He is, as a matter of fact, giving it, and giving it thus out of respect for the intelligence of men. "Hee will not doe it without us, because wee are reasonable men and women, and God affords us meanes." [151] Consequently, the duty of any man in a Christian community is to use the means to the end for which they are intended:

> howsoever God promiseth to enable his people to doe all he commandeth, yet this shutteth not out their endeavour. His promise of enabling them is upon this supposition, that they doe indeavour in the use of the meanes he shall appoint them. The Lord in promising doth not meane that they should be idle, and look that he should doe all; but his promising includeth their endeavouring, and upon their endeavouring in the use of the meanes that God hath appointed, he hath promised to enable them to doe what he hath commanded.[152]

Hooker says that if persons have lived under a "powerful ministry" a half-dozen years or so and have not profited therefrom, "It is no absolute conclusion, but . . . it is a shrewd suspicion, I say, that God will send them downe to hell." [153] Consequently, it behooves us all not to lie back until the Lord comes to us, but to exert ourselves at once in accordance with the instructions of our pastor.

[149] *Works*, II, 31.

[150] Preston, *Saints Qualification*, 223.

[151] Hooker, "The Poore Doubting Christian," in *The Saints Cordials* (London, 1629), 361.

[152] Hooker, *Saintes Dignitie*, 82–83.

[153] *The Soules Implantation* (London, 1637), 77.

On these grounds the school carried on Perkins' tendency to reduce the actual intrusion of grace to a very minute point. They not only insisted that the tiniest particle is sufficient to start a man on the road to salvation, they even argued that before any faith is generated, a man can at least "prepare" himself for it. He can put himself in an attitude of receptivity, can resolve with himself not to turn down the covenant when it seems to be offered to him.[154] God may decree, but a man must find out whether the decree applies to himself; "the kingdom of heaven is taken with violence." [155] "You must not thinke to goe to heaven on a feather-bed; if you will be Christs disciples, you must take up his crosse, and it will make you sweat." [156] If any man excuse himself by the sophistry that Christ must work for him and that he cannot under his own power "bring forth fruit to him," that man despises Christ's honor, and in that act rejects the covenant of grace.[157]

In this respect, as in others, the covenant doctrine did not intend to depart from essential Calvinism; it did not openly inculcate free will. But by conceiving of grace as the readiness of God to join in covenant with

[154] In many passages describing the extent to which an unregenerate man may go in the work of preparation, some of these writers passed beyond any limits that could be reconciled with Calvinism. In New England clearly the most extreme was Thomas Hooker, who with great eloquence magnified the possibilities of a man's producing in himself the receptive frame of mind, bringing himself to be "willingly content that Jesus Christ should come into it" (*Soules Implantation*, 34), and dared to assert that he who could force himself to the point of readiness would certainly receive grace in time. "It is onely in the way to be ingrafted into Christ; but so that undoubtedly that soule which hath this worke upon it, shall have faith poured into it" (*Soules Preparation*, London, 1632, 155). "If ever you thinke to share in the salvation that Christ hath purchased . . . if you would have him dwell with you, and doe good to you, either prepare for him, or else never expect him . . . . Christ is marvellous ready to come, only he watcheth the time till your heart be ready to receive and entertaine him . . . . If the soule be broken and humbled, he will come presently" (*Soules Implantation*, 47). It is probably significant, therefore, that John Cotton's regard for consistency was more circumspect, and though he, no less than Hooker, argued that unregenerate man was responsible for his own state, he could not admit that before some experience of faith a man could undertake even to put himself in readiness: "for our first union, there are no steps unto the Altar" (*New Covenant*, 54). "There is no promise of life made to those that wait & seek in their own strength, who being driven to it, have taken it up by their own resolutions" (*New Covenant*, 196–97). Yet even in denying the possibilities of natural preparation, Cotton prefaces his remarks: "Reserving due honour to such gracious and precious Saints as may be otherwise minded" (*Treatise of the Covenant of Grace*, 35). Under the circumstances this may very possibly be a reference to Hooker, and the difference of opinion between Hooker and Cotton on this important issue may throw some light upon the reasons why Hooker led the migration to Connecticut rather than remain in Massachusetts where Cotton had become installed as the principal interpreter of dogma (see pp. 25–27). However, Thomas Shepard was in agreement with Hooker, and his *Sincere Convert* was attacked by Giles Firmin for demanding too much of natural man before grace (Shepard, *Works*, I, clxxxvi; cf. *ibid.*, I, 160–63, 173; III, 308).

[155] Shepard, *Works*, II, 57.
[156] Hooker, *The Christians Two Chiefe Lessons* (London, 1640), 64.
[157] Shepard, *Works*, II, 224.

any man who does not actively refuse Him, this theory declared in effect that God has taken the initiative, that man can have only himself to blame if he does not accede to the divine proposal. This was indeed a marvellous stratagem for getting around a thorny difficulty in theology, a hazard which Calvin had simply taken in stride by asserting roundly that though God elects or rejects according to His pleasure, the responsibility for damnation is man's own. The generation of Peter Bulkley could no longer accept so brusque or unsophisticated an account as this. They were under greater compulsion to clear God of the charge of arbitrary condemnation and to place the responsibility for success or failure squarely on human shoulders. The result was the conception, not of conditional election, but of conditional covenant, according to which the absolute decree of God is defended, and yet the necessity of activity by man is asserted:

> The Lord doth not absolutely promise life unto any; he doth not say to any soule, I will save you and bring you to life, though you continue impenitent & unbelieving; but commands and works us to repent and believe, and then promises that in the way of faith and repentance, he will save us. He prescribes a way of life for us to walk in, that so wee may obtaine the salvation which he hath promised.[158]

The covenant involved ethics in the very stuff of grace itself:

> we must for our part assent unto the Covenant, not onely accepting the promise of it, but also submit to the duty required in it; or else there is no Covenant established betwixt God and us; we must as well accept of the condition as of the promise, if we will be in Covenant with God.[159]

The final outcome of the intricate system was a shamelessly pragmatic injunction. It permitted the minister to inform his congregation that if any man can fulfill the covenant, he is elected. The way for him to find out is to try and see: "Therefore goe on boldly, God hath promised to heare you, hee cannot deny you." [160] Whatever the differences among the various writers, there is a marvellous unanimity among them on the ultimate moral: "The way to grow in any grace is the exercise of that grace," said Preston.[161] "It is not so much the having of grace, as grace in exercise, that preserves the soul," said Sibbes.[162] And John Cotton said in Boston: "If thou hast but a thirsty soule, and longest for grace under sense of thine owne droughtinesse, then God will not deny the holy Ghost to them that aske him." [163]

The conclusion toward which the doctrine of the covenant shapes is always the practical one that activity is the essence of a Christian life, that deeds are not merely the concomitants of faith, but can even be in them-

---

[158] Bulkley, *Gospel-Covenant*, 313.

[159] Bulkley, *Gospel-Covenant*, 316; cf. part IV, *passim*.

[160] Preston, *New Creature*, 30–31.

[161] *The Saints Daily Exercise* (London, 1630), 35.

[162] *Works*, I, 199.

[163] *Way of Life*, 11–12.

selves the beginning of faith. Some kind of revision of Calvinism seemed absolutely inevitable if the doctrine of justification by faith were not to eventuate in a complete disregard of moral performance. The covenant theology was the form that that revision took among this particular group of thinkers. It was the preliminary to their proving that faith without performance is an impossibility, a contradiction in terms, and that that which must be performed is the moral law, the law which reason and common sense know to be good in itself. In dogmatic Calvinism morality could exist only as a series of divine commands. It has no other basis, and to Calvin it needed no other. The covenant theology is a recognition on the part of a subsequent generation that this basis was inadequate, that it reduced morality to an arbitrary fiat, that it presented no inducement to men other than the whip and lash of an angry God. Consequently, in New England morality was first of all the specific terms of a compact between God and man, and rested, therefore, not upon mere injunction but upon a mutual covenant in which man plays the positive role of a coöperator with the Lord. In the second place morality was also that which can be considered good and just.

x

This conception was of tremendous value to the leaders of Massachusetts, not only in the realm of faith and personal conduct, but just as much in the realm of politics and society. The sphere of moral conduct includes more than such matters as individual honesty or chastity; it includes participation in the corporate organization and the regulation of men in the body politic. The covenant theology becomes, therefore, the theoretical foundation both for metaphysics and for the state and the church in New England. An exhaustive study of the social theory would lead too far afield for the purposes of this paper, but a brief indication of the connection between it and the theology will demonstrate that without understanding this background we shall misread even such a familiar classic as Winthrop's speech of 1645 on liberty. That address is not what it is most often described as being — an expression of pure Calvinism. All that strictly Calvinistic political theory needs to contain is in the fourth book of the *Institutes*. It amounts in effect to the mandate that men must submit to magistrates because God orders them to submit, to the assertion that the power of the governor is of God, never of the people. But Winthrop outlines a much more subtle conception in his account, and by invoking the covenant theory secures the sway of morality in the state in precisely the same fashion in which the theologians secured it in the religious life. He distinguishes between the liberty all men have in the state of nature, the liberty to do anything they wish, which generally means something bad, and the liberty men exercise in society:

The other kind of liberty I call civil or federal, it may also be termed moral, in reference to the covenant between God and man, in the moral law, and the politic covenants and constitutions, amongst men themselves. This liberty is the proper end and object of authority, and cannot subsist without it; and it is a liberty to that only which is good, just, and honest.[164]

The real connotation of Winthrop's words has not been recognized in modern accounts. He is saying that just as the covenant between God and man is a coming to terms, and as the validity of that which is by its nature good, just, and honest rests not upon its intrinsic quality but upon its being agreed to by the contractors, so also in the state, the rule of law rests upon a similar agreement among the participants. The covenant theory can not claim for that which is inherently good the force of a cosmic law, because the universe and man are corrupted; it can not identify the good completely with the thought of God, because God transcends all systematic formulations. But being arrived at by compact, the good then acquires the power to compel obedience from those who have covenanted to observe it, be they gods or men. The personal covenant of the soul with God is impaled on the same axis as the social, like a small circle within a larger. Before entering into both the personal and social covenants men have a liberty to go their own gait; afterwards they have renounced their liberty to do anything but that which has been agreed upon. The mutual consenting involved in a covenant, says Hooker, is the "sement" which solders together all societies, political or ecclesiastical; "for there is no man constrained to enter into such a condition, unlesse he will: and he that will enter, must also willingly binde and ingage himself to each member of that society to promote the good of the whole, or else a member actually he is not." [165] The implanting of grace, being by definition an acceptance of the covenant, produces by the same token a people prepared and ready to be disciplined in a holy society. "The same Spirit quickneth us unto holy duties; so that . . . the Spirit sanctifying draweth us into an holy Confederacy to serve God in family, Church, & Common-wealth." [166] Peter Bulkley illustrates the paralleling of the social and political covenants which is characteristic of New England theory by insisting that he who accepts the covenant must obey its terms, exactly "as in a Common-wealth or Kingdome, none hath the benefit of the Law, but those that subject themselves to the Law: none have the protection of authority, but those that obey it." [167] Since grace takes the form of enabling men to embrace the covenant, the regenerate automatically obey the law of God both in personal life and in social relations:

Where the Lord sets himselfe over a people, he frames them unto a willing and voluntary subjection unto him, that they desire nothing more than to be under his government . . . . when the Lord is in Covenant with a people, they

---

[164] Winthrop, *Journal*, Hosmer, ed., II, 239.
[165] *Survey*, part I, 50.
[166] Cotton, *New Covenant*, 34.
[167] *Gospel-Covenant*, 346.

follow him not forcedly, but as farre as they are sanctified by grace, they submit willingly to his regiment.[168]

The covenant upon which a Congregational church was founded was viewed by the theologians in the same light as the political compact. It was held to be a miniature edition of the divine covenant. The saints come together and formally agree to carry out in ecclesiastical life the obligations to which they stand individually bound by their covenant with God. The duties and requirements are those determined in the covenant of grace. The church compact is the agreement of the people in a body to constitute an institution which will facilitate the achievement of these ends. "The rule bindes such to the duties of their places and relations, yet it is certain, it requires that they should *first freely ingage* themselves in such covenants, and *then* be carefull to fulfill such duties." [169] The creation of a church by the saints is necessary, furthermore, because the church makes possible the machinery of "means." The argument from the covenant, therefore, clinched the theoretical justification for the existence of a formal ecclesiastical order, for the dispensing of sacraments, and for the application of such regulatory measures as censure and excommunication, while at the same time protecting the liberty of God to enter into covenant with anyone He chose, inside or outside the church. Yet as long as it seemed that God would normally work through the regular means, He would therefore generally dispense grace through the ordinances of the church. Consequently the children of the saints should be baptized as a means toward their conversion, and should be taken into the church covenant:

The Covenant of Grace is to be considered, either according to the *benefits* of saving grace *given* in it, or according to the *means* of grace *offered*. . . . [The church covenant] is not the Covenant of the Gospel in the first sense; but it is

[168] Gospel-Covenant, 219–20. There can hardly be any doubt that the development of the covenant theology is in some fashion connected with the amplification of the social compact engineered by the lawyers and parliamentarians with whom the Puritans were associated in the struggle with the Crown. It is impossible to tell, without further research in the lives of such men as Preston and Sibbes and their associates, whether the political theory was the father of the theology, or the theology of the theory. It is clear, however, that the two ideas were developed *pari passu*. Certainly, in expounding the theological covenant the writers were constantly illustrating it by the analogy of the political, once more revealing the extremely legalistic cast of their minds.

"The Covenant which passeth betwixt God and us, is like that which passeth between a King and his people; the King promiseth to rule and govern in mercy and righteousnesse; and they againe promise to obey in loyalty and faithfulnesse" (*Gospel-Covenant*, 345–46). "Such a covenant there is usually in all well governed Common-wealths, unlesse the King comes in by way of Conquest and Tyranny, but in well settled Common-wealths, there is a Covenant and Oath between Prince and People" (Cotton, *Christ the Fountaine*, 34). From the political point of view this theology was a strategic assistance to parliament; it made God a constitutional monarch, so that James and Charles might feel no indignity in becoming such a ruler as well.

[169] Hooker, *Survey*, part I, 69.

within the verge, and contained within the compasse of the Covenant in the second sense.[170]

In this distinction between the covenant as faith and the covenant as the
provision of means for the engendering of faith were contained the seeds of
the difficulties which later produced the halfway covenant. But in the first
decades of New England history no difficulties were anticipated because
the theologians were so supremely confident that grace would almost
inevitably accompany the means. "God delights in us, when we are in his
Covenant, his Covenant reacheth to his Church, and wee being members
of that Church: Hence it comes to passe, that we partake of all the pleasant
springs of Gods love." [171]

Thus the sign of true faith is not only a desire on the part of the regenerate individual to fulfill the moral law, but it is also a determination to join
in the setting up of the one and only polity which Christ has outlined in
Scripture. For this reason New England was settled: "When faith is stirring, it longs and desires much after the strongest, purest, and liveliest
Ministery, and every Ordinance in the greatest purity." [172]

XI

I have not attempted in this acount of the covenant theology to give
more than a rapid survey; the summary of each point could easily be amplified, and revealing quotations multiplied indefinitely. But in even as com-
pressed a treatment as this, the bent of the thought becomes clear. In
every position there is a remarkable consistency of tone, a resolute determination to solve the riddles of Calvinist theology, as far as may be possible
by the ingenuity of man or the subterfuges of metaphysics, in a reasonable,
comprehensible fashion, and yet at the same time to preserve, in form at
least, the essential structure of Calvinism. To understand why these men
should have been driven by this urgency, it is necessary to remember what
was taking place in the intellectual life of Europe at the time, in science, in
politics, in the work of Bacon, of Descartes, and of Hobbes. Within the
limits of their particular theology, within the framework of their creed,
these Puritans were responding to the same impulses as their philosophical
contemporaries. They were seeking to understand, to draw up explicable
laws, to form clear and distinct ideas, to bring order and logic into the
universe. They could not interpret it as extension and movement as
did Descartes. They could not reduce it to atoms as did Hobbes. They
could not deify its natural construction as did the Newtonians. But oddly
enough they could take many steps in the same direction once they had
seized upon their fundamental discovery that God has voluntarily engaged

[170] Hooker, *Survey*, part I, 78.
[171] Cotton, *Covenant of Gods Free Grace*, 22.
[172] Cotton, *Way of Life*, 357.

Himself to regular, ascertainable procedures. The rest followed surely and easily from this premise: the validity of reason in man, the regularity of secondary causes in nature, the harmony of knowledge and faith, the coincidence of the arbitrary with inherent goodness, the intimate connection between grace and the incitements that generate grace, the necessity for moral responsibility and activity. Everywhere along the line the method of the divine dispensation, while authorized only by God and remaining under His constant control, is actually synchronized with a completely scientific account. God works grace in the soul, not by compulsion, but by persuasion and reasonable inducements, by the sermon of the minister which penetrates the sinner's mind. Was the real cause God working through the sermon, or was it the sermon itself? The authors had no hesitancy in saying that the sermon was simply the efficient cause and that God was the final cause, but they were delighted to find that God's activity could take the form of a natural stimulus. This seemed to make religion doubly secure and to enhance it by the addition of comprehensibility.

Yet there is a caution to be observed before we rest in this conclusion. By marshaling from the works of Cotton and Hooker passages which deal only with the covenant and its implications, an impression could easily be created that New England thought had ceased to have any affinities with Calvinism, that there was really no difference between the Puritans of the covenant school and the rational theologians of the century who, like John Smith listening to the Arminians at Dort, had bidden Calvin good night. To imply that there is an essential unanimity between Preston and Chillingworth, Cotton and Whichcote, would be to misread the whole history of Puritanism. For reasonable as this system was, coherent and uniform as was its cosmology, sequential as was its theory of causation, in the final analysis the basis of every contention, the goal of every proposition, was still the transcendent, omnipotent Divinity.

The achievement of this theology was that it did everything that could be done to confine the unconfinable God in human terms. It transformed the revealed Word from an exaction arbitrarily imposed by a conqueror into a treaty of mutual obligation. But it never forgot that at the long last God is not to be fathomed, understood, or described with absolute certainty. Such certainty as we do have is temporary, the result of an agreement, of God's having consented to be bound in the main by such and such conditions, of His condescending for the moment to speak the language of men. There is no absolute guarantee that *all* His manifestations will appear within the scope of the covenant. The essence of Calvinism and the essence of Puritanism is the hidden God, the unknowable, the unpredictable. In this sense the Puritans were indeed Calvinists. They hedged the undiscoverable Essence about with a much more elaborate frame than did Calvin. They muffled it and cloaked it (to borrow Cotton's phrase), they cabined it and circumscribed it up to a point; and though the point was far beyond anything Calvin would have allowed, there was still a limit beyond which even the federal theologians could not go. They could not say that natural law was immutable and eternal, though they might say it was generally reliable. They might say that God's justice was for all intents and purposes the same as human justice, but they could not say that it was invariably the same. Always they had to leave a loophole, they had to be wary and circumspect; for behind the panorama of the world, behind the covenant and behind the Scriptures there loomed an inconceivable being about whom no man could confidently predict anything, who might day in and day out deal with man in stated forms and then suddenly strike without warning and scatter the world into bits. There was no telling with unqualified certitude what He might do; there was only the rule of thumb, the working agreement that by and large He would save and reject according to reason and justice as we understand the words. For ordinary purposes this was enough; we could feel fairly secure, we need not be too distraught. But the Puritan, as long as he remained a Puritan, could never banish entirely from his mind the sense of something mysterious and terrible, of something that leaped when least expected, something that upset all regularizations and defied all logic, something behind appearances that could not be tamed and brought to heel by men. The covenant thought kept this divine liberty at several removes, placed it on a theoretical plane, robbed it of much of its terror, but it could not do away with it entirely.

The respects in which these men, for all their efforts at intellectualization, remained essentially Puritans may perhaps appear if we briefly compare the Puritan reasonableness of John Preston with the Anglican reasonableness of Jeremy Taylor. In the *Ductor Dubitantium* Taylor's exposition of the law of nature and his determination of the segment of it that is also moral law are so very close to the pronouncements of Preston and Thomas Shepard that at first sight there seems to be no philosophical conflict between them. But for Taylor the conclusions reached by right reason, the dictates of justice, and the ideals of goodness cannot be invested with divine sanction merely because God, out of sovereign pleasure, elected to give them a binding force when He might just as well have enacted rules contrary to all human expectations. Taylor denies that it is even remotely possible that there remain a hidden God, outside and above reason. God *is* reason. There cannot be one justice on earth and another in heaven:

how can we understand Him so, but by the measures of justice? and how shall we know that, if there be two justices, one that we know, and one that we know not, one contrary to another? If they be contrary, they are not justice; for justice can be no more opposed by justice, than truth to truth: if they be not contrary, then that which we understand to be just in us is just in God, and that which is just once is just for ever in the same case and circumstances.[173]

The measure of all virtue must be the same for God as for us. God cannot have a secret will distinct from his revealed one. He does not commit Him-

[173] *Works*, Reginald Heber, ed. (London, 1851), IX, 67.

self to any rules simply through choice; the rules in themselves must be good, and God must inevitably, inescapably, instinctively follow them and no others. There can be no such thing as an offer of the covenant, an invitation to all men, and yet a secret withholding of grace without which man cannot respond. Taylor satirizes the Puritan position with telling irony; the Puritan, as he portrays him, is forced to cry:

It is true, O God, that Thou dost call us, but dost never intend we should come, that Thy open will is loving and plausible, but Thy secret will is cruel, decretory, and destructive to us whom Thou hast reprobated; that Thy open will is ineffective, but Thy secret will only is operative, and productive of a material event, and therefore although we are taught to say, Thou art just, and true in all Thy sayings; yet certainly it is not that justice which Thou has commanded us to imitate and practise, it is not that sincerity which we can safely use to one another, and therefore either we men are not just when we think we are, or else Thou art not just who doest and speakest contrary things, or else there are two contrary things which may be called justice.[174]

For Preston and the Puritan theologians of the covenant it was enough that God had consented to reason and had made an effort to fit His will to the requirements of abstract justice. They would not dogmatize further about His essence, and they felt that no man had a right to. They would expound the laws of reason and the laws of nature step by step with Taylor, they would extol justice and virtue as much as he, but they would not affirm that these human constructions, these intellectual values, were necessarily part and parcel of the cosmos. God's will coincides roughly with such conceptions, but not always exactly. The universe is almost always regular and orderly, but there is the one chance in a million, the one inexplicable accident, the one fact that will not fit into any scheme. There is every so often the apparently good man who cannot be saved or the hopeless wretch who is lifted from the gutter to glory in spite of all that we think appropriate. "If he take pleasure to breathe in a man, there is nothing can hinder him, it will blow upon the most noysome dunghill in any place, and be never a whit the more defiled." [175] In a Christian community the machinery of conversion is set up, the covenant proposed, the terms made explicit, the means set in order, and yet in spite of all the best intentions this or that individual may never be able to join the covenant. And there is no explaining why, except that it is God's pleasure to withhold the ability from that particular man. Even the godly, after they have become partakers of the covenant, will not dwell in happiness and comfort. Their existence, as much as that of other men, will be hard and full of anguish:

It will be a vaine thing for men to think to escape scot-free from afflictions, and yet live a godly and an holy life; it never fell out otherwise, but as sure as thou art sprinkled with the water of Baptisme, so sure thou shalt be drenched in affliction.[176]

---

[174] *Works*, 67–68.
[175] Cotton, *Way of Life*, 113.
[176] Cotton, *Way of Life*, 477.

It is this sense of the exceptional that always can happen, of the incomprehensible, of the margin of human error in grasping ultimate truth, that perpetually exists in the back of the Puritan's mind; all his attempts at expounding proceed upon the recognition that all exposition is bound to fail of complete explanation:

there is something of the Essence of *God*, that may not bee inquired into, ... Looke not for a full knowledge of him, but onely for a small degree of it. . . . We should learne from hence, not to be searching and prying into the counsels of *God*; as to inquire why so many are damned, and so few saved; how the infallibilitie of *Gods* will and the libertie of mans will can stand together. . . . These, and all other such, we must be content to be ignorant of; for he doth not reveale himself fully in this life . . . We should be content to let *God* alone, not to inquire into all his actions, into the ground and reason of all his works . . . We should doe thus, stand upon the shore, (as it were) and behold his infinite Essence . . . and goe no further; as a man that stands upon the sea-shore, and sees the vastnesse of the sea, but dares goe no further, for if he goes into the deepe, he is drowned: You may looke into *Gods* Essence, and see and admire it; but to thinke that thou couldest comprehend *God* is as if a man should think to hold the whole sea in the hollow of his hand.[177]

The Puritan wished to bring his theology into harmony with science and reason wherever they might be made to coincide, but he could never lose his hunger for the inward exultation that came from a union with God which, though it might be brought about by natural causes, was yet something supernatural, something different from the causes, something which was bestowed only at the pleasure of God. Faith adds no new doctrine, teaches us no new facts, is not an addition to the contents of the mind. It is a glow of inspiration that quickens knowledge, and for that reason is all the more valuable and indispensable:

There is indeed a common faith, which the others may have, and thou mayest have, but the strong faith ariseth from the Spirit, *God* dispenseth it where he pleaseth; this infused faith is not gotten by strength of argument, or perspicuitie of the understanding; it is not brought in by custome, but *God* doth worke it; it is not all the antecedent preparation that will doe it, but *God* must first worke it, and then you are able to beleeve these principles of faith, and able to beleeve them to the purpose.[178]

Morality and God's decree may, as we have seen Shepard saying, kiss each other and agree, but the Puritan could never forget that the agreement comes of God's own choice, and Shepard must add that the agreement is not always perfect, that the will of God remains superior to the demands of human equity. "When they [moral precepts] are called perpetual and unchangeable, we must understand them in respect of God's ordinary dispensation; for he who is the great Lawgiver may, and doth sometimes ex-

---

[177] Preston, *Life Eternall*, 100–02.
[178] Preston, *Life Eternall*, 68–69.

traordinarily dispense with moral laws." [179] The Puritan temperament is nowhere so well illustrated as in the contrast between the tenor of these passages and the tendency of the Puritan metaphysic. As far as possible Puritans would explain, draw diagrams, plot the course of God's will, and generalize upon His character. But it would be the end of Puritanism if they ever succeeded completely in penetrating the ultimate secret, if they could reach the point of saying that thus and so is not simply the way God does behave, but the way in which He must behave for these and those reasons. If the covenant theology is, as I think it is, a characteristic product of the Puritan mind, then we are perhaps justified in describing Puritanism as a willingness to follow nature and reason as far as possible, but not completely; for though Puritanism will use reason and enjoy nature, it can never overcome a fundamental distrust. As Hooker says upon a chapter from the Gospel according to John:

For there be some depths in some passages of the verse which are fitter to be admired, than comprehended, and exceed the reach, and discovery of the most Judicious Interpreter, that I can look into, and indeed, seem to be reserved for another world, when the fruition of the good here mentioned will prove the best interpretation. We will study to be wise unto sobriety.[180]

To be wise unto sobriety was the purpose of this theology, to elucidate the laws of God's universe, but to keep a wary eye upon the unpredictability, the mystery of God. The evidence of subsequent history, both in England and in New England, would seem to be that it failed. Eventually the ideas which it introduced into the creed, reinforced by the triumph of Newtonian physics, displaced the theology in the estimation of such men as Charles Chauncy. The moral of this episode in the story is, I think, that the Calvinism to which the Puritans were ostensibly dedicated was already in the process of far-reaching modification at the hands of English theologians before it was transported to Massachusetts. The men who directed the intellectual life of seventeenth-cenutry New England left Cambridge and London when their tradition was in the first flush of transformation. They did not depart until into that tradition, under the guise of a doctrine of covenants made by God with man, there had been injected many ideas which derived, not from theology and revelation, but from law, from the study of nature, from the principles of a reason and common sense. As time went on, the incompatibility of these ideas with the official confession was bound to become more apparent. Seen in this light, the development of rationalism in eighteenth-century New England is not a phenomenon produced entirely by the stimulation of imported ideas. The intellectual life of American Puritans in the seventeenth century was by no means so sparse and monotonous as it has sometimes been accused of being. The pristine doctrine was not rigorous, ironclad, and inflexible; it had in it

[179] *Works*, III, 35.
[180] *Christs Last Prayer*, 110.

the elements of complexity, the seeds of future growth, making for diversity and contradiction. That period which is sometimes spoken of as the "glacial age" was not an era of intellectual dearth and philosophical sterility, but one of slow progression toward the ultimate separation of the diverse attitudes which had somehow been awkwardly and unwittingly put together in the covenant theology of Ames, Preston, and Sibbes. It was, therefore, no accident, no violent break in the course of New England thought, that John Wise should shift the grounds for defending Congregationalism from the Bible to the laws of reason and nature and to the character of the social compact. It is also not surprising to find that when Jonathan Edwards came to feel that rationalism and ethics had stifled the doctrine of God's sovereignty and dethroned the doctrine of grace, he threw over the whole covenant scheme, repudiated the conception of transmission of sin by judicial imputation, declared God unfettered by any agreement or obligation, made grace irresistible, and annihilated the natural ability of man. It was Jonathan Edwards who went back to the doctrine from which the tradition had started; went back, not to what the first generation of New Englanders had held, but to Calvin, and who became, therefore, the first consistent and authentic Calvinist in New England.

CHAPTER IV

RELIGION AND SOCIETY IN THE EARLY
LITERATURE OF VIRGINIA

[As I have remarked, children of the New England tradition — especially those who more recently have devoted themselves with conspicuous success to finance rather than to theology — are unhappy when reminded that their ancestors were so impractical as to be worried about religious matters. Those of the Virginia tradition, however, are confident that from the beginning only material ambitions of empire, profit, tobacco, and real estate occupied their pioneers. Historians who think exclusively in terms of economic incentives are relieved when they turn from New England, with its annoying proclivities for theology and polity, to a Virginia where no such nonsense supervenes.

If together with this comfortable persuasion, chroniclers were also required to show that into the Virginian wilderness was transported a spirit of chivalric nobility, the two themes have seldom shown signs of incompatibility.

Modern scholarship has long since rid itself of the legend of a "cavalier" origin. Having achieved that liberation, it consequently fights the more resolutely against any argument that in Virginia we have not to deal with a preponderant economic motive, in all its naked beauty. This motive, so blatantly advertised in the propaganda of the company, could not possibly have been cradled, these historians insist, in the teleological and (in that sense of the word) religious cosmology of the seventeenth century.

My contention is that such a view, though correct in specific details, does not allow for the larger assumptions of the promoters and settlers. Obviously, the desire of achieving a holy city was less explicit in the dreams of the Virginia Company than in those of Winthrop; still, the colonizing impulse was fulfilled within the same frame of universal relevance as the Puritans assumed. Whether the effort of seeing the settlement in terms of its original mental setting is worth making may be doubted — especially since in Virginia, as against either Pennsylvania or New England, the purely economic account is so eminently satisfactory to the sluggard intellect of this century. But history would be a dull business were it not occasionally called upon for an exercise of the historical imagination. Shakespeare himself would be merely an antiquarian curiosity if we had no appreciation whatsoever of the universe he took so hugely for granted. Hence

I contend that the Virginia settlement, no less than the New England, lends itself to little more than a bare chronicle unless the cosmological and religious premises of the epoch are taken into account. These governed the search for wealth, and in that regard defined, even for investors, the errand that Virginia was running into the wilderness.

This discussion was originally printed as two installments in *The William and Mary Quarterly* (October 1948, 5.492–522; January 1949, 6:24–41), and is here reprinted with permission.]

I

THE settlement of Virginia, so historians tell us, was a mercantile adventure, a purely business proposition. Behind it lay no organized religious interest as in Maryland or Massachusetts Bay, no Utopian expectation as in Pennsylvania, not even so vague a dream of philanthropy as created Georgia. It attracted no clique of intellectuals like the Puritan clergy, yet somehow, in its first tumultuous years, under the rule of a joint-stock company and amid administrative confusion, it produced a literature. If we include in this literature, as legitimately we may, not only documents written in the colony but those produced in England by persons no less vitally concerned in the project, we can gather a small but substantial body of expression. Historians have treated this literature, most of it propaganda, much of dubious accuracy, a large part merely rhetoric, as possessing value only for documentation; literary critics cull out a few gems, and are condescending toward the remainder. I venture to suggest that there is an aspect to the material that has been overlooked: the men who wrote for and about Virginia, precisely because they were not dogmatists or visionaries, gave expression to a kind of averageness of the age that is worth serious study. Actually, if we take all this literature in review, put aside for the moment its utility as source material and regard it as an index, often an unwitting or inadvertent revelation, or what ordinary men, financiers, investors, or planters assumed were cosmological conditions under which the enterprise was perforce conducted, then the Virginia literature becomes one of the most eloquent, even poignant, episodes in the emergence of the modern spirit. A great theme, vaster in conception than any of the writers could have framed by himself, elevates even the most ephemeral of these productions into a realm of universal meaning, and the philosophical student may, if he asks the right questions, find in them not only illumination of the pattern of mind out of which America emerged, but a profound comment upon the transformation of western European culture from a medieval to a modern (though in 1624 still a bewildered) conception of life and society.

Examined in this perspective, the literature as it stands tells a strange story; to take it at face value — and to the extent that it is literature, we may take it exactly that way — it exhibits a set of principles for guiding not a mercantile investment but a medieval pilgrimage. Whatever were the calculations of the city, the cosmos expounded in the Virginia pamphlets is one where the principal human concern is neither the rate of interest nor the discovery of gold, but the will of God. The intellectual affinities of the writers, of even the most blatant propagandists, are not with Thomas Jefferson or with the Franklin of *A Way to Wealth*, but with Calvin and Loyola. In fact, professions of Virginia adventurers sound much like those of Massachusetts Puritans, however heretical this may appear to modern Virginians! Not only in broadsides, but more emphatically in thoughts and in reported actions, religion *seems* the compelling, or at least the pervading, force. I am not, let me insist, concerned with events, but with ideas, for history is often more instructive as it considers what men conceived they were doing rather than what, in brute fact, they did. In this literature, expedience and convenience are not the criteria — had they been, fewer lives would have been lost — but the theological virtues. Planters and promoters present themselves as only secondarily merchants and exploiters, only secondarily Englishmen; in their own conception of themselves, they are first and foremost Christians, and above all militant Protestants. They are an inspired band marching out, in a world disfigured by the ravages of sin, including their own, for the glory of God, in whose sign they are confident of conquering not only the wilderness but themselves.

I submit this analysis of material already threshed and winnowed by historians in order to propose a thesis: within the framework of the Virginia Company, along with the desire for profits or for estates, along with nationilistic projects, another and determining, if not always specific, motive was at work. For men of 1600 to 1625, the new land was redemption even as it was also riches; the working out of society and the institutions cannot be understood (and it has not been understood), except as an effort toward salvation. Religion, in short, was the really energizing propulsion in this settlement, as in others.

II

The most obvious theme in this literature is the announced intention of converting Indians. In the Charter of 1606 King James declared that he incorporated the Company for the glory he would achieve "in propagating of Christian religion to such people, as yet live in darkness and miserable ignorance of the true knowledge and worship of God." [1] The *Phoenix* brought back from Virginia in 1608, along with a cargo of cedar, John Smith's *A True Relation*, which the company rushed into print with a preface by one "I. H." asserting that the hardest part was done, that the remaining action was purely "honorable, and the end to the high glory

[1] Alexander Brown, *The Genesis of the United States* (Boston, 1890), 53.

of God, to the erecting of true religion among Infidells, to the ouerthrow of superstition and idolatrie, to the winning of many thousands of wandering sheepe, vnto Christs fold, who now, and till now, haue strayed in the vnknowne paths of Paganisme, Idolatrie, and superstition." [2] "What glory! What honour to our Sovereign! What comfort to those subjects who shall be means of furthering of so happy a work!" cried Crakanthorpe in a sermon preached at Paul's Cross in 1609 at the crest of the Virginia enthusiasm.[3] In 1613, Strachey, like a sound Protestant, reasoned that good works, while not the cause of our salvation, are *"con sectaria* (as the schoolmen saieth)," and that thus even a Protestant may speak of this labor as "meritoryous." [4] In a court masque at the marriage of the Princess Elizabeth and the Prince Palatine — the fateful union which was shortly to involve Europe in thirty years of bloody warfare over the question of whether work were the cause or the "con sectaria" of faith — Indian medicine men were enjoined by "Eunomia" to renounce superstition and pay homage to England's king,

> whose bright skie
> Enlighted with a Christian piety
> Is never subject to black error's night.[5]

Courtiers applauded, and canny British merchants were beguiled into purchasing more shares in the Virginia Company, though it had not yet paid a penny on all the pounds invested.

Three hundred years of European imperialism, which was ultimately to become an immense organization of hypocrisy, have made us skeptical of such professions. We are wearily familiar with a pattern of conquest in which the missionary precedes the gunboat. We suspect that the literature was simply propaganda, as did the Spanish ambassador in 1609: he reported that the merchants "have actually made the ministers in their sermons dwell upon the importance of filling the world with their religion." [6] The interpretation put upon the enterprise by modern historians reinforces our disposition to see in the published intention a sanctimonious masquerade, especially in the publications issued under Sandys' rule. This gentleman, while doggedly pursuing a ruinous policy, suppressed letters from Virginia that told the true conditions, and instead issued seductive lies that lured hundreds to their doom,[7] among which were pious sermons

[2] Edwin Arber and A. G. Bradley, eds., John Smith, *Works* (Edinburgh, 1910), 4.

[3] Brown, *Genesis*, 256.

[4] William Strachey, *The Historie of Travaile into Virginia Britannia*, ed. Richard Henry Major (London, 1849), 12.

[5] Brown, *Genesis*, 605.

[6] Brown, *Genesis*, 258–59; see the Catholice satire on the pious professions of the company in John Floyd, *The Overthrow of the Protestant Pulpit-Babels*, in Brown, *First Republic*, 183–84.

[7] Wesley Frank Craven, *Dissolution of the Virginia Company* (New York, 1932), 214.

and further dedications to the missionary purpose. Captain John Smith got his revenge by telling posterity of the Company's fantastic instructions to the men on the spot: "We did admire how it was possible such wise men could so torment themselves and us with such strange absurdities and impossibilities: making Religion their colour, when all their aime was nothing but present profit." [8] The knight-errant who could proclaim no pleasure comparable to a generous spirit and employment in noble actions could also speak a language familiar to the twentieth century: "For, I am not so simple to thinke, that euer any other motiue then wealth, will euer erect there a Commonweale." [9] This being, it seems to us, the bald truth, we are ready to set aside as so much cant publications which assert that the primary motive in Virginia was evangelical.

Yet it is clearly impossible so to dismiss the piety of the first Virginians, for the records offer ample testimony to the power of religion in their lives. Even if the project was basically a commercial affair, the men engaged in it, not merely ministers but soldiers, gave homage to religion. Though John Smith asserted that only wealth would entice men to America, yet when he reviewed his career, he said that though he had lived for thirty-seven years amid wars, pestilence, and famine, and now had nothing but his pains for his reward, still he had "much reason both privately and publikely to acknowledge it and give God thankes, whose omnipotent power onely delivered me, to doe the utmost of my best to make his name knowne in those remote parts of the world, and his loving mercy to such a miserable sinner." [10]

The first ministers were men who took the evangelical aim seriously. The Reverend Robert Hunt, whom Smith adored and called "an honest, religious, and couragious Divine," demonstrated his saintly character a hundred times in tending the sick and dying, in composing quarrels, and, in 1608, when a fire destroyed his library and all his possessions but the clothes on his back, "yet [did] none ever see him repine at his losse." [11] And Alexander Whitaker wrote from his post at Henrico that the most grievous hardship of pioneer life was ignorance of spiritual matters, the utter lack of village churches, to be remedied only by the hearing of Christian wisdom: "And this is the almes which may bee most profitable vnto this barbarous Countrey of *Virginia*, where the name of God hath beene yet scarce heard of." [12]

The secular commanders paid no less tribute to the power of religion. When Lord De La Warr arrived, just in time to save the colony, his first act, even before his commission was read, was to hear "a sermon made by

[8] Smith, *Works*, 928.
[9] Smith, *Works*, 212.
[10] Smith, *Works*, 945.
[11] Smith, *Works*, 958, 90, 103.
[12] Alexander Whitaker, *Good Newes from Virginia* (London, 1613), ed. Wesley F. Craven (New York, 1937), 15.

Mr. Buck." [13] As Richard Rich reported in verses hawked on the streets of London,

> He comforts them, and cheeres their hearts,
>   That they abound with joy;
> He feedes them full, and feedes their soules
>   With God's word every day.[14]

Sir Thomas Dale, landing the next year, also immediately repaired to the church for a sermon.[15] and wrote to a friend in London that he was engaged in a *"religious* Warfare," with no thought of reward *"but from him in whose* vineyard *I labor, whose* Church *with greedy appetite I desire to erect."* [16] Sandys' lieutenants were the Ferrars, conspicuous even in a religious epoch for the extravagance of their piety; one of them wrote to the colony in 1621, in the face of the agony which his and Sandys' policy was inflicting upon it, that God still had a hand in it.[17] When Yeardley was leaving, after three years of attempting to put into effect the impossible schemes of Sandys and the Ferrars, he never blamed them, but exhibited the spirt of his age by bowing to the will of God:

> What am I that I should be able to do anything against which the Lord of Lords hath otherwise disposed, or what are we all that we should gainsay the Allmighty, and although as I do acknowledge all things have been most effectually and wisely projected, yet if the Lord will lay his hand upon us and cross us with sickness and mortality, and so appoint in his providence a longer time for the bringing those matters to pass which are by men determined of, what then shall he say unto these things but that it is the Lord, let him do what he please, and although he kill yet still to trust in him, not doubting but there is a time wherein he will be merciful.[18]

Whenever we allow for the conventions of a period when men of affairs made parade of their religion, nevertheless Yeardley's letter comes from conviction, not from formality.

Public observances in pioneer Virginia manifested a power of religion that again was not mere ritual. During the horrible years 1607–1609, in the worst of the "starving time," the garrison of Jamestown dragged themselves to hear a sermon every Sunday.[19] Sir Thomas Dale, "a martiall

---

[13] Brown, *Genesis*, 407.

[14] Richard Rich, *Newes from Virginia. The Lost Flocke Triumphant* (1610), in Brown, *Genesis*, 424.

[15] Brown, *Genesis*, 491.

[16] Raphe Hamor, *A Trve Discourse of the Present Estate of Virginia* (London, 1615), 51.

[17] Craven, *Dissolution*, 185.

[18] Craven, *Dissolution*, 186.

[19] Edward Maria Wingfield, *A Discourse of Virginia* (1608), ed. Charles Deane, *Archaeologia Americana*, IV (American Antiquarian Society, 1860), 90–91; Smith, *Works*, 36, 39, 118; Philip Alexander Bruce, *Institutional History of Virginia in the Seventeenth Century* (New York, 1910), I, 11–12.

man," had spent his life in the camp but was yet "a man of great knowledge in Diuinity, and of a good conscience in all his doing"; under his rule, Whitaker reported, there was preaching every Sunday in the forenoon and catechizing in the afternoon, while "Euery Saturday at night I exercise in Sir Thomas Dales house"; once a month they had communion and every year a solemn fast.[20] When the Assembly convened, its first concern was for religion; professing that "men's affaires doe little prosper where God's service is neglected," the Burgesses heard a prayer by Mr. Buck and thereupon enacted a series of religious laws that are a match for anything to be found in Puritan societies. Ministers were to hold services every Sunday; attendance was compulsory; the moral law was enacted into statute; idleness, gaming, drunkenness, excess in apparel were heavily fined; ministers and churchwardens were instructed to present "all ungodly disorders . . . as suspicions of whordomes, dishonest company keeping with woemen and such like" to the judgment of the church, and if an offender did not amend, he was to be excommunicated and his goods confiscated. Further legislation in the next two decades made the code still more drastic: observance of the Sabbath was enforced by laws as rigorous as those of New England, in fact even more rigorous, and persons could be presented for such minute violation as carrying a gun, shelling corn, or fetching a pair of shoes. All inhabitants paid taxes for the support of the church and the clergy, and those who objected suffered a double levy.[21]

If we are astonished to find in Virginia the legislation of a New England "theocracy," it is only because we forget that both communities were legatees of the Reformation, and that much we consider distinctively Puritan was really the spirit of the times. No nation of Europe had yet divided the state from the church; no government had yet imagined that religion could be left to the individual conscience. Society, economics, and the will of God were one and the same, and the ultimate authority in human relations was the ethic of Christendom. All the transactions of this world held their rank in a hierarchical structure, with salvation, to which all other activities ministered, at the apex. The legislation of Virginia, whether imposed by the Company or enacted by the Burgesses, was designed to repeat in America the political philosophy of Europe, which was still medieval and still demanded enforcement by the state of the moral as well as the civil code. Officers of the company utilized the evangelical appeal to attract investors and settlers; they were of course interested in profits, but they exemplified the coincidence of the spiritual and the practical which was then assumed in every walk of life. They were incapable of

[20] Hamor, *Trve Discourse*, 60.
[21] *Proceedings of the Virginia Assembly* (1619), in Lyon Gardiner Tyler, ed., *Narratives of Early Virginia* (New York, 1907), 251, 265, 271–72, etc., Bruce, *Institutional History*, I, 13, 18, 28–38, 42, 97, 186; William Waller Hening, *The Statutes at Large* (New York, 1819–1823), I, 144, 156–60.

pursuing a purely economic program which would have left religion in the hands of private citizens.

III

The Virginia Company, being an English enterprise, was not only Christian but specifically Protestant, and being blessed by the Crown, was resolved that the ecclesiastical order in Virginia should be that of the Church of England. The king instructed the first governors to make certain that "the true word, and service of God and Christian faith be preached, planted, and used, . . . according to the doctrine, rights, and religion now professed and established within our realme of England." [22] The Company's publications advertised that no papists or recusants were admitted,[23] and that no man or women would be sent out who could not "bring or render some good testimony of his religion to God." [24] The first Assembly, after Mr. Buck's prayer, took the oath of supremacy, "none staggering at it," [25] and required the ministers to read the service every Sunday "according to the Ecclesiastical lawes and orders of the churche of Englande." [26] In 1624 the Assembly more specifically demanded "that there be an uniformity in our church as neere as may be to the canons in England." [27]

Yet there is the fact to be noted: while the Virginia Company professed adherence to the Church of England, its ecclesiastical complexion always shows itself more "low" than "high," and therefore not radically different from that of many Puritans. Virginians enacted the canons of England, creating a state church, but the quality of their piety, their sense of their relation to God, was so thoroughly Protestant as to be virtually indistinguishable from the Puritan. The most elaborate of the sermons before the Company, William Crashaw's, was a Puritan discourse which reviewed the basic dogmas of election, faith, perseverance, and assurance of salvation. His final word upon the migration was that if it aimed solely at profit, God would defeat it. In the colony itself the literature exhibits an even deeper feeling for the Puritan conception of the universe, wherein a Calvinist God and His awful decrees are realities of experience, and the facts of sin and innate depravity, the premises of all action. Under the military rule of the soldier-governors, under De La Warr, Gates, Dale, and Argall, the captains of the guard were required to lead their platoons

[22] Brown, *Genesis*, 67–68.

[23] *Nova Britannia*: *Offering Most Excellent Fruits by Planting in Virginia* (London, 1609), ed. George Humphrey (Rochester, New York, 1897), 19–20. See William Symonds, *Virginia, A Sermon Preached at White-Chapel* (London, 1609), A3.

[24] Brown, *Genesis*, 352–53.

[25] *Proceedings of the Virginia Assembly*, 251.

[26] *Proceedings of the Virginia Assembly*, 271.

[27] Hening, *Statutes*, I, 123.

to prayer both morning and evening, and to lift up their voices from the wilderness to heaven, confessing that all had sinned against God,

through our blindnesse of mind, profanesse of spirit, hardnesse of heart, selfe loue, worldlinesse, carnall lusts, hypocrisie, pride, vanitie, vnthankfulnesse, infidelitie, and other our natiue corruptions.

This prayer, in length and substance the equal of any Puritan supplication, ends with a plea for mercy and a request that the God of Israel will cast down the idols of Dagon, that He will "let such swine still wallow in their mire." [28] When soldiers and laborers were fed daily upon such reflections we may well believe Alexander Whitaker's report that several had declared, "All we haue, euen life it selfe, will we willingly giue, and consecrate to God, that the Gospell may bee preached, and the name of Iesus Christ called vpon in *Virginia*." [29] That many who listened to the prescribed prayer were the ragtag and bobtail of England, that they were dissolute and lazy, or that the leaders quarreled among themselves and almost wrecked the settlement, does not alter the fact that all conceived of the undertaking as a mission for the glory of God.

The personal history of John Rolfe gives a still better insight into the piety of the settlers, an example all the more instructive because this worthy showed the way to profit from tobacco, which was first to save the community and then to transform it into something entirely other than a holy and dedicated state. The legend of Pocahontas is a classic of American mythology, but Rolfe's own version of his love for the Indian maiden is less widely known. In 1613 she was captured by a stratagem and held at Jamestown as a hostage, where Rolfe learned to love her (the competition was not numerous). His letter to Sir Thomas Dale requesting permission to marry her takes us across the chasm that separates modern sensibility from the seventeenth century's, and shows us how men actually felt in a day when redemption was the ultimate issue. Rolfe cannot for a moment entertain the thought of this marriage unless he is certain that he is "called hereunto by the spirit of God," no matter how much he fancies himself in love. He protests before heaven that he is not led "with the vnbridled desire of carnall affection: but for the good of this plantation, for the honour of our countrie, for the glory of God, for my owne saluation, and for conuerting to the true knowledge of God and Iesus Christ, an vnbeleeuing creature." His English heart and thoughts have for long been tangled with thoughts of her, he has become "inthralled in so intricate a laborinth, I was euen awearied to vnwinde my selfe thereout"; yet he could not make his way out by the pragmatic argument that because he loved the girl he should marry her. When the notion first occurred to him, good Protestant that he was, he was horrified, for he

[28] *For the Colony in Virginea Britannia, Lawes Diuine, Morall and Martiall, &c.* (London, 1612), 90–96.

[29] Whitaker, *Good Newes*, C3 recto.

remembered that God forbade Israelites to marry strangers, and he told himself, "Surely these are wicked instigations, hatched by him who seeketh and delighteth in mans destruction." By dint of prayer and fasting Rolfe overcame these "diabolical assaults." But then an idea came to him: why should he not convert her? This seemed an authentically divine prompting because it dawned upon him after he had been separated from her for some weeks, "which in common reason (were it not an vndoubted worke of God) might breede forgetfulnesse of a farre more worthie creature." Only when he sees the marriage in this light does he feel justified, only then can he be assured that he may seek his own welfare in doing the Lord's work. He asks himself why he was created, and answers as any primitive Virginian should:

If not for transitory pleasures and worldly vanities, but to labour in the Lords vineyard, there to sow and plant, to nourish and increase the fruites thereof, daily adding with the good husband in the Gospell, somewhat to the tallent, that in the end the fruites may be reaped, to the comfort of the laborer in this life, and his saluation in the world to come?

If he converts her, marries her, and becomes the means of saving her soul — and incidentally manages an accommodation between her father and the colony, thus bringing peace to God's people — then he feels that he is guided by heavenly grace. If marrying Pocahontas be the labor to which he is called, Rolfe concludes on the heights of resignation, let the Lord do with His own what He will, "and I will never cease, (God assisting me) vntill I haue accomplished, & brought to perfection so holy a worke, in which I will daily pray God to blesse me, to mine, and her eternall happines." [30]

To discover a courtship conducted in this spirit beside the James is to realize that however much Virginia and New England differed in ecclesiastical polities, they were both recruited from the same type of Englishmen, pious, hard-working, middle-class, accepting literally and solemnly the tenets of Puritanism — original sin, predestination, and election — who could conceive of the society they were erecting in America only within a religious framework. In the fullness of time the differing church polities of Virginia and New England became institutional dresses for diverging characters, but at the beginning the two had much in common. The leaders of Jamestown were not "saints" as were Bradford and Winthrop, yet they, too, proceeded to set up a church and regulate their lives by it. In a famous passage, John Smith tells how, upon the very day of the landing, they hung up an old sail for an awning, used fallen trees for pews, and made a pulpit out of a bar of wood nailed to two trees, and "This was our Church, till wee built a homely thing like a barne, set upon Cratchets, covered with rafts, sedge, and earth." [31]

Undoubtedly the publicists worked the evangelical argument for all it

[30] Hamor, *True Discourse*, 62–68.

[31] Smith, *Works*, 957.

was worth: the important fact is that for Englishmen at the beginning of the seventeenth century it was worth a great deal. John Donne was more of a Laudian than either Sandys or Rolfe, yet in the sermon he delivered before the Company in 1622, when that body was torn by dissension and the colony almost wiped out by the massacre, the familiar theme reappeared, not only untarnished by these considerations, but even more exalted by his cadences. Whatever action aims at spreading the Gospel, he said, is an apostolical action, and before the end of the world shall come, God's kingdom must be extended over it:

Before the end of the world come, before this mortality shall put on immortality, before the creature shall be delivered of the bondage of corruption under which it groans, before the martyrs under the altar shall be silenced, before all things shall be subdued to Christ, his kingdom perfected, and the last enemy death destroyed; the Gospel must be preached to those men to whom ye send; to all men; further and hasten you this blessed, this joyful, this glorious consummation of all, and happy reunion of all bodies to their souls, by preaching the Gospel to those men.[32]

John Rolfe is a crude rhetorician beside John Donne, but his address to King James in 1616 exhibits the same spirit, urging that no man can look upon these wretched Indians without pity, "seeing they beare the image of our Heavenlie Creator, and we and they come from one and the same mould," that every Christian heart should desire that they be purged of their ignorance and settled in the paths of righteousness "to serve the King of Heaven." [33]

The event, as we know, proved otherwise. Pagans and Christians had to fight it out, and even John Rolfe died by the tomahawk; missionaries were diverted into raising tobacco, and the company disintegrated. But we should not be deceived by these facts into supposing that the profession of a missionizing aim was a fraud. Even though most of the writing is propaganda, it exhibits a mental universe in which religion was the main ingredient in human motive. The discrepancy between profession and performance was, to be sure, immense. How great and how distressing that contrast appeared to the protagonists themselves we may better understand if we read more deeply into the literature, to determine what part the intention played in their total scheme of things.

IV

The first premise of all the Virginia writers, whether in London or in Jamestown, is the providence of God. The natural universe, in which Virginia took its place, conformed to a "law of nature," but that law was simply God's customary way of acting. He was free to disregard it when-

[32] John Donne, "A Sermon upon the eighth verse of the first chapter of the Acts of the Apostles," Works, ed. Henry Alford (London, 1836), VI, 240–41.

[33] John Rolfe, A Relation of the State of Virginia (1616), in The Virginia Historical Register and Literary Advertiser, I (July, 1848), 111–12.

ever He wished. Events were not produced by the blind operations of cause and effect, economic motives, or human contrivances; these were "second causes" through which God worked. The "first cause" was always His will. He decreed whether the much-needed supply ships would founder or arrive, whether Powhatan should be friendly or hostile, whether corn should grow or rats consume it, whether Virginia was to succeed or fail. "It pleased God," said John Smith, to move the Indians; God, "the absolute disposer of all heartes," changed their minds; "by Gods assistance" we procured corn; He who is "the guider of all good actions" brought the ship into harbor; He who is "the patron of all good indeavours" sent relief when He had "seene our misery sufficient." [34] In 1624, revising his earlier books for *The Generall Historie*, Smith inserted verses to point the moral of the providential theme:

> Thus the Almightie was the bringer on,
> The guide, path, terme, all which was God alone.[35]

Smith, like all the authors, held up Virginia to the admiring gaze of the world as a particularly clear instance of God's will in action, and a company broadside in 1610 told of recent events as "the reuealed counsell of God." [36]

When men look upon the universe and see in it not the impersonal workings of physical law but the manipulations of an intelligent being, their conceptions of what they are doing inevitably differ from those of a scientific age. It mattered little to the Virginia theorists whether the expedition could be traced to natural causes and economic incentives or to pure miracle; in either case God was at work. England, for instance, was overpopulated; but was not this fact simply a divine contrivance in order that the Gospel should be carried to America? Preachers to the Company dwelt long, even enthusiastically, upon the economic crisis: "The people, blessed be God, doe swarme in the land, as yong bees in a hiue in June; insomuch that there is very hardly roome for one man to liue by another." [37] Though all the tenderhearted are grieved, said Copland in 1622, to see men starve daily in the streets of London, though it is sad that laborers who rise early and tear their flesh all day and go late to bed "are scarce able to put bread in their mouthes at the weekes end, and cloathes on their backes at the yeares end," nevertheless there has been a design in these misfortunes, because now a labor supply is available for the plantation.[38]

[34] Smith, *Works*, 8, 10, 12, 91, 95, 159.

[35] Smith, *Works*, 404; see George Percy, *Observations gathered out of a Discourse of the Plantation of the Southerne Colonie in Virginia* (1607), in *Narratives of Early Virginia*, 22; Brown, *Genesis*, 107.

[36] *A Trve Declaration of the Estate of the Colonie in Virginia* (London, 1610), 19, in Peter Force, ed., *Tracts* (New York, 1844), III.

[37] Symonds, *Virginia*, 19.

[38] Patrick Copland, *Virginia's God be Thanked, or A Sermon of Thanksgiving for the Happie successe of the affayres in Virginia this last yeare* (London, 1622), 34.

Of course, God does not always need to work by such devious mehods; men can be directly inspired by "the powerfull perswasion of Gods spirit to their consciences." [39] Many went, according to the divines, without thought or hope of profit, simply because they knew that God was working "to some higher end then ordinary." [40] The ministers who chose Virginia rather than a comfortable vicarage in England professed that "the God of heauen found vs out, and made vs readie to our hands, able and fit men, for the Ministeriall function in this Plantation." [41] Hence the colonizing of Virginia could be no ordinary commercial transaction; it was an act in the economy of redemption, a special and supernatural summons, a maneuver which the wisdom of God had made inevitable from the beginning of time and was now carrying to its foreordained completion.[42]

Further evidence that God had a hand in the plantation was provided in generous measure when Europe was enthralled by the story of the wreck of Somers and Gates upon the islands of Bermuda in 1609, of the long sojourn of the crew of the foundered *Sea Venture* upon those mysterious strands, their construction of new ships, their arrival at Jamestown long after they had been given up for lost, their decision to abandon the colony, and then — to crown the work — just as they were putting out to sea, their marvellous meeting with the relieving fleet of Lord De La Warr at the mouth of the James. Had they left one day before, or had De La Warr arrived one day later, all would have been lost and savages would have stalked through the empty and rotting wharfs of Jamestown. To the seventeenth century this was the supremely "special" providence of all time. The impact upon its imagination can be gauged by Shakespeare's *The Tempest*, and still more by the tracts which the company rushed into print to exploit the sensation. "The finger of God hath been the onely true worker heere," wrote Whitaker from Virginia,[43] and Crashaw in London agreed: "If euer the hand of God appeared in action of man, it was heere most euident: for when man had forsaken this businesse, God tooke it in hand." [44]

Unfortunately in a universe presided over by a Protestant God,[45] events

[39] William Crashaw, *A Sermon Preached in London before the right honorable Lord La warre, Lord Gouernour and Captaine Generall of Virginea* (London, 1610), I2 verso.

[40] Whitaker, *Good Newes*, B3 verso.

[41] Whitaker, *Good Newes*, C1 verso.

[42] Strachey, *Historie*, 153.

[43] Whitaker, *Good Newes*, 23.

[44] Crashaw, in Whitaker, *Good Newes*, B2 recto.

[45] It should be noted that the conception of God presiding through His providence over the settling of America was fully as strong and articulated among the Catholics of Maryland as among the settlers of Virginia and New England. For example, "Thus we were in feare of imminent death . . . till at length it pleased God to send some ease. . . . This deliverie in a manner assured us of Gods mercy towards us, and those infideels Conversion of Maryland," in Clayton C. Hall, ed., *Narratives of Early Maryland* (New York, 1910), 31. The Jesuit fathers could report as many divine provi-

do not always make their meanings so clear. The Protestant Reformation impressed upon the popular mind a sense of the majesty and sovereignty of God. The elaborate proof of His rationality and of the intelligibility of nature built up by the Scholastic doctors of the thirteenth century was swept aside by a dogmatic assertion that He was transcendent, terrible, incomprehensible, even while good and merciful. The Laudian party, reacting against the Calvinism which captured the church under Elizabeth, turned back to scholastic conceptions and celebrated a God of reason and of beauty, the God of Richard Hooker's "Laws" and of Herbert's poetry. Among Puritans such a God was suspect, for to them the primary fact about the creator and governor of the universe was not His rationality or His benevolence but His power, and among the mass of those whom we have called "low church" Anglicans, God was more often conceived in the manner of Calvin than of Herbert.

The deity who by His providence governed early Virginia was at times, as in the wreck of the *Sea Venture*, considerate, but at other times inscrutable. He permitted sinful and incompetent men to mismanage the colony and Company; He afflicted the planters with famine and disease; He hardened the hearts of the Indians against His own Gospel and turned the fiends loose upon His faithful and unprepared saints. If men's faith wavered under these shocks, if investors began to doubt whether they had a vocation to throw away their savings, Protestant leaders could point out that Virginia was merely encountering the sort of difficulties which the Protestant God, for reasons best known to Himself, frequently put in the way of His chosen. All excellent things, said Alderman Johnson in 1612, are "accompanied with manifold difficulties, crosses and disasters, being such as are appointed by the highest providence." [46] Perhaps God's purpose in so encumbering them might be surmised, if not positively demonstrated; probably He wished to exercise the patience of the managers and make them more wise. In any event, the company assured its stockholders, "It is but a golden slumber, that dream of any humane felicity, which is not sauced with some contingent miserie. . . . Griefe and pleasure are the crosse sailes of the worlds euer-turning windmill." [47] By 1616 the affair was definitely languishing, shares were going begging, and stockholders would not pay another assessment. Again the Company turned to the providential philosophy; six years ago, it recollected, no earthly means were lacking, but "such was the will of Almighty God, as the world well knoweth, that this great hope and preparation, by many disasters on Sea and Land, . . . was in a manner cleane defeated." Yet for men now to give over and abandon hope was clearly a sinful error; lukewarm investors would have sacrificed the lives of the settlers "had not Gods secret purpose

dences in winning souls to their church as could the Protestants (*ibid.*, 120, 126, 133, 138–39).

[46] *The New Life of Virginea* (London, 1612), A3 recto.

[47] *A True Declaration*, 24.

beene more strongly fixed to uphold the same" by stirring up a few of the faithful to send over more supplies.[48] When Sandys, Southampton, and the Ferrars took the direction, there was a resurgence of confidence in divine favor, with a new series of sermons preached at the quarter-courts; Sandys inspired a sort of religious revival, and the work went forward with new zeal.[49]

Divine inscrutability did not leave men of that age altogether in the dark as to why holy undertakings suffered afflictions. Even in strict Calvinism, there were possible explanations of how, in spite of absolute decrees, men were required to do their utmost, as though all depended upon them and not on foreordination. In the looser forms of Calvinism there was less difficulty in asserting at one and the same time that God determines but man must perform. Divine wisdom foresees and ordains every action, said the Company in 1610, and the best that human prudence can do is to propose religious, noble, and "feasable" ends; but because men do not share the wisdom of God, there can be no absolute assurance that even the most pious of men will choose the proper ways and means. "And the higher the quality, and nature, and more removed from ordinary action (such as this is of which we discourse) the more perplexed and misty are the pathes there-unto." [50]

Even though an enterprise be holy, there may be reasons operating entirely outside it which generate chastisements. Here the Virginia apologists told how Columbus had offered Henry VII the chance to underwrite his voyage and how England had failed its opportunity; so God struck a nice balance between punishment and favor by reserving for the English "an excellent portion" of the new world, yet making their conquest of it difficult.[51] Biblical precedents for such treatment of a chosen people were not lacking; the wandering of the Israelites was the classic example, and Virginia writers told and retold the episode of the twelve scouts sent to inspect Canaan, of whom ten reported it no land of milk and honey and only two, Caleb and Joshua, spoke the truth; wherefore because of the mendacity of ten God afflicted the people, but for the virtue of two he succored them. Like Caleb and Joshua, said John Rolfe, those who have not allowed themselves to become discouraged by the mysterious workings of God's providence "have mightilie upheld this Christian cause — for God, even our owne God, did helpe them." [52]

Of course, if the way appeared strewn with difficulty, there was another being at work in the universe who could be blamed. The religious quality

[48] Brown, *Genesis*, 775.
[49] *A Declaration of the State of the Colonie and Affaires in Virginia* (London, 1620), 3, in Force's *Tracts*, III. See Copland, *Virginia's God*, 11.
[50] Brown, *Genesis*, 339.
[51] *Nova Britannia*, 27; Robert Gray, *A Good Speed to Virginia* (London, 1609), ed. Wesley F. Craven, Scholars' Facsimiles and Reprints (New York, 1937), B1 verso.
[52] Rolfe, *Relation*, 112.

of the early Virginia mind is nowhere more evident than in the readiness with which adventurers and planters felt in every disaster the hoof of the Devil. Satan inspired and circulated the slanders, false reports, doubts and objections that discouraged investors, and quite understandably, "for we goe to disherit him of his ancient freehold, and to deliuer from out of his bondage the soules, which he hath kept so many yeeres in thraldome." [53] We are therefore to expect that he will move all the infernal powers against us. The devout Whitaker was serene in the face of trouble, for he reflected, "wheresoeuer any goodnesse shall begin to bud forth, the Diuell will labour by all meanes to nip it in the head." The vices and squabbles of the settlers were instigated by him — "some striuing for superioritie, others by murmurings, mutinies, & plaine treasons; & others by fornication, prophanenes, idlenes, and such monstrous sinnes; that he had almost thrust vs out of this kingdome, and indeed quitted this Land of vs." [54] To men of the Reformation, to Protestants, the Devil was no abstraction; he was an ever-present force for evil, and to their eyes it seemed obvious that his last stronghold was the wilderness of America, inhabited by his imps. The morale of Virginians, as of other colonists, was sustained by this conviction.

It could be so sustained, because in Protestant theology the Devil exists on sufferance. God permits Satan to work, but for purposes of His own, for the unnamable purposes of His secret will. When Satan sifts us most narrowly, then is Christ most near, as to Whitaker it seemed evident that at the worst moments, God "(as one awaked out of sleepe) stood vp and set vs meanes of great helpe, when we needed most, and expected least reliefe." [55]

In the final analysis, the effect of the doctrine of divine providence for pioneers in America was not to disguise the economic motive, as twentieth-century historians are fond of supposing; instead, it gave them a conviction that the visible universe is intelligible and significant, that it is directed by a consciousness who orders all things for the best, even though in many instances the benefit is not immediately obvious. Those versions of history which see in the founding of Virginia an assertion of individualism sin against history most unforgivably by leaving out of account the cosmology of the colonists. Those who see in it only the beginnings of capitalist imperialism sin even 'more by their ignorance of the teleological world in which the seventeenth century lived, a world where every action found its rationale, not in politics or in economics, but in religion. When the Company heard of the deliverance of Somers and Gates, these businessmen interpreted the specific providence according to the general conception that presided over the founding of Virginia:

He that shall but turne vp his eye, and behold the spangled Canopie of heauen, shall but cast down his eye, and consider the imbroidered Carpet of the earth, and

---

[53] Crashaw, *Sermon*, H1 verso.
[54] Whitaker, *Good Newes*, D2 recto 22.
[55] Whitaker, *Good Newes*, D2 recto 22.

withall shall marke, how the heauens beare the earth, the earth beare the corne and oyle, and they relieue the necessities of man, that man wil acknowledge Gods infinite prouidence. But hee that shall further obserue, how God inclineth all casuall euents, to worke the necessary helpe of his Saints, must needs adore the Lords infinite goodnesse.[56]

When the English undertook to plant colonies in America, they commenced — whatever they ended with — not with propositions about the rights of man or with the gospel of wealth, but with absolute certainties concerning the providence of God.

V

In the face of some particular disaster, the colonist often could only bow his head, as did Sir George Yeardley over his recall in 1621. If there was a reason, he confessed himself unable to perceive it. But in more general terms, in the full perspective of time, the design of God was not obscure to him, and from contemplation of it, the colonist could always derive consolation and encouragement. The doctrine of providence meant that God governed the universe not only in space but also in time, and as there was an intelligent purpose in each enactment, so all events were connected in a long-range program which men call history.

In this program, the colonization of Virginia had a definite place. God had not kept America hidden for centuries that men should now supinely admire it; He had disclosed it at this moment in order to inform the present age what was required of it. The New World was to be the scene of the next great act in the history of redemption. A philosophy of history followed as an inevitable corollary from the doctrine of providence; the great theologians fashion it, and a peculiar adaptation was achieved in New England, but the substance of its appears in the Virginia pamphlets. Perhaps the best statement is in Purchas,[57] and the force of the conception was so great that he could not begin an account of European migration to the New World without expounding a Christian version of history. In the story of Virginia, which was the first and still, in 1625, the principal English colony, he had to go back to Adam and Eve, and show how God had so managed the past that English colonization in the present was the fulfillment of His plan.

He had to begin with Adam because Adam had determined, not only the fate of humanity, but the progress of geography. Had he not fallen, a virtuous race would have peaceably expanded over the globe to view the creation, and America need not have been concealed. Had Adam not sinned, man would have lived everywhere in Eden, holding sway over all creatures and enjoying all fruits of the field. But Adam fell, and a curse

[56] *A True Declaration,* 19.
[57] *Hakluytus Posthumus or Purchas His Pilgrims* (London, 1625; Glasgow, 1905–1906), I, 1–45, XIX, 218–67.

fell upon mankind and upon the earth; the design of God seemed balked by the creature. Had depraved men then been left to themselves, they would not have multiplied over the globe in peace and innocence, but would have slaughtered each other. In all justice, God could have left them so to perish, or He could have regenerated them at once by an act of power. Instead, He chose another, a cleverer course; he worked out a "scheme" by Which He could carry out His original plan and yet administer their punishment. He made their very depravity the instrument of their obedience. To keep them from killing each other, He dispersed them in tribes and countries over the face of the earth, and shut them up in ignorance of each other's existence. For seventeenth-century colonizers, the story of the Tower of Babel was of central importance: hereby God artfully turned the greatest curse into the greatest blessing, and, as the Virginia Company moralized in 1610, "by confusion of tongues, kept them from confusion of states; scattering those clouen people, into as many colonies ouer the face of the earth, as there are diuersities of languages in the earth." [58] But the earth being now accursed, the peoples went forth not to enjoy and to admire, but to labor in the sweat of their brows; they went out to find the land which had been man's fee simple by deed of gift "possessed & wrongfully usurped by wild beasts, and unreasonable creatures." [59]

To keep these wanderers in some degree of order, God graciously bestowed upon them the "law of nature," allowing them to retain a modicum of the original wisdom. Insofar as the Indians have laws, said Purchas, "God himself is the Law giver, and hath written by the stile of Nature this Law in the hearts of men," to which all kingdoms and even all kings are subject. By it they allot their people public and private tenures. In addition, that men may not utterly starve in a now hostile world, God gives to all people, even the most barbaric, some knowledge of the arts of agriculture and carpentry, so that they may eat and build, though of course He gives them enough only for the barest subsistence. He deprives them of the supreme felicity of life, true religion, but He leaves in them just enough hunger for divinity that they expend themselves in an unavailing worship of Satan. This fact, that they still grope after God, even under misconceptions, proves that they retain something of the image of God, just as even in the benighted wilderness they still retain dominion over the creatures.

With the Fall, Purchas explained, man's tenure became, instead of a "free-hold," a "villenage"; yet because man still possesses the faculties of the soul, he may still exercise command over the "torpid, vegetative, and all unreasonable creatures." His supremacy is "continued to him by that Charter of Reason." Before the Fall, man used the creatures only for the glory of God; now he misuses them; still, he does use them, and they exist to be used. "God even in the sentencing of that judgement remembring mercy, added thornes, and thistles, and sorrow, and sweate, but tooke not

---

[58] *A Trve Declaration*, 4. See Symonds, *Virginia*.
[59] Gray, *Good Speed*, B1 verso.

away the use." By that same charter, by the light of nature, savage and heathen men have a right to their lands and their implements; the tenure of infidels is warranted by Christ and cannot be taken away by violence. One comes from a reading of the Virginia literature persuaded that historians have so failed in historical imagination that they have not done justice either to the grandeur or the humility of a conception which was at the very center of the impetus to Christian imperialism.

As seventeenth-century imperialists saw it, the fallen races had unwittingly begun a laborious fulfillment of God's unchangeable decree, a long ascent back to the integrity they lost in Eden. Men wilfully threw away the chance of walking through history with God's aid; therefore God contrived that, after being dispersed to the ends of the earth, they must walk alone, or with no more assistance than the "light of nature." They had to reachieve unity by themselves. This was a terrible task, but that they might have some hints of how they should proceed, God — who is ever merciful — diversified the products of the earth, so that different commodities are no longer found all in one place, as they were at the creation. Because products man desires are scattered over land and sea, commerce becomes inevitable, and in the wake of commerce, salvation. International trade was conceived in the bed of religion, and Virginia, in its first two decades, was faithful to the inheritance.

God has made men, continued Purchas, all of one blood, and "would still they should bee as fellow members one of another." Their natural inclination would be to hate each other, to avoid or to murder each other, but God circumvented them. He decreed "that there should still remaine mutual Necessitie, the Mother of mutuall Commerce, that one should not bee hungry, and another drunken, but the superflueitie of one Countrey, should supply the necessities of another, in exchange for such things, which are here also necessary, and there abound." Thus is mankind compelled, in its own despite, to be one body, "each communicating with other for publike good." (Before the century was out, this magnificent conception of Christian community would be secularized and vulgarized into the unabashed nationalistic egoism of "mercantilism.") The ingenuity of divine Providence — which the most grasping of the time would confess far outruns human calculation — was shown when it withheld Columbus until commerce had made Europe one economic family and until Europeans had learned, in God's school, enough of the arts of navigation to manage a trade across the terrible ocean.[60]

Then, because one of the parties to this commerce conducted according to the law of nature happens to be a Christian people, the crowning touch in God's intricate scheme is applied: as they go forth to trade and colonize, Christians automatically carry the Gospel with them, and when mankind has been once more united by the merchants, it can be made one in profession by the preachers. The conversion of the world is not to be

[60] See Strachey, *Historie*, 138.

worked "by myracle," said Strachey, because in the course of international exchange the "sacred word will have a powerfull passage throughout the world," and all nations may "be reduced to the kingdome of grace." [61]

Hence the Virginia Company and all Christian enterprises must be exceedingly careful: they must adventure for profit, but in the spirit of faith. If they, like pagans, think it enough to observe only the law of nature, and if they use the bounty of God for their selfish pleasures, He will curse them — and they will go bankrupt. They must seek the needed commodities, but must recognize that traffic in worldly commodities is but a means to spiritual. Merely because we are Christians, Purchas continued, we have by that token no title to estates superior to that of savages, but we do have the chance, once we get them, to use them correctly. We may acquire riches only if we do not set our hearts upon them, and if Virginia has suffered, the reason must be clear: "But how the loving our selves more then God, hath detained so great blessings from us to Virginia, and from Virginia to us." But if the prescribed conditions be scrupulously observed, then will our enterprise be both lawful and blessed, then will even a joint-stock trading venture become a holy venture, for we have a commission from Him to plant the land, from the Alpha and Omega of Virginia. If Englishmen go in the right spirit, they may be sure that they will succeed, for the rationale of history requires that they prevail. And to induce them into doing what they must do, a wily God attracts them with the promise of economic reward:

God goeth before us, and hath given Virginia so rich a portion, to allure and assure our loves; in multiplying our people, and thereby our necessities enforcing a vent: in endowing Virginia with so large a jointure, so temperate, so commodious for the climate.

The settlers of Virginia went forth having been told — and believing — that "when they looked to heauen they saw a promise, and looking to earthward they saw a blessing." [62]

I have thus summarized Purchas's argument because his theology, so deeply imbedded in his immense narrative as to elude the appreciation of historians, provides the best exposition in the literature of Virginia of the theory upon which the more fugitive pamphlets were constructed. Without an understanding of this theory, these publications are scarcely intelligible. When we turn from this cosmic perspective to the more delimited pleading of the Virginia apologists, we also find in Purchas the beginnings of another idea that figures in their works, one which was later to be more extensively elaborated in New England, but which may be read in either literature as a peculiar addition made by the English genius to Protestant philosophy. Since Englishmen were now called in the providence of God to set out on commercial expeditions, they naturally looked to the Bible

---

[61] Strachey, *Historie*, 21.
[62] *The New Life of Virginea*, B3 recto.

for precedent, and both the Virginia Company and the Massachusetts Bay Company found an ideal prototype in Abraham. "Then here must wee know, that what inducement Abraham had, to goe out of his Countrey, by a generall calling, the same doth binde all his sonnes, according to the faith, to goe likewise abroad, when God doth not otherwise call them to some special affaires." [63] But Abraham, going forth in the explicit knowledge of God, did not flee headlong into the wilderness like the crazed sinners of Babel; he went upon an explicit arrangement with God, an engagemen to Jehovah and of Jehovah to him. In so many words, God promised Abraham that he would become a great nation, that he would be given "the good things of this present world," that the estates of the heathen would be disposed of according to their courtesy toward Abraham.[64] He went forth, not under the normal compulsion of mere nature, but under a unique, an explicit, a conscious contract with God, under a "covenant," in which he promised to do certain things for God in return for which God pledged Himself to recompense Abraham. So the English migration to Virginia was not merely an event in nature, but over and above that, it was a going forth, as John Rolfe put it, of "a peculiar people, marked and chosen by the finger of God, to possess it, for undoubtedly he is with us." [65] This was not simply an economic transaction; it proceeded "from the extraordinary motion of Gods Spirit." [66] Hence this colony was to play its special part in the scheme of history not blindly, as do ordinary men, but intelligently, as do the regenerate.

To the legalistic minds of seventeenth-century English Protestants, there was an irresistible charm in this notion of a covenant, by which both God and man were bound to respect certain avowed terms. To the Puritans of New England it was exceedingly attractive, but to Virginians, who were almost if not quite Puritans, it was also enticing. It could serve as a prod and inducement to faithful service, and could provide a ready explanation for mishaps. If Virginia was afflicted with famine and massacre, then it was obvious that it had failed to live up to the terms of its covenant, and God was justly punishing it. Even the rugged John Smith could see in God's righteous anger the cause of his difficulties.[67] God binds Himself, said the preachers, "to him that receiueth his Couenant," and those who truly love God will prosper.[68] Whitaker could write in 1611 that the sins of the English in Virginia had been intolerable, and he marveled that God had not swept them away at once.[69] By 1622 Patrick Copland in London reminded the company that God had not been too tender, and told them

[63] Symonds, *Virginia*, 8–9. See Gray, *Good Speed*; Crashaw, *Sermon*, F2 verso–F4 recto.

[64] Symonds, *Virginia*, 4–5.

[65] Rolfe, *Relation*, 113.

[66] Crashaw, in Whitaker, *Good Newes*, B4 recto.

[67] Smith, *Works*, 8, 598.

[68] Symonds, *Virginia*, 38ff.

[69] Brown, *Genesis*, 499.

that both the company and the settlers had suffered so heavily because they had failed their covenant, the adventurers having too much affected gain, and the settlers, "most of them at the first, beeing the very scumme of the Land, and great pity it was that no better at that time could be had," neglecting God's worship and living in idleness and vice.[70] When news of the massacre of 1622 was received in London, the officials straightway discerned the vengeance of God, and suggested that the best precaution hereafter would be a reform "of those two enormous excesses of apparel and drinking, the cry whereof cannot but have gone up to heaven, since the infamy hath spread itself to all that have but heard the name of Virginia." [71]

Even though this doctrine of a special covenant between a chosen people and their Jehovah blinded the leaders to the material reasons of their defeats, or prevented officials from blaming themselves rather than the sins of the settlers, yet in the long run it was a source of strength. Even in the starving times or during the massacre, Virginians could feel that their sufferings were not meaningless, that their griefs were actually testimonies to their special importance in the universe, since God took such extraordinary measures to chastise them. And then there was always the promise, guaranteed by the infallible word of God, that if they did behave well, they would acquire riches. This promise, explained one of the preachers, is "an example of that sweete sanction of the law, when the Lord doth allure men to keepe it, by the abundance of his blessings." [72] No one can ever tell how many among those whom Copland called "the very scumme of the Land," went to Virginia and died there in the belief that their agony was a juridical punishment for violating their covenant with God; but the idea of the covenant did play a part in the philosophy of the settlement, and left a heritage of self-esteem, even after Virginians ceased to think of themselves as the modern analogy to Israel.

In all things God wrought His will by the use of "means." Without interrupting or inhibiting "second causes," He guided them to their effects, just as He guided the winds that blew the *Sea Venture* ashore on the Bermudas. Even in the salvation of souls God did not bring men to repentance by an immediate infusion of the Holy Ghost, striking them blind in an instant; He offered them the "means" of grace, the church, the sermon, and prayer, through which they might receive their vocation. Protestantism found in this conception a counterpoise to the Catholic doctrine of the sacraments, for it permitted even the strictest predestinarian to argue that while salvation comes by faith, God engenders faith in His

---

[70] Copland, *Virginia's God*, 24.

[71] Craven, *Dissolution*, 203. See Virginia legislation of 1632 requiring church-wardens to enforce moral regulations, "as they will answer before God for such evills and plagues wherewith Almighty God may iustlie punish his people for neglectinge this good and wholesome lawe" (Hening, *Statutes*, I, 155).

[72] Symonds, *Virginia*, 26.

elect by the means supplied through the true church. As Protestantism revivified the theory of providence, so it popularized that of means, and then extended it from the method of conversion to the mechanism of physics and commerce. Crashaw expounded to the company the doctrine that a man's conversion is in God's hands, but at the same time is in his own, because God vouchsafes him "the meanes of vocation and conuersion." [73] Captains of the guard in Virginia confessed the fault that brought the vengeance of God upon them: "wee haue outstood the gracious time and meanes of our conuersion." [74] If God governed the world through means, then whatever forces or instruments fulfilled His will were appointed means. The motives of men, for instance, were means: men thought themselves the authors of their ambitions or their desires, but actually these were instigated by God, so that, acting under their own conceit, they did what He wanted. Virginia's function in the divine program was obvious; the desire for profit which led men to invest or to settle was a divinely authorized means. "As many actions both good in themselves and in their success, have been performed with bad intents, so in this case, howsoever our naughtiness of mind may sway very much, yet God may have the honor, and his kingdom advanced in the action done." [75] Though He might summon a few exceptional saints to Virginia by an inward motion of conscience, He lured the majority by economic hopes and further prevailed upon them by assurances of success. He has provided us, said Crashaw, the means to discover the land and a hospitable reception from the Indians, a people inclinable to civility and so to religion: "These meanes and opportunities, I say, being offered by Gods prouidence vnto vs, it not only shewes vs the *possibility*, but laies vpon vs a *necessity* of seeking their conuersions, and consequentlie of setting forward this plantation, without which the former cannot be." [76] The desire for wealth, the opportunity to procure it, the ships and the tools, England's need of Virginia's commodities, these were all stratagems within the providence of God to make certain that the Gospel be carried to America.

Whenever God wished, any man or object might become a means, but Christians differed from heathens in that when required to serve as instruments, they responded consciously and willingly. [77] Caesar had been a blind instrument of civilizing Britain, unaware that God was employing him for ends quite different from those he imagined; a Christian acted with complete understanding. Whether aware or not, men could effect only the predetermined result, but a Christian proved his faith by doing the inevitable with a cheerful consent. The pamphleteers rested their case finally upon the argument that by trading with the Indians, setting up a colony

[73] Crashaw, *Sermon*, B4 verso–C1 recto.
[74] *Lawes*, 90.
[75] *Nova Britannia*, 11.
[76] Crashaw, *Sermon*, C3 verso.
[77] Crashaw, *Sermon*, B4 verso; Strachey, *Historie*, 12–13.

that would produce staples for England, and by returning the investors a profit of 20 per cent, the Company would consciously and deliberately become the means of bringing faith and civility to America. The Gospel must be preached to all the world, the Company reasoned in 1610, but how? It can no longer be delivered "Apostolically, without the helpe of man," because God no longer disseminates it miraculously; the "commission of the Apostles is expired," and nowadays there is no way but "mixtly, by discouerie, and trade of marchants; where all temporall meanes are vsed for defence, and security." We go "by way of marchandizing and trade" to buy from the Indians the pearls of the earth and to "sell to them the pearles of heauen." [78] Strachey quoted Augustine to prove that the Gospel must be spread not alone by preachers, but by those who go abroad for "temporall endes." "Yf so, why then besides these alleaged divine motives, politique and rationall respects, even common trade and hope of profitt might make us forward to be adventurers." [79] We can perform the duties of a means, the Company reflected, only if we possess part of the Indians' land and dwell with them, there being no other "moderate, and mixt course, to bring them to conuersion, but by dailie conuersation, where they may see the life, and learne the language each of other." [80] If the depravity of the Indians should prove so incurable that they resist moderate means, then God will allow us to employ more forceful ones. After the massacre of 1622 one writer even tried to prove that the situation was improved, "Because our hands which before were tied with gentlenesse and faire vsage, are now set at liberty," and "the way of conquering them is much more easie than of ciuilizing them by faire meanes." [81] In either event, whether the English recovered the lost sheep of America by the means of sermons or of bullets, they were doing the will of God, serving as the agents through which providence was completing its vast design.[82] The course of Christian history, like the grace of God, was irresistible.

VI

To modern eyes the theory of the Virginia promoters seems remarkable because it prohibited them from advocating the enterprise on frankly secular or economic grounds, although the strength of the economic motive emerges clearly enough from their pages. They could not argue that men should go to Virginia merely for estates, for staples, or for England's welfare; instead they had to find methods of subordinating these aims to the higher interests of Christendom. They could justify the Company only

[78] *A Trve Declaration,* 5–6.

[79] Strachey, *Historie,* 15. See Hamor, *Trve Discovrse,* 46–47.

[80] *A Trve Declaration,* 6; *The New Life,* 20.

[81] Edward Waterhouse, *A Declaration of the State of the Colony and Affaires in Virginia* (London, 1622), 22, 24.

[82] *Nova Britannia,* 12.

by an appeal to Protestant theology, to providence, the epic of Christian history, the Fall of man, and the scheme of regeneration, to a divine covenant and the means of grace. What may seem to us a needlessly roundabout procedure was imposed upon the age by its allegiance to certain Christian assumptions, by its yet unshaken belief in the unity of the world in the single purpose of God. Only when they could shelter economic and national ambitions under spiritual warrants were they free to pursue them. John Smith had his moments of realistic insight, in which he saw wealth and not religion as the dominant consideration; more often he combined them in the mannor of his contemporaries:

So then here is a place a nurse for souldiers, a practise for marriners, a trade for marchants, a reward for the good, and that which is most of all, a businesse (most acceptable to God) to bring such poore infidels to the true knoweldge of God and his holy Gospell.[83]

Official publications of the Company fused the divine and the earthly by pointing out that the action concerned "God, and the advancement of religion, the present ease, future honor and safety of the Kingdome, the strength of our Navy, the visible hope of a great and rich trade, and many secrett blessings not yet discovered." [84] Alderman Johnson was a businessman who at the conclusion of his *Nova Britannia* would not "hold you longer with many words (being near exchange time, as I take it)." He was no otherworldly ascetic, and could appraise the buccaneering voyages of the Elizabethans for their financial worth: "the days and reign of Queen Elizabeth brought forth the highest degree of wealth, happiness and honor that ever England had," but he, no less than the clerical writers, took care to warn his fellows that they would fail if under the pretense of religion "that bitter root of greedy gain be not so settled in our hearts"; there is indeed an "assured hope of gain" in the business, but "look it be not chief in your thoughts." [85]

Sermons delivered in London, like Crashaw's in 1610, or in Virginia, like Whitaker's *Good Newes from Virginia*, the text of which was sent to London in 1613, illustrate more fully the manner in which secular ambitions were interwoven with religious. Profit is the last end of the voyage, said Crashaw; though assuredly it will be profitable in time. The potential return depends entirely upon our most directly seeking it: "Now the high way to obtaine that, is to forget our own affectiones, & to neglect our own priuate profit in respect of Gods glorie, . . . and he that seekes only or principally *spirituall* things, God will reward him both with those *spirituall and temporal* things." Neither can we rest upon the assurance that God, intending the colonization of America, will support us whatever our motives, for He can accomplish His purpose without us: "God will stirre

[83] Smith, *Works*, 64.
[84] Brown, *Genesis*, 253, 463.
[85] *Nova Britannia*, 27, 5, 11–12.

vp our children after vs, who will learne by our example to follow it in more holy manner, and so bring it to that perfection which we for our sinnes and prophanenesse could not doe." [86] Whitkaer's sermon was on the well-tried theme of casting bread upon waters. He was less confident than Crashaw about the present rewards, because the three intervening years had cost the shareholders several fortunes, and so he explained that God does not reward charity all at once, but only in His appointed time. If He repaid good works immediately, "who then would not be a prodigall giuer, who then would bee a faithful giuer?" But if the Company will persist in this pious undertaking, "I dare affirme, that by Gods assistance, your profitable returnes shall be of more certainty, and much shorter expectation"; though God might defer temporal reward for a season, "be assured that in the end you shall find riches and honour in this world, and blessed immortality in the world to come." [87]

The greatest name in the literature of early Virginia is John Donne, whose sermon in 1622 harped upon the old theme even when the Company was staggering to its collapse and the hope of profit was about to be lost forever. Yet in his somber periods there is no trace of hypocrisy; his faith in the method of God's providence was undisturbed, and again the Company heard, with an eloquence beyond any to which it ever listened, that God's intention was to give it the riches and commodities of this world, not now, not at once, but hereafter.

> Be not you discouraged, if the promises which you have made to yourselves, or to others, be not so soon discharged; though you see not your money, though you see not your men, though a flood, a flood of blood have broken in upon them, be not discouraged. . . . Only let your principal end be the propagation of the glorious Gospel.

Though the plantation had not yet discharged expenses, Donne reminded his hearers, it had conduced to great uses, redeemed many from the hands of the executioner, swept the streets of idle persons and their children. "It is already, not only a spleen, to drain the ill humours of the body, but a liver, to breed good blood." But above all, he informed them that the interest of profit and religion "may well consist together," and that if they would study first to advance religion they still need not worry about the profits:

> You shall, when the Holy Ghost is come upon you; that is, when the instinct, the influence, the emotions of the Holy Ghost enables your conscience to say, that your principal end is not gain, nor glory, but to gain souls to the glory of God, this seals the great seal, this justifies itself, this authorises authority, and gives power to strength itself.[88]

[86] Crashaw, *Sermon*, G3 recto, L1 verso.
[87] Whitaker, *Good Newes*, 29, 32–33, 44.
[88] Donne, *Sermon*, 231–32, 235. Precisely the same reasoning as employed by Crashaw, Whitaker, and Donne is to be found among the letters of the Jesuit Fathers

We may suspect that by their interminable insistence the preachers were obliquely confessing that few of Alderman Johnson's colleagues were up to making their end the gain of souls instead of pounds. The preachers did indeed admit that a number of the investors failed to achieve the proper balance. Robert Gray in 1609 told those who held back for fear of losing their wealth that they were under the curse of Simon Nagus;[89] Crashaw said that those who did not empty their purses on Sir Thomas Smith's counter were "unconuerted & vnsanctified men, and seeke meerely the world and themselues, and no further"; they would bite at anything that promised "XX in the C," but "tell them of planting a Church, of conuerting 10000 soules to God, they are senslesse as stones: . . . nay they smile at the simplicities, and laugh in their sleeues at the sillinesse of such as ingage themselues in such matters."[90] Whitaker had to confess that "Some of our Aduenturers in *London* haue been most miserable couetous men, sold ouer to Vsurie, Extortion and Oppression," while of those sent to Virginia many "haue bin Murtherers, Theeues, Adulterers, idle persons, and what not besides";[91] it was difficult for such persons to appreciate a scheme in which they would be economically recompensed only if they did not directly seek economic rewards.

Thus we should be sadly mistaken if we supposed, because the propagandists rationalized the Virginia Company in terms of Christian cosmology, demanding that they expend their lives and fortunes in an enterprise which might never repay them and find compensation in the contemplation of their own sanctity, that therefore the founders of Virginia were saints and martyrs. There is altogether too much evidence that they were not, to go no further than Captain John Smith. But the point is that a cynical unscrupulousness among the businessmen of London, or a mercenary spirit among the settlers, was not incompatible with their belief in the validity of the transcendent standard or in a cosmology by which their actions were sins. Sharp practices, schemes for quick returns, unethical business methods could flourish despite Christian morality. Businessmen and pioneers fell short of their profession, then as now; they acted in specific situations in opposition to their belief. Yet when they came to say what they did believe, to express not merely their formal morality but, more important, their conception of the world in which they were succeeding or failing as moral beings, they used the language of the Virginia pamphlets, and so acknowledged that all their activity was inevitably turned in God's direction, whether they would or no.

---

in Maryland: "Yet we trust in the goodness of God and the piety of the Catholics that, while we sow spiritual seed, we shall reap carnal things in abundance, and that to those who seek the kingdom of God the other things shall be added" (*Narratives of Early Maryland*, 143–44).

[89] Gray, *Good Speed*, D1 verso.
[90] Crashaw, *Sermon*, C2 recto.
[91] Whitaker, *Good Newes*, 11.

Of one thing we may be certain, that if men who thus believed still fell short of perfection, they attributed it to sheer recalcitrancy, to sin and the fall of Adam. And sinners had no excuse. The greed of merchants or the laziness of settlers were defects which could not be extenuated by any philosophy of nature or of society. The London businessman had as yet no way of arguing, in the face of a sermon by Crashaw or Donne, that he had a natural right to invest his money where he could get the best rate of interest regardless of the kingdom of Christ. The settler had no idea that he might refuse to pray with his captain or deny that he was depraved, carnal, and corrupt; he could not assert that his religion was no business of the state's, that he had a right to cultivate his own lands in his own way, to make money however he might, as long as he payed his taxes and got into no trouble with the police. The literature testifies not only to a cosmology and a philosophy of history, but to a social and political ethic. Just as religion and economics were fused into one conception in statements of the company's aim, so within the original Virginia — the first permanent English settlement in the New World — the government was formed by a conscious and powerful intention to merge the society with the purposes of God.

VII

In January 1619, the Virginia Company dispatched Sir George Yeardley to govern its hitherto not very successful colony, and armed him with a set of instructions. Accordingly, he summoned the first meeting of the House of Burgesses at Jamestown on July 30. Posterity has elevated these instructions into a charter of liberty no less momentous than Magna Charta, and has idealized the Burgesses, cloaked and plumed, swords at their sides, seated in "the Quire of the Church," into forerunners of Patrick Henry. The classic statement is Alexander Brown's, which even to repeat is to feel its thrill of conviction: "The seedling," he said, after being fostered at home by "advanced statesmen," grew on this soil into the political system of the new nation, "until our forefathers could rest under its shade, and under its expanding branches the sons of cavaliers learned to defend the liberties of the subject from the encroachments of the crown."

At the moment Sir George set sail, a faction within the Company, led by Sir Edwin Sandys, was wresting control from the group that had ruled since the beginning under Sir Thomas Smith. Therefore it seemed evident to Brown and to nineteenth-century narrators that Sandys was the "advanced statesman" who issued the instructions. The creation of the first local representative body was for a long time ascribed to him, and the ultimate achievement of American independence has even been termed, with an irresistible, dramatic flourish, the fulfillment of "the dream of Sir Edwin Sandys." [92]

---

[92] Alexander Brown, *The First Republic in America* (Boston, 1898), 650.

During the hectic life of the Company, especially from 1609 to 1616, and again after Sandys took over, 1619 to 1622, the interest of Englishmen in Virginia was expressed in, and excited by, a flood of publications, some from promoters in London, some by the more infatuated settlers themselves. There were poems, broadsides, sermons, letters, reports, even plays and masques. When this literature was interpreted in the spirit of Alexander Brown, it readily yielded up evidences of a "struggle" between the liberal Sandys and the autocratic Smith; hence men who stood with Sandys became heroes and prophets of 1776, and by the same token his opponents were villains and Tories. James I defeated Sandys, dissolved the Company in 1624, and made Virginia a royal colony; but the Virginians — so runs the legend — tenaciously guarded the heritage of Sandys. Thus the literature of the seventeenth century was rediscovered, and was presented to the nineteenth century as though already informed with the ideals of individualism, *laissez faire*, and democracy.

Now, of course, that conception has been challenged, and a less exciting but more objective version has been substituted.[93] In this view, the Company is no longer a disinterested effort to plant a race of freemen in the wilderness; instead, it is a straight commercial proposition, initiated by merchants who wanted a monetary return on their investment, encouraged by a parsimonious king who hoped his businessmen would save him the trouble of erecting an outpost against Spain. The colony is no longer a symbol of liberalism, but of expanding capitalism and nascent nationalism. Sandys himself turns out to say that making the business pay was "that whereon all men's eyes were fixed." [94] His quarrels with Smith were not the conflicts of a republican with a cabal of royalists, but of one businessman with another over the quickest way to get rich, and neither of them was a minion of the crown.

By 1619 Sandys thought the profits were overdue, as indeed they were. He organized an opposition among the stockholders and got control of the Company; he more or less had to try a new policy. By the lights of a business office in London, it was obvious what had gone wrong: the colony was growing too much tobacco and was not diversifying crops and industries. Sandys attempted to reverse these tendencies by measures that proved disastrous. He poured several thousand ill-equipped settlers into the colony, and despite Yeardley's frantic protests, continued obstinately putting men and women ashore at Jamestown, where, without food to nourish them or houses to shelter them, three out of four perished from disease or from the tomahawk. Under his regime the squabble between the factions in London grew even more violent; the adventurers, instead of consulting for the good of the colony, dissipated their sessions "in invectives one against

---

[93] The classic statement of the modern thesis is Craven, *Dissolution*, Charles M. Andrews, *The Colonial Period of American History* (New Haven, 1934), I, chaps. 5–10, generalizes Craven's discussion.

[94] Craven, *Dissolution*, 24–25.

another, with great sharpnes and bitternes to the great prejudice of the Plantation." [95] When King James stepped in, he saved Virginia, though that may be a difficult lesson for the partisans of democracy, either in the legend or today, to accept.

Far from resenting this "usurpation," the inhabitants were grateful. In 1642, the Virginia Assembly earnestly opposed a movement to revive the Company, assuring the King that they loved a "monarchical government" and had no wish ever again to live under "a popular and tumultuary government depending upon the greatest number of votes of persons of several humors and dispositions as this of a company must be granted to be." [96] To the extent that a joint-stock company may be described as a democracy among shareholders, the story of the Virginia Company is a portentous record of the failure of a businessman's democracy to cope with the problem of governing a society.

As for the Assembly, that now appears to have been as much the work of Sir Thomas Smith as of Sandys, since Yeardley sailed before Sandys made his coup, and Smith helped to compose the famous instructions.[97] Furthermore, the Company decided on an Assembly not in order to give Virginians the delights of representative government but to expedite the new economic program.[98] When the King took over, he showed no disposition to subvert the "free institutions" of Virginia. He apparently never gave them any thought at all; he was simply determined to halt the murderous policy and stop the disgraceful brawls of the Company. His aspersions upon the "democratical" form of government were directed at the joint-stock company,[99] not at the House of Burgesses. Once the demoralized Company was out of the way, King James sent Yeardley back to the colony, retained the old councilors, and was concerned only that the local government — any kind of government — maintain a semblance of functioning. Not until 1639 did Charles I get around to acknowledging that something called an Assembly was in existence. The great institution survived through sheer neglect — which may perhaps be one of the glories of the English system. Certainly, to read the first writings as prefigurements of the Declaration of Independence, to find in them precocious ideals of democracy, is totally to misunderstand the origins of America.

Thanks to the competence and wit of Professor Craven, the new version is now the generally accepted reading of the record. However, in the literature which he employed for establishing the record there are also declarations, often uttered with fervor, of what the promoters and settlers announced as their motives. It seems unlikely that further discoveries will

[95] *Considerations Against a New Virginia Company* (1631), in *Virginia Magazine of History and Biography*, VIII (1900–1901), 40.
[96] Hening, *Statutes*, I, 232–33.
[97] Craven, *Dissolution*, 44–46.
[98] Craven, *Dissolution*, 47–50.
[99] Craven, *Dissolution*, 331. Cf. Smith, *Works*, 526.

alter the picture, and if a deeper understanding of this small but important enterprise is to be attained, it must come from a fresh reading of familiar materials. Therefore, I have put aside for the moment the interpretation of social historians and attempted, as an exercise in intellectual history, to read the literature for what it says rather than for what it conceals. Examined in such a spirit, it may just possibly tell us something of the mental processes which actually did govern the undertaking, or at least of the conception to which the participants gave some sort of service, even if only of the lip.

In the dominant Christian tradition of government as it existed when Virginia was settled, there were, I think it fair to say, no elements which in modern parlance can be called liberal or democratic. Political philosophy had as yet been little concerned about the rights of man or the protection of the individual, and the most radical had only recently proposed a conception of the rights of the religious conscience against a sovereign of a different creed. European society, both Catholic and Protestant (each assuming that the state should be devoted to a specific confession), took for granted that the aim of any government is absolute control over the subject's life. Why it had to exercise such power was not far to seek: as in every department of theory, the political doctrine was founded on the premise of original sin. Had Adam not fallen, government would have been superfluous except as a council of the righteous; men would instinctively have observed the moral law and done unto others as they would be done unto. But by the depravity into which Adam's disobedience precipitated the race, every man was the enemy of every other man. To keep men in order, God instituted government; thus, even the government of infidel savages had a divine sanction, and every civil authority had both a negative and positive function. On the one hand, it was to restrain the evil passions and the rapacity of men, in business as well as in the street, in the home, in the countinghouse, as well as in the army, because if it did not, the social scene would become chaos and rapine. On the other hand, it was actively to lead men in the paths of righteousness, to maintain religion, to force the observance of divine services, to compel support of the true church, and to suppress heresy and schism by the sword. No one in 1607 (except possibly one or two visionaries) had yet called these assumptions into question; the Virginia Company took them as self-evident truths when it set out to erect a commonweal in the wilderness.

The Virginia literature is too occasional to give this political ideal the full expression it received in the more systematic literature of Massachusetts Bay, but the pivotal point was confessed in several of the sermons, and was made wholly explicit in the legislation. For example, Robert Gray in his *A Good Speed to Virginia* of 1609 declared that "arts" are not invented by man but given him from God, and "forasmuch as of all humane Artes Political gouernment is the chiefest, there must be a speciall care in the Magistrate how to carry himselfe in his place and order." In this conception, a magistrate is not limited to enforcing police regulations and does not allow men to pursue private interests without public control; on the contrary, he places the public welfare above individual interests, and takes into his charge the moral welfare of the community. He punishes the "vile and vitious" and advances the "painfull and industrious"; he will "establish true religion, and he will represse heresies and schismes; he wil releeue the weake and impotent, and he will suppresse the mutinous and insolent; so that God will giue a blessing, & al things wil prosper vnder his gouernment." The brevity and casualness of this summary indicates not that Gray was proposing anything novel, but that he was running over basic premises upon which he and the age were so much in accord that the propositions needed only summary statement in order to appear conclusive.

Hence, Gray continues with a picture of a coöperation between church and state so intimate that the state itself becomes a sort of church. The minister must be subject to the magistrate, but "the Magistrate must bee carefull to yeeld him countenance to keepe him from neglect, and maintenance to incourage him in his ministry." The civil authority must enforce unity of the spirit, since all dissensions are apt to "open a gappe to schisme and contempt of religion." [100] At every point the theory expected the worst of mankind: "the greater part," said Crashaw in terms that jibe with Governor Winthrop's famous estimate, "generally is the worst part." [101] To make the mass of sinful men serve the purposes of divine providence was the ultimate function of government, and it could use any means that would serve.

As a matter of fact, the Virginia Company stood guilty in the opinion of contemporaries — in contrast to the opinion of today — for foolishly neglecting the wisdom of Christianity and for permitting the colonists far too much liberty. The regime improvised in 1607 was an aristocracy with a president to be chosen out of the council: the unhappy result can be followed in the pages of Captain John Smith, or in the account of John Rolfe, who remembered that in 1607–1609 "dissentions and jarres were daily sowne amongst them, that they choaked the seed and blasted the fruits of all men's labors." [102] The councilors quarreled and conspired against each other, the planters ran riot, and all gave conclusive testimony to the awful truth of innate depravity. In a region remote from civilization and authority, John Smith declared, men's minds become so untoward "as neither do well themselues, nor suffer others"; where everyone can seek his own profit, there is no chance to effect the public good. Experience proved that if men could live as freely as they listed, they would live as brutes.[103] To the settlers of Massachusetts in 1630 Smith delivered the moral of his experience: "the maintainers of good Orders and Lawes is the best preservation

---

[100] Gray, *Good Speed*, D2 recto–D3 recto.
[101] Crashaw, *Sermon*, F2 recto.
[102] Rolfe, *Relation*, 104.
[103] Smith, *Works*, 96, 127–28, 162, 170, 455.

next God of a Kingdome." [104] If the defective government of these two years had not sufficiently proved the need for absolute control over human wickedness, the still more horrible winter of 1609–10 sealed it; in that time the legal authority was cast away on the Bermudas, John Smith was deposed, and for several months Jamestown was anarchy — the natural man unchecked. The colonists made a greater wreck of the society than the winds had made of the *Sea Venture,* wrote Strachey; the "headlesse multitude" would not even "sowe Corne for their owne bellies" and would devour their fish raw "rather then they would goe a stones cast to fetch wood and dresse it." [105] The Company had to confess its mistake, declaring in 1610 that if many had hitherto perished, it was not from the climate of Virginia, but because "licence, sedition, and furie, are the fruits of a headie, daring, and vnruly multitude." [106]

Out of this experience the Company, reorganized under the second charter in 1609, resolved to observe more faithfully the traditional principles of political science, and sent Lord De La Warr to govern Virginia with an absolute commission.[107] Such severe measures were deemed the more necessary because so many of the settlers were, as was publicly admitted, the scum of England, gathered, according to Sir Thomas Dale, "in sutch riotous, lasie, and infected places," a concourse of "sutch disordered persons, so prophane, so riotous, so full of Mutenie and treasonable Intendments, as . . . in a parcell of 300 . . . not many give testimonie beside their names that they are Christians." [108] However, the remedy was now prepared, "since all necessarie things are prouided, an absolute and powerfull gouernment." [109] Crashaw's sermon, delivered before the departing governor, informed him in no uncertain terms: "The principal (if not the only) wound in this businesse hath been the *want of gouernment,* there is now care taken, that (by the blessing of God) there neuer shall bee want of that againe." An adequate government would not look to profit, but to "the high and better ends that concerne the kingdome of God"; it would not tolerate Papists or Separatists, and it would "make Atheisme and other blasphemie capitall, and let that bee the first law made in *Virginia.*" It would expel lewd and licentious men, and its laws would be strict, "especially against swearing and other prophanenesse"; the Sabbath would be scrupulously observed and the laws relentlessly enforced — "let none stand for scarre-crowes." If these instructions were observed, Crashaw was confident that even the refuse of England could be made to serve the purposes of God: "The basest and worst men trained vp in seuere discipline, sharpe

---

[104] Smith, *Works,* 959.

[105] William Strachey, *A True Reportory of the wracke, and redemption of Sir Thomas Gates,* in Purchas, XIX, 47–48. See also Whitaker, *Good Newes,* B2 verso.

[106] *A Trve Declaration,* 15.

[107] Brown, *Genesis,* 379. See also Strachey, *Historie,* 84–85.

[108] Sir Thomas Dale, "Letter to Salisbury, August 17, 1611," in Brown, *Genesis,* 506–07.

[109] *A Trve Declaration,* 18.

lawes, a hard life, and much labour, do proue good members of a Common-wealth." If we have resolute governors and preaching of the Word, we need not worry about the "generalitie," since even the most disordered, "if you will, the very *excrements*, of a full and swelling State," put under firm discipline in a new country, "wanting pleasures, and subiect to some pinching miseries," will become new men, "good and worthie instruments and members of a Common-wealth." [110]

Crashaw's sermon is an epitome of a theory of government that had during many centuries been perfected by Christian philosophers but which was particularly developed by Protestant writers in the first century of the Reformation. Because Protestantism put a renewed emphasis upon the concept of original sin, and then replaced the medieval ritual with a doctrine of the ordinances of God as the means of conversion, it quickly focused upon the absolute state not merely for a restraint upon sinful lusts but for a positive force to regenerate men whether they would or no. If there is a liberalism that has emerged out of certain Protestant premises, in the seventeenth century there was a political authoritarianism that seemed the logical consequence of a theology of depravity and enslavement of the will, a social concept that was exemplified equally in the legislation of Massachusetts Bay and of Virginia.

The Virginia code, the *Lawes Diuine, Morall and Martiall*, shocks posterity; because Sandys repealed it in 1619, he again appears the liberal. Its chief authors, Gates and Dale, were hard-bitten campaigners from Holland, and it was long supposed that they transferred the regulations of the Dutch army to Virginia, although recent investigation can find no analogues in Holland.[111] It should, I believe, be explained more simply as a result of the bitter experiences of 1607–1609 and as an application to a desperate situation of the pure Protestant concept of the state. William Strachey published the code in London in 1612 as an advertisement! Much of it obviously has a theological background, and the parallel with the enactments of free legislatures in New England is striking. No doubt the penalties were severe, but the authorities pled that they were obliged to take extreme measures because the case was urgent. The populace were sensible only of bodily torments — "the feare of a cruell, painefull and vnusuall death, more restrains them then death it selfe." [112] In this respect alone was the code exceptional, not in its underlying principle. Sir Thomas Smith later said that the laws were framed "in some cases *ad terrorem*, and in some to be truly executed." [113] Alderman Johnson praised the code in 1612 because of its great care "for the honour and seruice of God, for daily frequenting the Church, the house of prayer, at the toling of the bell, for preaching, catechizing, and the religious obseruation of the Sabbath day," for its punishment of

[110] Crashaw, *Sermon*, G2 recto, K4 verso–L1 recto, E4 verso.

[111] Andrews, *The Colonial Period*, I, 115.

[112] Hamor, *Trve Discourse*, 27–28.

[113] Brown, *Genesis*, 530.

blasphemy, dishonor of the Word and heresy, and for the assured propriety of undertakings "wherein God is thus before." [114]

The *Lawes* propound the Protestant conception of the state: mankind was created that they might learn both to govern and to obey, "since without order and gouernement, (the onely hendges, whereupon, not onely the safety, but the being of all states doe turne and depend) what society may possibly subsist, or commutatiue goodnesse be practised?" [115] The governor was to rule in imitation of the king of England, who "hath in his owne Realmes a principall care of true Religion, and reuerence to God." [116] The state must enforce the religious life, because man's highest duty is to God; [117] to resist the civil magistrate, the representative of God on earth, is contrary to the Bible, "which tyes euery particular and priuate man, for conscience sake to obedience, and duty of the Magistrate, and such as shall be placed in authoritie ouer them." [118] The local officer was to be the more active in supervising religious behavior because, according to the doctrine of the covenant, "all the crimes and trespasses of his people vnder him shall bee exacted at his hands, not onely by his superior officer and Iudge here, but by the great Iudge of Iudges, who leaues not vnpunished the sinnes of the people, vpon the Magistrates, in whose hands the power and sword of Iustice and authority is committed, to restraine them from all delinquences, misdeeds and trespasses." The magistrate's charge extends not alone to "ciuill duties," but to anything "contrary to the diuine prescriptions of Piety and Religion." Especially in Virginia, the *Lawes* declared, he must remember these obligations, for Virginia is a holy experiment with "no other ends but such as may punctually aduance the glory, and propagation of the heauenly goodnesse." [119] What to modern eyes has seemed an attempt to transport Stuart "absolutism" to America was, to the eyes of the seventeenth century, the strict application to a particularly violent situation of the principles of the Christian state.

To this manner of thinking any notion of a republic was inconceivable, and still more foreign was any love for democracy. The Virginia literature assumes at every point what Tawney calls "the functional view of class organization." [120] The importance of this concept in every American colony of the seventeenth century can hardly be overstressed. It maintained that society is made up of ranks eternally fixed by the divine will, and that the internal subordination is the very essence of a community.

> Take but degree away, untune that string,
> And hark, what discord follows.

[114] *The New Life of Virginea*, D1 recto–verso.
[115] *Lawes*, A3 recto.
[116] *Lawes*, B1 recto.
[117] *Lawes*, 2.
[118] *Lawes*, 6–7.
[119] *Lawes*, 55–56.
[120] R. H. Tawney, *Religion and the Rise of Capitalism* (New York, 1926), 22.

Persons of low as well as of high degree accepted the fact of their station, and one George Alsop, who for four years was an indentured servant in Maryland, reflected in 1666 that because, in the original wisdom of all things, it was ordained "That there should be Degrees and Diversities amongst the Sons of men, in acknowledging of a Superiority from Inferiors to Superiors," the servant was as bound to wait upon his master with a reverent obedience as the subject upon his prince.[121]

Again and again statements of the ideal employed the analogy of the body; like Menenius in *Coriolanus*, the governor of Virginia declared in the preface to his *Lawes*:

Sithence, as in euery liuing creature, there be many and sundry members, & those distinct in place and office, and all yet vnder the regiment of the soule, and heart, so in euery army, commonwealth, or Colonie (all bodies a like compounded) it cannot be otherwise for the establishment of the same in perfect order and vertue, but that there should be many differing parts, which directed by the chiefe, should helpe to gouerne and administer Iustice vnder him.[122]

He intended, he said, to create in Virginia a society "like our natiue country," and England was a society of gradations, a hierarchy which men took to be a visible embodiment of the hierarchy of values that God established in all things, natural or social. Leaders of the colony petitioned in 1621, when Yeardley was to retire, for the appointment of another nobleman as governor, because to such "by Nature every man subordinate is ready to yield a willing submission without contempt or repyning," whereas they will never obey "a meane man" or "one no better than selected out of their own Ranke." [123] The first philosophy of Virginia, in short, accepted inequality of rank and birth as a fact, not merely of experience but of eternal decree; democracy was as abhorrent to the founders as to King James, and if anything of their doing subsequently worked out to the advantage of the democratic idea, this was entirely beside their intention.

VIII

THE one action which did, in spite of themselves, become a republican and even a democratic engine was the Assembly. After this excursion, we may then return to our first question of how the Assembly was conceived in the context of the age. Orthodox as the martial code was in principle, it was indeed harsh, even for a harsh epoch; nevertheless, it might have stood, and have become the model for future colonies, if only the autocratic regime had been able to make the company a profit. Nine years of it increased the debt, and in 1619 the Sandys faction were ready to try a new policy.

---

[121] George Alsop, *A Character of the Province of Maryland* (London, 1666), in *Narratives of Early Maryland*, 354.

[122] *Lawes*, 47–48.

[123] Brown, *First Republic*, 392.

They were not rejecting the basic philosophy of authoritarianism, religious uniformity, and class distinctions, but they had to do something to get the results which the military government had failed to produce. So obvious was the need that both factions, Smith's and Sandys', agreed to the change, though a few years later, when the fight became bitter, Sandys made what capital he could out of the financial failures of Smith's conduct, and accused him of imposing "bloudy Lawes." Sandys took credit unto himself for granting "the libertie of a Generall assembly," but only on the grounds that it was a sensible economic device: "Whereby they find out and execute those things as might best tend to their good." [124] Smith denied that he had anything to do with framing the *Lawes,* which were entirely the work of "those worthye governours" in Virginia, but he pointed out that they could be justified by the laws of England.[125] However, the charge which was in fact merely a tactic in factional recrimination was picked up in an era when bloody laws were automatically assumed to be reprehensible, and Smith has borne the obloquy of a "tyrannical" rule.

Yeardley's commission inaugurated the new policy, the intention of which was to strengthen the colony by attracting settlers of a better class than jailbirds and unskilled laborers; to procure artisans and yeomen the colony needed peace and freedom, diversified industries and crops, schools, inns, hospitals, and housing. The last of the military governors, Argall, abused his powers; hence, when the Company cast about for a better system they looked upon their own organization and transferred the joint-stock idea to the colony itself, setting up a legislature, not to defend the rights of man, but, as Sandys said, in order that men on the spot might find out and execute those measures that would best tend to their own prosperity. If they did good for themselves, they would induce good men to leave England, and would eventually produce the commodities England needed and the company longed for.[126]

The new leaders expounded their motive in a pamphlet of 1620, stating it so baldly that cultivators of the legend have had to call its honesty in question in order to maintain against it the secret reason that supposedly lay in the heart of Sandys. *A Declaration of the State of the Colonie and Affaires in Virginia* is an appeal to prospective immigrants on the ground that the colony has now been reduced "into a regular course" and "beginneth now to haue the face and fashion of an orderly State," that such a state "is likely to grow and prosper," and hence none need be frightened by rumors of a military regime. "The rigour of Martiall Law, wherewith before they were gouerned, is reduced within the limits prescribed by his Maiesty: and the laudable forme of Iustice and gouernment vsed in this Realme, established, and followed as neere as may be." Thanks to this stability, the settlers are now constructing guesthouses for new arrivals,

[124] *The Discourse of the Old Company* (1625), in Tyler, *Narratives,* 435.

[125] Andrews, *The Colonial Period,* I, 114.

[126] Andrews, *The Colonial Period,* I, 182; Craven, *Dissolution,* 68–69.

planting vineyards, and "pursuing of the Staple Commodities furnished and commended from hence." Sandys was claiming as already accomplished what he was still hoping might be the results of an Assembly, but his language makes clear the manner in which he and Smith were thinking when they decided to abandon the profitless line of military dictatorship and to experiment with local self-government. They were not composing charters of liberty; they were devising propaganda. Surely, they said, sober citizens or solid yeomen could not object to emigrating once they were assured that in Virginia they would enjoy "the religious and happy gouernment of their natiue Countrey." [127]

However, it is true that although the Assembly was primarily a tactical device to further the prosperity of the enterprise, once it was organized, another element in the intellectual heritage was now emphasized, namely, "the rights of Englishmen." Here again, the student must exercise caution, and properly to appreciate the situation must not interpret this conception as meaning in 1619 what it came to signify only after 1689. As a matter of fact, the rights of Englishmen were recognized in the charters and directives from the beginning. The charters of 1606 and 1609 declared that men in Virginia were to have "all liberties, franchises, and immunities . . . to all intents and purposes, as if they had been abiding and born, within this our realm of England." The settlers were to live in the fear and worship of God, but at the same time to be governed by laws as close as possible to those of England.[128] Even the absolute power entrusted to De La Warr was qualified by the instruction that his proceedings should "as neere as convenientlie maybe, be agreeable to the Laws, Statutes, Government and Policie of this his Majesties Realme of England." [129] The idea that there existed certain peculiar exemptions which were the unique prerogative of Englishmen was already a conviction of the English mind when Virginia was founded. As we look back upon the period from the vantage point of today, there seems to be a tension, if not a contradiction, between this concept and the Christian theory of the state as a bulwark against original sin, but actually to the mentality of 1610 or 1620, the two beliefs were far from incompatible.

We must remind ourselves that the struggle between the crown and parliament was only beginning to take shape, and the Civil Wars, let alone the Glorious Revolution, were still inconceivable. Hence in the context of the moment, the rights of Englishmen meant only those rights that as a matter of brute fact (which was the providence of God) happened, upon the basis solely of custom and precedent, to be granted to Englishmen. These rights were not philosophical abstractions, not eternal verities or universals sanctioned by a law of nature, but only those opportunities which English society permitted its citizens. As Andrews says, "They have nothing

---

[127] *A Declaration of the State of the Colonie and Affaires in Virginia*, 5–6.

[128] Brown, *Genesis*, 61. See also 236.

[129] Brown, *Genesis*, 377.

to do with civil liberty, self-government, or democracy; they were strictly legal, tenurial, and financial in their application." [130] They were chiefly valued for the precise reason that prompted the Company to pay increased respect to them in 1619, for their utility. Captain John Smith bluntly expressed it, "No man wil go from hence,to haue lesse freedome there then here." If liberty, profit, honor, and prosperity, he explained — the conjunction of terms reveals how the age was thinking — can be found in Virginia, the settlers will be more devoted to the cause than if they expect "bondage, violence, tyranny, ingratitude and such double dealing, as bindes freemen to become slaues, and honest men [to] turn knaues." [131] These rights did not yet include the right to vote; the settlers were not so much interested in lawmaking as in administration.[132]

Nor was the existence of such rights incompatible with the code of religious authoritarianism and of the corporate social hierarchy; they were not yet slogans to be invoked against the doctrine of an omnicompetent state. Though Protestant theory held that God is the author of all government, it also declared that God had never decreed any particular form of government to be used everywhere by all men. He left the race at liberty to vary the pattern in accordance with circumstances, to set up republics or monarchies, aristocracies or oligarchies, or even democracies (though all theologians agreed that democracy was the worst form), because whatever intelligent adjustment to a situation men were capable of making was what God intended, by the prodding and hinting of His providence, they should do. Hence if the experience of England indicated that certain privileges or grants were the most efficient way of conducting its business, then this course of events had been God's way of suggesting these ideas to Englishmen. In this sense alone Englishmen lay claim to certain prescriptive rights, and in this sense alone were they carried to America. The military code curtailed some of these rights, because the circumstances demanded departures from English custom; but as soon as the code failed to produce a profitable colony, then God had shown that it was not the proper response. Hence the company undertook a reform that would bring Virginia more into line with English custom in the hope of stimulating dividends (with divine blessing), but not with any faraway dream of a liberal America.

Even this effort failed. By 1624 the Company was in a worse state than in 1619. The King dissolved the corporation and took the colony into his royal charge, but nobody knew what was to be done with it, or how, in the name of the King or of Heaven, it was to be conducted. The vast structure of propaganda collapsed; demonstrations of Virginia's role in the scheme of providence were refuted by stubborn facts, and the holy edifice was a ruin. The dissolution of the Virginia Company was a momentous event in the intellectual history of modern Europe, though none at the

[130] Andrews, *The Colonial Period*, I, 86, 181.
[131] Smith, *Works*, 271, 216.
[132] Andrews, *The Colonial Period*, I, 197.

moment realized the implication: it was a turning point, not because a tyrannical king triumphed over a liberal Sandys, but because it shattered the immense conception of the colonial impulse which the Virginia writers had constructed in terms of a medieval, hierarchical, providential universe. They had dedicated Virginia to a special sanctity, to a divine designation in terms of a teleological reading of human history. Crashaw had explained that this was a holy action, "euen such a one as in the performance whereof a man may bee assured that hee pleaseth God, and shall haue a bountifull reward from the mercie of God: and this is peculiar to this voiage aboue other." In the ordinary joint-stock company we "may shew our selues good commonwealthsmen: by this good Christians. By others we may inrich our purses: but by this our consciences." [133] The Company had worked upon the emotions of investors with the argument, "Doubt ye not but God hath determined, and demonstrated (by the wondrous preseruation of those principal persons which fell vpon the Bermudos) that he will raise our state, and build his Church in that excellent climate, if the action be seconded with resolution and Religion." [134] The soldier-governors had exhorted the band to remember that they were partakers of the promise, "that they which lead others in Righteousnesse, shal shine like the starres in the firmament," [135] and the ministers had told them, "it is Gods cause you haue taken in hand. It may therefore be hindred, but cannot bee ouerthrowne." [136] Now, despite these assurances, it was overthrown, and not by a slow and almost imperceptible evolution, such as that through which the Massachusetts Zion was subtly transformed into a mercantile society, but by a dramatic failure which, in implication, overthrew the entire ideological rationalization.

In spite of every exertion, the staples could not be produced; in spite of every restraint, tobacco was planted. The weed alone offered any return to the stricken planters. Officers and ministers might fulminate and invoke the cosmic plan, assuring settlers that if they would hasten the iron and glass works and "restraine the quantitie of Tobacco," [137] they would inevitably prosper: pioneers had perforce learned a different lesson. In 1623 a hostile critic reported that the projects for glass and iron were abandoned, that when the pamphlets in which Sandys set forth the grandiose aims of the colony arrived in Virginia, they "were laughed to scorne, and every base fellow boldly gave them the Lye in divers perticulers." In simple fact, the glorious mission of Virginia came down to growing a weed: "Tobacco onely was the buisines and for ought I could here every man madded upon that, and lyttle thought or looked for any thinge else." [138] When he took over the leadership, Sandys himself condemned tobacco and promised more re-

---

[133] Crashaw, *Sermon*, I1 recto.

[134] *A Trve Declaration*, 27.

[135] *Lawes*, 36.

[136] Crashaw, in Whitaker, *Good Newes*, C4 recto.

[137] Copland, *Virginia's God*, 13; Waterhouse, *A Declaration*, 7.

[138] Nathaniel Butler, *The Unmasking of Virginia* (1623), in Tyler, *Narratives*, 416.

spectable products; the Assembly was to be his means of getting them. Now he was convicted of failure, and the Assembly, instead of being his dream, was his defeat. The cool-tempered Francis Bacon, whose detachment from the prejudices of his day is always terrifying, moralized in a secular vein a century in advance of his contemporaries, that before we plant colonies we might speculate less about the will of God and more about what the soil will actually yield, "(so it be not, as was said, to the untimely prejudice of the main business,) as it hath fared with tobacco in Virginia." [139]

The great and noble intention of converting the Indians eventuated in the massacre of 1622 and the complete debacle of all missionizing projects. It was all very well for Purchas to argue that if the Indians would not observe the law of nature, Christians could justifiably chastise them; [140] real frontiersmen, those who survived a massacre, went after the Indians not with theories of conversion but with the intention of exterminating vermin. After 1622 the evangelical argument fell, along with the argument for staples,[141] and in London the preachers "that had begun in this latter Governement to pray continually for Virginia" now omitted it from their prayers, "finding the Action to growe either odious or contemptible in mens minds." [142] John Donne had assured the company that if they attempted to establish a temporal kingdom, if the planters proposed to live at their liberty and to seek merely a sudden way to get rich, they would not be in the right way.[143] Liberty and abundance, not having been the aims of the Apostles, should not be sought in Virginia. Well, now the company was fallen, the college wiped out, the missionary spirit dead; providence seemed clearly to call upon men in Virginia not to emulate the Apostles but to seek liberty and abundance, especially the great abundance that could be procured if the price of tobacco remained at five shillings the pound.

For the historian, the contrast between the contemporaneous statements of Bacon and Donne may well be taken as symbolic of the moment and of the fashion in which the modern mind emerged from the medieval. The dissolution of the company changed Virginia from a holy experiment to a commercial plantation. Even before Massachusetts Bay was settled by a people who believed still more rigorously in the ideas of providence, the covenant of grace, and the means of conversion, who set out more deliberately to create a holy commonwealth, Virginia had already gone through the cycle of exploration, religious dedication, disillusionment, and then reconcilation to a world in which making a living was the ultimate reality.

Few if any appreciated in 1624 the epochal significance of the failure

[139] "Of Plantations," in *Works*, ed. Spedding, Ellis, and Heath (Boston, 1857), XII, 196.

[140] Purchas, I, 41–45; XIX, 220–22, 224, 229.

[141] Bruce, *Institutional History*, I, 5–8.

[142] *Discourse of the Old Company*, 439.

[143] Donne, *Sermon*, 229.

of the Virginia Company. England was shortly too much concerned at home to wonder about the theological implications of a tobacco colony. But as we review the story, conscious of what was to happen in England and in Europe during the next hundred years, the Virginia literature takes on a prophetic character.

In the 1640's England fought the Civil Wars, a battle between two absolutes, each trying to make the will of God prevail; neither the Puritans nor the Royalists were prepared for the defeat of the ideal on which they both agreed, the ideal of a state in which Christian morality is the final authority, where the church gives rules for politics and business, where the state enforces uniformity and conformity. Neither could even imagine, at the beginning of the conflict, that when their wars were over, the wars that "brought nothing about," church and state would be separated, reason would usurp the place of revelation, and physics would become a better expositor of the divine mind than theology. Neither could foresee a society in which uniformity would give way to a program of toleration inspired not by religious conviction but by indifference. Instead of being primarily concerned over right and wrong, men would learn, while fighting over these issues, that political arithmetic could be substituted for ethics, that they could live more peaceably by a calculus of forces than by the spirit. At the end of the seventeenth century, the medieval synthesis, in which all activities were gradations within a coherent organization of existence, was broken apart. Into this new world, the world of reason and commerce, Virginia was prepared to enter as early as 1624; it was stripped of its medieval notions and was started on the road which led from teleology to competition and expedience, where the decisive factor would be, not the example of the Apostles, but the price per pound of tobacco.

What, one may ask, out of all the experiments of the Virginia Company, could survive or be found useful in the new universe? Which of the themes enunciated in the early laws and literature could be adapted to the revolutionized situation? When Sir George Yeardley appeared before the Privy Council, after the death of James I, to help it decide what to do with a colony that it found upon its hands, he presented the only answer Virginians could offer to these questions. He asked the Council "to avoid the oppression of Governors there, that their liberty of Generall Assemblyes may be continued and confirmed, and that they may have a voice in the election of officers, as in other Corporations." [144] In a world where the ancient landmarks were fading, where the will of God was becoming ambiguous to man's reading, the one remaining certainty, the one institution which could plead at least the excuse of utility, was the organized rights of Englishmen, exercised and protected in an elective assembly.

[144] Thomas J. Wertenbaker, *Virginia under the Stuarts* (Princeton, 1914), 62.

CHAPTER V

THE PURITAN STATE AND PURITAN SOCIETY

[A short two decades ago, the effort to expound Puritan political doctrine put upon the conscientious historian an obligation to make painfully clear that it was not at all "liberal." There was then an obstinate holdover from the myth constructed by patriotic orators of the nineteenth century, by filial pietists who were determined to find in the Puritans prophets of the American Constitution and of the Bill of Rights. Hence it was natural for students of the sources to insist upon the authoritarian, the totalitarian elements in a complex and sophisticated philosophy.

With the change that has supposedly come over the ruling temper of the nation, the temptation becomes exactly contrary: to dwell upon the inherent individualism, the respect for private conscience, the implications of revolution, nurtured by the Puritan doctrine.

From neither resistance to the *Zeitgeist* will come more than a partial apprehension of the reality. This article was originally written as preface to a chapter of selections of political utterances in *The Puritans*, which Thomas H. Johnson and I edited in 1938. That volume, having served its purpose, is now out of print, but students have asked me to salvage this discourse. Since it is now unsupported by accompanying texts, I have re-written the concluding paragraphs in order to indicate, briefly, the evolutionary thesis that was implicit in the extracts themselves.]

IT has often been said that the end of the seventeenth and the beginning of the eighteenth century mark the first real break with the Middle Ages in the history of European thought. Even though the Renaissance and Reformation transformed many aspects of the Western intellect, still it was not until the time of Newton that the modern scientific era began; only then could men commence to regard life in this world as something more than preparation for life beyond the grave. Certainly if the eighteenth century inaugurated the modern epoch in natural sciences, so also did it in the political and social sciences. For the first time since the fall of the Roman Empire religion could be separated from politics, doctrinal orthodoxy divorced from loyalty to the state, and the citizens of a nation be permitted to worship in diverse churches and to believe different creeds without endangering the public peace. Various factors contributed to effecting this revolution; the triumph of scientific method and of rationalism made impossible the older belief that government was of divine origin; the rise of capitalism, of the middle class, and eventually of democracy, necessitated new conceptions of the role of the state. Social leadership in England and America was assumed by a group of gentlemen who were, by and large, deists or skeptics, and to them all religious issues had become supremely boring. At the same time the churches themselves, particularly the newer evangelical denominations, were swinging round to a theology that made religious belief the subjective experience of individual men, entirely unrelated to any particular political philosophy or social theory.

In order to understand Puritanism we must go behind these eighteenth-century developments to an age when the unity of religion and politics was so axiomatic that very few men would even have grasped the idea that church and state could be distinct. For the Puritan mind it was not possible to segregate a man's spiritual life from his communal life. Massachusetts was settled for religious reasons, but as John Winthrop announced, religious reasons included "a due forme of Government both ciuill and ecclesiasticall," and the civil was quite as important in his eyes as the ecclesiastical. Only in recent years has it become possible for us to view the political aspects of Puritanism with something like comprehension and justice. For two centuries our social thinking has been dominated by ideas that were generated in the course of a sweeping revolt against everything for which the Puritans stood; the political beliefs of the Puritans were forgotten, or, if remembered at all, either deplored or condemned as unfortunate remnants of medievalism. Puritanism has been viewed mainly as a religious and ethical movement. But of late years the standards of the eighteenth century have for the first time come under serious criticism and in many quarters are showing the strain. In these circumstances the social philosophy of Puritanism takes on a new interest, and quite possibly becomes for us the most instructive and valuable portion of the Puritan heritage.

The Puritan theory of the state began with the hypothesis of original sin. Had Adam transmitted undiminished to his descendants the image of God in which he had been created, no government would ever have been necessary among men; they would all then have done justice to each other without the supervision of a judge, they would have respected each other's rights without the intervention of a policeman. But the Bible said — and experience proved — that since the Fall, without the policeman, the judge, the jail, the law, and the magistrate, men will rob, murder, and fight among themselves; without a coercive state to restrain evil impulses and administer punishments, no life will be safe, no property secure, no honor observed. Therefore, upon Adam's apostasy, God Himself instituted governments among men. He left the particular form to be determined by circumstance — this was one important human art on which the Puritans said the Bible was *not* an absolute and imperious law-giver — but He enacted that all men should be under some sort of corporate rule, that they should all submit to the sway of their superiors, that no man should live apart from his fellows, that the government should have full power to enforce obedience and to inflict every punishment that the crimes of men deserved.

There was, it is true, a strong element of individualism in the Puritan creed; every man had to work out his own salvation, each soul had to face his maker alone. But at the same time, the Puritan philosophy demanded that in society all men, at least all regenerate men, be marshaled into one united array. The lone horseman, the single trapper, the solitary hunter was not a figure of the Puritan frontier; Puritans moved in groups and towns, settled in whole communities, and maintained firm government over all units. Neither were the individualistic business man, the shopkeeper who seized every opportunity to enlarge his profits, the speculator who contrived to gain wealth at the expense of his fellows, neither were these typical figures of the original Puritan society. Puritan opinion was at the opposite pole from Jefferson's feeling that the best government governs as little as possible. The theorists of New England thought of society as a unit, bound together by inviolable ties; they thought of it not as an aggregation of individuals but as an organism, functioning for a definite purpose, with all parts subordinate to the whole, all members contributing a definite share, every person occupying a particular status. "Society in all sorts of humane affaires is better then Solitariness," said John Cotton. The society of early New England was decidedly "regimented." Puritans did not think that the state was merely an umpire, standing on the side lines of a contest, limited to checking egregious fouls but otherwise allowing men free play according to their abilities and the breaks of the game. They would have expected *laissez faire* to result in a reign of rapine and horror. The state to them was an active instrument of leadership, discipline, and, wherever necessary, of coercion; it legislated over any or all aspects of human behavior, it not merely regulated misconduct but undertook to inspire and direct all conduct. The commanders were not to trim their policies by the desires of the people, but to drive ahead upon the predetermined course; the people were all to turn out as they were ordered, and together they were to crowd sail to the full capacity of the vessel. The officers were above the common men, as the quarter-deck is above the forecastle. There was no idea of the equality of all men. There was no questioning that men who would not serve the purposes of the society should be whipped into line. The objectives were clear and unmistakable; any one's disinclination to dedicate himself to them was obviously so much recalcitrancy and depravity. The government of Massachusetts, and of Connecticut as well, was a dictatorship, and never pretended to be anything else; it was a dictatorship, not of a single tyrant, or of an economic class, or of a political faction, but of the holy and regenerate. Those who did not hold with the ideals entertained by the righteous, or who believed God had preached other principles, or who desired that in religious belief, morality, and ecclesiastical preferences all men should be left at liberty to do as they wished — such persons had every liberty, as Nathaniel Ward said, to stay away from New England. If they did come, they were expected to keep their opinions to themselves; if they discussed them in public or attempted to act upon them, they were exiled; if they persisted in returning, they were cast out again; if they still came back, as did four Quakers, they were hanged on Boston Common. And from the Puritan point of view, it was good riddance.

These views of the nature and function of the state were not peculiar to the Puritans of New England; they were the heritage of the past, the ideals, if not always the actuality, of the previous centuries. That government was established by God in order to save depraved men from their own depravity had been orthodox Christian teaching for centuries; that men should be arranged in serried ranks, inferiors obeying superiors, was the essence of feudalism; that men should live a social life, that profit-making should be restrained within the limits of the "just price," that the welfare of the whole took precedence over any individual advantage, was the doctrine of the medieval church, and of the Church of England in the early seventeenth century. Furthermore, in addition to these general principles, there were two or three more doctrines in the New England philosophy which also were common to the age and the background: all the world at that moment believed with them that the church was to be maintained and protected by the civil authority, and a certain part of the world was contending that government must be limited by fundamental law and that it takes its origin from the consent of the people.

Every respectable state in the Western world assumed that it could allow only one church to exist within its borders, that every citizen should be compelled to attend it and conform to its requirements, and that all inhabitants should pay taxes for its support. When the Puritans came to New England the idea had not yet dawned that a government could safely permit several creeds to exist side by side within the confines of a single nation. They had not been fighting in England for any milk-and-water toleration, and had they been offered such religious freedom as dissenters now enjoy in Great Britain they would have scorned to accept the terms. Only a hypocrite, a person who did not really believe what he professed, would be content to practice his religion under those conditions. The Puritans were assured that they alone knew the exact truth, as it was contained in the written word of God, and they were fighting to enthrone it in England and to extirpate utterly and mercilessly all other pretended versions of Christianity. When they could not succeed at home, they came to America, where they could establish a society in which the one and only truth should reign forever. There is nothing so idle as to praise the Puritans for being in any sense conscious or deliberate pioneers of religious liberty — unless, indeed, it is still more idle to berate them because in America they persecuted dissenters for their beliefs after themselves had undergone persecution for differing with the bishops. To allow no dissent from the truth was exactly the reason they had come to America. They maintained here precisely what they had maintained in England, and if they exiled, fined, jailed, whipped, or hanged those who disagreed with them in New England, they would have done the same thing in England could they have secured the power. It is almost pathetic to trace the puzzlement of New England leaders at the end of the seventeenth century, when the idea of toleration was becoming more and more respectable in European thought. They could hardly understand what was happening in the world, and they could not for a long time be persuaded that they had any reason to be ashamed of their record of so many Quakers whipped, blasphemers punished by the amputation of ears, Antinomians exiled, Anabaptists fined, or witches executed. By all the lights which had prevailed in Europe at the time the Puritans had left, these were achievements to which any government could point with pride. In 1681 a congregation of Anabaptists, who led a stormy and precarious existence for several years in Charlestown, published an attack upon the government of Massachusetts Bay; they justified themselves by appealing to the example of the first settlers, claiming that like themselves the founders had been nonconformists and had fled to New England to establish a refuge for persecuted consciences. When Samuel Willard, minister of the Third Church in Boston, read this, he could hardly believe his eyes; he hastened to assure the authors that they did not know what they were talking about:

I perceive they are mistaken in the design of our first Planters, whose business was not Toleration; but were professed Enemies of it, and could leave the World professing they *died no Libertines*. Their business was to settle, and (as much as in them lay) secure Religion to Posterity, according to that way which they believed was of God.

For the pamphlet in which Willard penned these lines Increase Mather wrote an approving preface. Forty years later, he and his son Cotton participated in the ordination of a Baptist minister in Boston, and he then preached on the need for harmony between differing sects. But by that time much water had gone under the bridge, the old charter had been revoked, there was danger that the Church of England might be made the established church of the colonies, theology had come to be of less importance in men's minds than morality, the tone of the eighteenth century was beginning to influence opinion — even in Boston. Increase was old and weary. Puritanism, in the true sense of the word, was dead.

Of course, the whole Puritan philosophy of church and state rested upon the assumption that the Word of God was clear and explicit, that the divines had interpreted it correctly, and that no one who was not either a knave or a fool could deny their demonstrations. *Ergo*, it seemed plain, those who did deny them should be punished for being obstinate. John

Cotton said that offenders should not be disciplined for their wrong opinions, but for persisting in them; he said that Roger Williams was turned out of Massachusetts not for his conscience but for sinning against his own conscience. Roger Williams and John Cotton debated the question of "persecution" through several hundred pages; after they had finished, I think it is very doubtful whether Cotton had even begun to see his adversary's point. And still today it is hard to make clear the exact grounds upon which Roger Williams became the great apostle of religious liberty. Williams was not, like Thomas Jefferson, a man to whom theology and divine grace had become stuff and nonsense; on the contrary he was pious with a fervor and passion that went beyond most of his contemporaries. So exalted was his conception of the spiritual life that he could not bear to have it polluted with earthly considerations. He did not believe that any man could determine the precise intention of Scripture with such dreadful certainty as the New England clergy claimed to possess. Furthermore, it seemed to him that even if their version were true, submission to truth itself was worth nothing at all when forced upon men by the sword. Williams evolved from an orthodox Puritan into the champion of religious liberty because he came to see spiritual truth as so rare, so elevated, so supernal a loveliness that it could not be chained to a worldly establishment and a vested interest. He was a libertarian because he contemned the world, and he wanted to separate church and state so that the church would not be contaminated by the state; Thomas Jefferson loved the world and was dubious about the spirit, and he sought to separate church and state so that the state would not be contaminated by the church. But John Cotton believed that the state and church were partners in furthering the cause of truth; he knew that the truth was clear, definite, reasonable, and undeniable; he expected all good men to live by it voluntarily, and he was sure that all men who did not do so were obviously bad men. Bad men were criminals, whether their offense was theft or a belief in the "inner light," and they should be punished. Moses and Aaron, the priest and the statesman, were equally the vice-regents of God, and the notion that one could contaminate the other was utter insanity.

The two other ideas derived from the background of the age, rule by fundamental law and the social compact, were also special tenets of English Puritanism. For three decades before the settlement of Massachusetts the Puritan party in England had been working hand in glove with the Parliament against the King. The absolutist Stuarts were allied with the bishops, and the Puritan agitator and the Parliamentary leader made common cause against them both. As a result of this combination, the Puritan theorists had taken over the essentials of the Parliamentary conception of society, the contention that the power of the ruler should be exercised in accordance with established fundamental law, and that the government should owe its existence to a compact of the governed. Because these ideas were strategically invaluable in England, they became ingrained in the

Puritan consciousness; they were carried to the New England wilderness and were preached from every pulpit in the land.

The Puritans did not see any conflict between them and their religious intentions. In New England the fundamental law was the Bible. The magistrates were to have full power to rule men for the specific purposes to which the society was dedicated; but they as well as their subordinates were tied to the specific purposes, and could not go beyond the prescribed limits. The Bible was clear and definite on the form of the church, on the code of punishments for crimes, on the general purposes of social existence; its specifications were binding on all, magistrates, ministers, and citizens. Consequently, the Puritans did not find it difficult to conclude that in those matters upon which the Bible left men free to follow their own discretion, the society itself should establish basic rules. The New England leaders and the people frequently disagreed about what these rules were, or how detailed they should be made, but neither side ever doubted that the community must abide by whatever laws had been enacted, either by God or by the state. The government of New England was, as I have said, a dictatorship, but the dictators were not absolute and irresponsible. John Cotton was the clerical spokesman for the Massachusetts rulers, but he stoutly demanded "that all power that is on earth be limited."

The belief that government originated in the consent of the governed was equally congenial to the Puritan creed. The theology is often enough described as deterministic, because it held that men were predestined to Heaven or Hell; but we are always in danger of forgetting that the life of the Puritan was completely voluntaristic. The natural man was indeed bound in slavery to sin and unable to make exertions toward his own salvation; but the man into whose soul grace had been infused was liberated from that bondage and made free to undertake the responsibilities and obligations of virtue and decency. The holy society was erected upon the belief that the right sort of men could of their own free will and choice carry through the creation and administration of the right sort of community. The churches of New England were made up of "saints," who came into the church because they wanted membership, not because they were born in it, or were forced into it, or joined because of policy and convention. Though every resident was obliged to attend and to pay taxes for the support of the churches, no one became an actual member who did not signify his strong desire to be one. The saints were expected to act positively because they had in them a spirit of God that made them capable of every exertion. No doubt the Puritans maintained that government originated in the consent of the people because that theory was an implement for chastening the absolutism of the Stuarts; but they maintained it also because they did not believe that any society, civil or ecclesiastical, into which men did not enter of themselves was worthy of the name.

Consequently, the social theory of Puritanism, based upon the law of God, was posited also upon the voluntary submission of the citizens.

As men exist in nature, said Thomas Hooker, no one person has any power over another; "there must of necessity be a mutuall ingagement, each of the other, by their free consent, before by any rule of God they have any right or power, or can exercise either, each towards the other." This truth appears, he argues, from all relations among men, that of husband and wife, master and servant; there must be a compact drawn up and sealed between them.

From *mutuall acts* of consenting and ingaging each of other, there is an impression of *ingagement* results, as a *relative bond,* betwixt the contractours and confederatours, wherein the *formalis ratio,* or *specificall nature* of the covenant lieth, in all the former instances especially *that of* corporations. So that however it is true, the rule bindes such to the duties of their places and relations, yet it is certain, it requires that they should *first freely ingage* themselves in such covenants, and *then* be carefull to fullfill such duties. A man is allowed freely to make choice of his wife, and she of her husband, before they need or should perform the duties of husband and wife one towards another.

The rules and regulations of society, the objectives and the duties, are erected by God; but in a healthy state the citizens must first agree to abide by those regulations, must first create the society by willing consent and active participation.

These ideas, of a uniform church supported by the civil authority, of rule by explicit law, of the derivation of the state from the consent of the people, were transported to the wilderness because they were the stock ideas of the time and place. What the New England Puritans added of their own was the unique fashion in which they combined them into one coherent and rounded theory. The classic expression of this theory is the speech on liberty delivered by John Winthrop to the General Court in 1645. In that year Winthrop was serving as lieutenant governor, and as such was a justice of the peace; a squabble broke out in the town of Hingham over the election of a militia officer; Winthrop intervened, committing one faction for contempt of court when they would not give bond to appear peaceably before the legislature and let the affair be adjudicated. Some of the citizens were enraged, and the lower house of the General Court impeached Winthrop for exceeding his commission and going beyond the basic law of the land. He was tried and acquitted; thereupon he pronounced his magnificent oration, setting before the people the unified theory of the Puritan commonwealth.

As he expounds it, the political doctrine becomes part and parcel of the theological, and the cord that binds all ideas together is the covenant. Winthrop argues that individuals, in a natural state, before grace has been given them, are at absolute liberty to do anything they can, to lie, steal, murder; obviously he is certain that natural men, being what they are, will do exactly these things unless prevented. But when men become regenerate they are then at "liberty" to do only what God commands. And God commands certain things for the group as a whole as well as for each individual. Regenerate men, therefore, by the very fact of being regenerate, come together, form churches and a state upon explicit agreements, in which they all promise to live with one another according to the laws and for the purposes of God. Thus the government is brought into being by the act of the people; but the people do not create just any sort of government, but the one kind of government which God has outlined. The governors are elected by the people, but elected into an office which has been established by God. God engenders the society by acting through the people, as in nature He secures His effects by guiding secondary causes; the collective will of regenerate men, bound together by the social compact, projects and continues the will of God into the state. As John Davenport expressed it, "In regular actings of the creature, God is the first Agent; there are not two several and distinct actings, one of God, another of the People: but in one and the same action, God, by the Peoples suffrages, makes such an one Governour, or Magistrate, and not another." So, when men have made a covenant with God they have thereby promised Him, in the very terms of that agreement, to compact among themselves in order to form a holy state in which His discipline will be practiced. As one of the ministers phrased it:

Where the Lord sets himselfe over a people, he frames them unto a willing and voluntary subjection unto him, that they desire nothing more then to be under his government . . . . When the Lord is in Covenant with a people, they follow him not forcedly, but as farre as they are sanctified by grace, they submit willingly to his regiment.

When men have entered these covenants, first with God, then with each other in the church and again in the state, they have thrice committed themselves to the rule of law and the control of authority. Winthrop can thus insist that though the government of Massachusetts is bound by fundamental law, and though it takes its rise from the people, and though the people elect the officials, still the people's liberty in Massachusetts consists in a "liberty to that only which is good, just and honest." By entering the covenant with God, and the covenant with each other, the citizens renounce all natural liberty, surrender the right to seek for anything that they themselves might lust after, and retain only the freedom that "is maintained and exercised in a way of subjection to authority."

The theory furnishes an excellent illustration of the intellectual ideal toward which all Puritan thought aspired; in the realm of government as of nature, the Puritan thinker strove to harmonize the determination of God with the exertion of men, the edicts of revelation with the counsels of reason and experience. On one side, this account exhibits the creation of society as flowing from the promptings and coaction of God; on the other side it attributes the origination to the teachings of nature and necessity. The social compact may be engineered by God, but it is also an eminently reasonable method of bringing a state into being. Delimitation of the ruler's power by basic law may be a divine ordinance to restrain the innate sinfulness of men, but it is also a very natural device to avoid oppression and despotism; the constitution may be promulgated to men from on high, but it is in fact very much the sort which, had they been left to their own devices, they might have contrived in the interests of efficiency and practicality. Men might conceivably have come upon the erection of governments through explicit compacts, in which they incorporated certain inviolable regulations and a guarantee of rights, quite as much by their own intelligence as by divine instruction. As always in Puritan thought, there was no intention to discredit either source, but rather to integrate the divine and the natural, revelation and reason, into a single inspiration. "Power of Civil Rule, by men orderly chosen, is Gods Ordinance," said John Davenport, even if "It is from the Light and Law of Nature," because "the Law of Nature is God's Law." The Puritan state was thus from one point of view purely and simply a "theocracy"; God was the sovereign; His fiats were law and His wishes took precedence over all other considerations; the magistrates and ministers were His viceroys. But from another point of view, the Puritan state was built upon reason and the law of nature; it was set up by the covenant of the people, the scope of its power was determined by the compact, and the magistrates and ministers were the commissioned servants of the people.

As this theory stands on paper it is, like so many edifices of the Puritan mind, almost perfect. When it was realized in practice, however, there were at least two difficulties that soon became apparent. For one, not all the people, even in New England, were regenerate; in fact, the provable elect were a minority, probably no more than one-fifth of the total population. But this did not dismay the original theorists, for they had never thought that mere numerical majorities proved anything. Consequently, though the social compact furnished the theoretical basis of society in New England, nevertheless it was confined to the special few; the election of officers and the passing of laws was given to those only who could demonstrate their justification and sanctification. The congregational system, with its membership limited to those who had proved before the church that they possessed the signs of grace, offered a ready machinery for winnowing the wheat from the chaff. Therefore, under the first charter the suffrage in Massachusetts was limited to the church members. In Connecticut the franchise was not officially restrained in this fashion, but other means served as well to keep the electorate pure and orthodox. The "citizens," as they were called, elected delegates to the General Court, chose judges, and passed laws. The others, the "inhabitants," had equality before the law, property rights, police protection; they were taxed no more than the citizens or submitted to no indignities, but they were allowed no voice in the government or in the choice of ministers, and only by the mere force of numbers gained any influence in town meetings.

The restriction of the franchise to church membership seemed to solve the first difficulty confronted by the Puritan theorists. But in time it only brought them face to face with the second and more serious problem: the whole structure of theory which Winthrop outlined in his speech, and which the sermons of the 1660's and 1670's reiterated, fell apart the moment the "citizens" were no longer really and ardently holy. Just as soon as the early zeal began to die down, and the distinction between the citizens and the inhabitants became difficult to discern, then the purely naturalistic, rational, practical aspect of the political theory became detached from the theological, began to stand alone and by itself. As the religious inspiration waned, there remained no reason why all the people should not be held partners to the social compact; the idea that God worked His ends through the covenant of the people grew vague and obscure, while the notion that all the people made the covenant for their own reasons and created the state for their own purposes took on more and more definite outlines. As toleration was forced upon the colonies by royal command, or became more estimable as religious passions abated, the necessity for the social bond being considered a commitment of the nation to the will of God disappeared. Instead, men perceived the charms and usefulness of claiming that the compact had been an agreement of the people, not to God's terms, but to their own terms. The divine ordinance and the spirit of God, which were supposed to have presided over the political process, vanished, leaving a government founded on the self-evident truths of the law of nature, brought into being by social compact, instituted not for the glory of God, but to secure men's "inalienable rights" of life, liberty, and the pursuit of happiness. Except that, until Jefferson rewrote the phrase, the sacred trinity of interests which government could not tamper with were more candidly summarized as life, liberty — and property.

After the new charter of 1691 — which Increase Mather negotiated and which for him was a diplomatic triumph, but which nevertheless was an imposition upon Massachusetts from the outside — leaders of the colony made various efforts to accommodate the orignal conception of social purpose to the constitutional requirements of the document. I have elsewhere described their flounderings (*The New England Mind: From Colony to Province*, 1953), and the literature of the eighteenth century clearly yields up the evolution of a political philosophy which, by the time of the revolution, was entirely perfected (see Alice M. Baldwin, *The New England Clergy and the American Revolution*, Durham, North Carolina, 1928). Historians now agree that the first clear break with the seventeenth-century complex was John Wise's *Vindication of the Government of the New England Churches* in 1717. Though actually this book had little or no effect on colonial thinking, and does not appear to have been cited even in the revolutionary debates, still it was far ahead of its own time in proclaiming that a contractual system of government, with inalienable rights preserved in society from the original state of nature, was the dictate of aboriginal reason, that it could be said to have only subsequently obtained "the Royal Approbation" of the Creator. The transformation of the doctrine of the founders into a weapon for burgeoning nationalism was virtually completed in 1750 when Jonathan Mayhew, preaching on the anniversary of the day on which the Puritans had decapitated Charles I, delivered "A Discourse Concerning Unlimited Subjection." To this enlightened Puritan it now appeared that the purposes of society are not at all those of the deity but of the subjects. The advantage to be derived from corporate existence is no longer the salvation but the well-being of the citizen. The power even of the Puritan God — and therefore, naturally, that of an English king — is bound by the terms of compact. New England's errand into the wilderness — having set out from the federal theology — had now developed into an assurance that God Himself would respect the laws we have agreed upon. As for King George, if he imposes a tax to which we do not ourselves consent, and if we thereupon resist him, "even to the dethroning him," we are not criminals: we have only taken "a reasonable way" of vindicating our natural rights.

In 1750 Mayhew's boldness still dismayed most of his contemporaries, as did also his theological liberalism, but it was only a matter of time before the community caught up with at least his political argument. Hence he is the most obvious link between Puritan and revolutionary ideas. However, in the excitement of embracing Mayhew's radicalism, few at the time of the war had the leisure or inclination to look back to Winthrop or to inquire how they had managed to travel the tortuous road from his doctrine of federal liberty to their constitutionalism. There ceased to survive even the faintest memory of an era when the social contract had incorporated absolute subjection to the ontological realities of the good, just, and honest — those anterior verities which existed from eternity, long before any peoples anywhere were gathered into societies and which no mere convention of the citizens could alter or redefine.

CHAPTER VI

JONATHAN EDWARDS AND THE GREAT AWAKENING

[The social historian, if he keeps strictly within the limits of his commitment, has difficulty in dealing with the Great Awakening of 1740. On the surface it seems an inexplicable outburst of neurotic energies which, in most if not all of the colonies, had not been bottled up, which assuredly needed no such spectacular vent. By the time the hysteria died down in the middle of the decade (except for sporadic heavings in Virginia and the Carolinas), it does not appear to have accomplished much in the history of America other than producing acrimonious divisions within the churches — generating "separatists" in New England and a split (ultimately healed) between the "Old" and the "New" sides in the Presbyterian synods of the middle colonies. Efforts have been made to identify the commotion with agrarian protest, with an uprising of debtors against creditors, of the common man against the gentry, or even with the sheer panic resulting from a sore-throat epidemic. None of these accounts offers an "explanation," either of the causes or of the consequences, that strikes one as more than peripheral.

Wherefore I am obliged to argue that this eruption came from sources that elude a merely sociological analysis. At the risk of sacrificing every pretense to scientific respectability, but out of respect for the theme of this volume, I am ready to say that the Great Awakening was the point at which the wilderness took over the task of defining the objectives of the Puritan errand. I am the more prepared to say this because Jonathan Edwards was a child of the wilderness as well as of Puritanism.

Thus there is a certain satisfaction in standing beside the greatest American leader of the Awakening, and trying to make out what he thought he was doing, or what he himself conceived that he had wrought, particularly because in 1750 he became the victim of whatever it was he had done.

Edwards is a mysterious being, and any effort to interpret the Awakening through his view of it comes to a dead stop before his reticence. This is true, even though in his revival tracts, above all in *A Treatise Concerning Religious Affections*, he analyzed the phenomenon in ultrascientific terms. Still, whatever light we can get upon the cataclysm from the enigmatic Edwards is worth having. This effort at a statement about his relation to the mysterious convulsion was the first in a series delivered at Bennington College in 1949, under the comprehensive title of "American Response to Crisis." My contribution is here reprinted from *America in Crisis*, edited by Daniel Aaron, copyrighted 1952 by Alfred A. Knopf, Inc.

Two or three of my colleagues objected that the Great Awakening was not, in historical terms, a "crisis," such as Nullification, John Brown's raid, or the closing of the banks in 1933. In that sense, it was not. Wherefore it remains something deeper than a specific event: it was a transformation, a blaze that consumed the theological universe of the seventeenth century, and left the American wilderness to rake the embers for a new concept of meaning. Jonathan Edwards survived the holocaust to put his final meditations on the social revolution into the subtle comment of *The Nature of True Virtue*. In the relation of that essay to the story I here briefly recount, we might say that *True Virtue* is almost a satire, utterly opposite in technique to Dr. Johnson's *Vanity of Human Wishes*, but oddly coincident in the lesson. If the absolute validity of the good, just, and honest would no longer prevail, in the wilderness of the Valley no less than in the turmoil of London, how then is modern man to find even the semblance of moral universality?

I have endeavored herein to point out a corollary of Edwards' thinking, though I do not for a moment suppose that he, could he read it, would agree.]

I

Although in the year 1740 some fairly flagrant scenes of emotional religion were being enacted in Boston, it was mainly in the Connecticut Valley that the frenzy raged and whence it spread like a pestilence to the civilized East. The Harvard faculty of that time would indeed have considered the Great Awakening a "crisis," because to them it threatened everything they meant by culture or religion or just common decency. It was a horrible business that should be suppressed and altogether forgotten. Certainly they would not have approved its being dignified as a starting point in a series of great American crises.

As far as they could see, it was nothing but an orgy of the emotions. They called it — in the lexicon of the Harvard faculty this word conveyed the utmost contempt — "enthusiasm." It was not a religious persuasion: it was an excitement of overstimulated passions that understandably slopped over into activities other than the ecclesiastical and increased the number of bastards in the Valley, where already there were too many. And above all, in the Valley lived their archenemy, the deliberate instigator of this crime, who not only fomented the frenzy but was so lost to shame that he brazenly defended it as a positive advance in American culture. To add insult to injury, he justified the Awakening by employing a science and a psychological conception with which nothing they had learned at Harvard had prepared them to cope.

It was certainly a weird performance. Edwards delivered his revival sermons — for example the goriest, the one at Enfield that goes by the title "Sinners in the Hands of an Angry God" and is all that most people nowadays associate with his name — to small audiences in country churches. In these rude structures (few towns had yet prospered enough to afford the Georgian churches of the later eighteenth century which are now the charm of the landscape) the people yelled and shrieked, they rolled in the aisles, they crowded up to the pulpit and begged him to stop, they cried for mercy. One who heard him described his method of preaching: he looked all the time at the bell rope (hanging down from the roof at the other end of the church) as though he would look it in two; he did not stoop to regard the screaming mass, much less to console them.

Of course, in a short time the opinion of the Harvard faculty appeared to be vindicated. In 1740 Edwards had writhing in the churches not only his own people but every congregation he spoke to, and he dominated the entire region. Ten years later he was exiled, thrown out of his church and town after a vicious squabble (the fight against him being instigated by certain of the first citizens, some of them his cousins, who by adroit propaganda mobilized "the people" against him), and no pulpit in New England would invite this terrifying figure. He had no choice but to escape to the frontier, as did so many misfits in American history. He went to Stockbridge, where he eked out his last years as a missionary to a lot of moth-eaten Indians. Because of the works he produced under these — shall we call them untoward? — circumstances, and because he was still the acknowledged leader of the revival movement, he was invited in 1758 to become president of the College of New Jersey (the present-day Princeton), but he died a few weeks after his inauguration, so that his life really belongs to the Connecticut Valley.

One may well ask what makes such a chronicle of frenzy and defeat a "crisis" in American history. From the point of view of the social historian and still more from that of the sociologist it was a phenomenon of mass behavior, of which poor Mr. Edwards was the deluded victim. No sociologically trained historian will for a moment accept it on Edwards' terms — which were, simply, that it was an outpouring of the Spirit of God upon the land. And so why should we, today, mark it as a turning point in our history, especially since thereafter religious revivals became a part of the American social pattern, while our intellectual life developed, on the whole, apart from these vulgar eruptions? The answer is that this first occurrence did actually involve all the interests of the community, and the definitions that arose out of it were profoundly decisive and meaningful. In that perspective Jonathan Edwards, being the most acute definer of the terms on which the revival was conducted and the issues on which it went astray, should be regarded — even by the social historian — as a formulator of propositions that the American society, having been shaken by this experience, was henceforth consciously to observe.

There is not space enough here to survey the Awakening through the vast reaches of the South and the Middle Colonies, nor even to list the intricate consequences for the social ordering of New England. The splintering of the churches and the increase of sectarianism suggest one way in which Americans "responded" to this crisis, and the impulse it gave to education, most notably in the founding of Princeton, is another. Such discussions, however valuable, are external and statistical. We come to a deeper understanding of what this crisis meant by examining more closely a revelation or two from the most self-conscious — not to say the most literate — theorist of the Awakening.

The theme I would here isolate is one with which Edwards dealt only by indirection. He was skilled in the art of presenting ideas not so much by expounding as by vivifying them, and he achieved his ends not only by explicit statement but more often by a subtle shift in emphasis. In this case, it is entirely a matter of divining nuances. Nevertheless, the issue was present throughout the Awakening and, after the temporary manifestations had abated, on this proposition a revolution was found to have been wrought that is one of the enduring responses of the American mind to crisis.

I mean specifically what it did to the conception of the relation of the ruler — political or ecclesiastical — to the body politic. However, before we can pin down this somewhat illusive development, we are confronted with the problem of whether the Great Awakening is properly to be viewed as a peculiarly American phenomenon at all. It would be possible to write about it — as has been done — as merely one variant of a universal occurrence in Western culture. Between about 1730 and 1760 practically all of Western Europe was swept by some kind of religious emotionalism. It was present in Germany, Holland, Switzerland, and France, and in Catholic circles there was an analogous movement that can be interpreted as an outcropping of the same thing: this the textbooks call "Quietism." And most dramatically, it was present in England with the Wesleys, Whitefield, and Methodism.

Once this international viewpoint is assumed, the American outburst becomes merely one among many — a colonial one at that — and we hesitate to speak about it as a crisis in a history specifically American. What was at work throughout the Western world is fairly obvious: the upper or the educated classes were tired of the religious squabbling of the seventeenth century, and turned to the more pleasing and not at all contentious generalities of eighteenth-century rationalism; the spiritual hungers of the lower classes or of what, for shorthand purposes, we may call "ordinary" folk were not satisfied by Newtonian demonstrations that design in the universe proved the existence of God. Their aspirations finally found vent in the revivals, and in each country we may date the end of a Calvinist or scholastic or, in short, a theological era by the appearance of these movements, and thereupon mark what is by now called the era of Pietism or Evangelicalism.

In this frame of reference, the Great Awakening was only incidentally American. It is merely necessary to translate the European language into the local terminology to have an adequate account. In this phraseology, the Great Awakening in New England was an uprising of the common people who declared that what Harvard and Yale graduates were teaching was too academic. This sort of rebellion has subsequently proved so continuous that one can hardly speak of it as a crisis. It is rather a chronic state of affairs. And in this view of it, the uprising of 1740 belongs to the international history of the eighteenth century rather than to any account of forces at work only on this continent.

Told in this way, the story will be perfectly true. Because we talk so much today of the unity of Western European culture, maybe we ought to tell it in these terms, and then stop. But on the other hand there is a curiously double aspect to the business. If we forget about Germany and Holland and even England — if we examine in detail the local history of Virginia, Pennsylvania, and New England — we will find that a coherent narrative can be constructed out of the cultural developments in each particular area. This Awakening can be seen as the culmination of factors long at work in each society, and as constituting, in that sense, a veritable crisis in the indigenous civilization.

II

The church polity established in New England was what today we call congregational. This meant, to put it crudely, that a church was conceived as being composed of people who could certify before other people that they had a religious experience, that they were qualified to become what the founders called "visible saints." The founders were never so foolish as to suppose that everybody who pretended to be a saint *was* a saint, but they believed that a rough approximation of the membership to the covenant of grace could be worked out. A church was composed of the congregation, but these were only the professing Christians. The rest of the community were to be rigorously excluded; the civil magistrate would, of course, compel them to come to the church and listen to the sermon, collect from them a tax to support the preacher, but they could not be actual members. Those who qualified were supposed to have had something happen to them that made them capable — as the reprobate was not — of swearing to the covenant of the church. They were able, as the others were not, *physically* to perform the act.

The basic contention of the founders was that a church is based upon the covenant. Isolated individuals might be Christians in their heart of hearts, but a corporate body could not come into being unless there was this preliminary clasping of hands, this taking of the official oath in the open and before all the community, saying in effect: "We abide by this faith, by this covenant." In scholastic language, the congregation were the "matter" but the covenant was the "form" of the church. They objected above all things to the practice in England whereby churches were made by geography; that a lot of people, merely because they resided in Little Willingdon, should make the church of Little Willingdon, seemed to them blasphemy. That principle was mechanical and unreal; there was no spiritual participation in it — no covenant.

That was why they (or at any rate the leaders and the theorists) came to New England. On the voyage over, in 1630, John Winthrop said to them: "For wee must Consider that wee shall be as a Citty vppon a Hill, the eies of all people are vppon us." They had been attempting in England to lead a revolution; after the King's dismissal of Parliament in 1629 it looked as though there was no longer any hope of revolution there, and so they migrated to New England, to build the revolutionary city, where they could exhibit to Englishmen an England that would be as all England should be.

The essence of this conception was the covenant. As soon as they were disembarked, as soon as they could collect in one spot enough people to examine each other and acknowledge that each seemed visibly capable of taking the oath, they incorporated churches — in Boston, Charlestown, and Watertown, and, even in the first decade, in the Connecticut Valley. But we must always remember that even in those first days, when conviction was at its height, and among so highly selected and dedicated numbers as made up the Great Migration, only about one fifth of the population were found able, or could find themselves able, to take the covenant. The rest of them — with astonishingly few exceptions — accepted their exclusion from the churches, knowing that they were not "enabled" and praying for the grace that might yet empower them.

From that point on, the story may seem somewhat peculiar, but after a little scrutiny it becomes an old and a familiar one: it is what happens to a successful revolution. The New Englanders did not have to fight on the barricades or at Marston Moor; by the act of migrating, they *had* their revolution. Obeying the Biblical command to increase and multiply, they had children — hordes of them. Despite the high rate of infant mortality, numbers of these children grew up in New England knowing nothing, except by hearsay and rumor, of the struggles in Europe, never having lived amid the tensions of England. This second generation were, for the most part, good people; but they simply did not have — they could not have — the kind of emotional experience that made them ready to stand up before the whole community and say: "On Friday the 19th, I was smitten while plowing Deacon Jones's meadow; I fell to the earth, and I knew that the grace of God was upon me." They were honest people, and they found it difficult to romanticize about themselves — even when they desperately wanted to.

In 1662 the churches of New England convoked a synod and announced that the children of the primitive church members were included in the covenant by the promise of God to Abraham. This solution was called at the time the halfway covenant, and the very phrase itself is an instructive demonstration of the New Englanders' awareness that their revolution was no longer revolutionary. These children, they decided, must be treated as members of the church, although they had not had the kind of experience that qualified their fathers. They must be subject to discipline and censures, because the body of the saints must be preserved. But just in case the authorities might be mistaken, they compromised by giving to these children only a "halfway" status, which made them members but did not admit them to the Lord's Supper.

This provision can easily be described as a pathetic, where it is not a ridiculous, device. It becomes more comprehensible when we realize that it was an accommodation to the successful revolution. Second and third generations grow up inheritors of a revolution, but are not themselves revolutionaries.

For the moment, in the 1660's and 1670's, the compromise worked, but the situation got worse. For one thing, New England suffered in King Philip's War, when the male population was decimated. Then, in 1684, the charter of Massachusetts was revoked, and after 1691 the colony had to adjust itself to the notion that its governor was imposed by the royal whim, not by the election of the saints. Furthermore, after 1715 all the colonies were prospering economically; inevitably they became more and more concerned with earthly things — rum, land, furs. On the whole they remained a pious people. Could one go back to Boston of 1710 or 1720 — when the ministers were asserting that it was as profligate as Babylon — I am sure that one would find it, compared with modern Hollywood, a strict and moral community. Nevertheless, everybody was convinced that the cause of religion had declined. Something had to be done.

As early as the 1670's the ministers had found something they could do: they could work upon the halfway members. They could say to these hesitants: "You were baptized in this church, and if you will now come before the body and 'own' the covenant, then your children can in turn be baptized." Gradually a whole segment of doctrine was formulated that was not in the original theory — which made it possible to address these citizens who were neither outside the pale nor yet snugly inside, which told them that however dubious they might be as saints, visible or invisible, they yet had sufficient will power to perform the public act of "owning the covenant."

With the increasing pressures of the late seventeenth and early eighteenth centuries, the practice of owning the covenant gradually became a communal rite. It was not enough that the minister labored separately with John or Elizabeth to make an acknowledgement the next Sunday: a day was appointed when all the Johns and Elizabeths would come to church

and do it in unison, the whole town looking on. It is not difficult to trace
through the increasing reënactments of this ceremony a mounting crescendo
of communal action that was, to say the least, wholly foreign to the original
Puritanism. The theology of the founders conceived of man as single and
alone, apart in a corner or in an empty field, wrestling with his sins; only
after he had survived this experience in solitude could he walk into the
church and by telling about it prove his right to the covenant. But this
communal confession — with everybody doing it together, under the
urgencies of an organized moment — this was something new, emerging
so imperceptibly that nobody recognized it as an innovation (or rather I
should say that some did, but they were shouted down) that by the turn
of the century was rapidly becoming the focus for the ordering of the
spiritual life of the town.

The grandfather of Jonathan Edwards, Solomon Stoddard of Northampton, was the first man who openly extended the practice or renewal of
covenant to those who had never been in it at all. In short, when these
occasions arose, or when he could precipitate them, he simply took into the
church and up to the Lord's Supper everyone who would or could come.
He called the periods when the community responded en masse his "har-
vests," of which he had five: 1679, 1683, 1696, 1712, 1718. The Mathers
attacked him for so completely letting down the bars, but in the Connecticut Valley his success was envied and imitated.

The Great Awakening of 1740, seen in the light of this devolopment,
was nothing more than an inevitable culmination. It was the point at
which the method of owning the covenant became most widely and exult-
ingly extended, in which the momentum of the appeal got out of hand,
and the ministers, led by Jonathan Edwards, were forced by the logic of
evolution not only to admit all those who would come, but to excite and to
drive as many as possible, by such rhetorical stimulations as "Sinners in
the Hands of an Angry God," into demanding entrance.

All of this, traced historically, seems natural enough. What 1740 did
was present a number of leading citizens, like the Harvard faculty, with
the results of a process that had been going on for decades but of which
they were utterly unaware until the explosion. Then they found themselves
trying to control it or censure it by standards that had in fact been out of
date for a century, although they had all that while professed them. In
this sense — which I regret to state has generally eluded the social historian
— the Great Awakening was a crisis in the New England society.

Professional patriots, especially those of New England descent, are fond
of celebrating the Puritans as the founders of the American tradition of
rugged individualism, freedom of conscience, popular education, and democracy. The Puritans were not rugged individualists; they did indeed
believe in education of a sort, but not in the "progressive" sense; they
abhorred freedom of conscience; and they did not believe at all in
democracy. They advertised again and again that their church polity was

not democratic. The fact that a church was founded on a covenant and that the minister happened to be elected by the mass of the church — this emphatically did not constitute a democracy. John Cotton made the position of the founders crystal clear when he told Lord Say and Seal that God never ordained democracy as a fit government for either church or commonwealth; although at first sight one might suppose that a congregational church was one, in that the people chose their governors, the truth was that "the government is not a democracy, if it be administered, not by the people, but by the governors." He meant, in short, that even though the people did select the person, the office was prescribed; they did not define its functions, nor was it responsible to the will or the whim of the electors. "In which respect it is, that church government is iustly denied . . . to be democratical, though the people choose their owne officers and rulers."

The conception ran through every department of the social thinking of New England in the seventeenth century, and persisted in the eighteenth up to the very outbreak of the Awakening. The essence of its always was that though officers may come into their office by the choice of the people, nevertheless the definition of the function, dignity, and prerogatives of the position does not depend upon the intentions or wishes of the electorate, but upon an abstract, divinely given, absolute prescription, which has nothing — in theory — to do with such practical or utilitarian considerations as may, at the moment of the election, be at work among the people.

The divine and immutable pattern of church government was set, once and for all, in the New Testament; likewise, the principles of political justice were given in an eternal and definitive form. The machinery by which a particular man was chosen to fulfill these directives (as the minister was elected by the vote of a congregation, or as John Winthrop was made governor of the Massachusetts Bay Company by a vote of the stockholders) was irrelevant. The exsitence of such machinery did not mean that the elected officer was in any sense responsible to the electorate. He knew what was expected of him from an entirely other source than their temporary passions; he knew what he, upon becoming such a being, should do — as such!

The classic statement, as is widely known, was the speech that John Winthrop delivered before the General Court on July 3, 1645. He informed the people that the liberty of the subject may sometimes include, as happily it did in Massachusetts, the privilege of selecting this or that person for office, but that it did not therefore mean the right to tell the officer what he should do once he was installed. The liberty that men enjoy in civil society, he said, "is the proper end and object of authority, and cannot subsist without it." It is not a liberty to do what you will, or to require the authority to do what you want: "It is a liberty to do that only which is good, just, and honest." Who defines the good, the just, and the honest? Obviously, the authority does.

In other words, the theory of early New England was basically medieval.

Behind it lay the conception of an authoritative scheme of things, in which basic principles are set down once and for all, entirely antecedent to, and utterly without regard for, political experience. The formulation of social wisdom had nothing to do with the specific problems of any one society. It was not devised by a committee on ways and means. Policy was not to be arrived at by a discussion of strategy — for example (in modern terms), shouldn't we use the atomic bomb now? This sort of argument was unavailing, because the function of government was to maintain by authority that which was inherently — and definably — the true, just, and honest.

In Hartford, Connecticut, Samuel Stone, colleague of the great Thomas Hooker, summarized the argument by declaring that congregationalism meant a silent democracy in the face of a speaking aristocracy. There might be something which we call democracy in the form of the church, but the congregation had to keep silent when the minister spoke. And yet, for a hundred years after the death of Hooker, this strange alteration went on inside the institution. The official theory remained, down to the time of Edwards, that the spokesman for the society — be he governor or minister — told the society, by right divine, what it should or should not do, without any regard to its immediate interests, whether emotional or economic. He had laid upon him, in fact, the duty of forgetting such wisdom as he might have accumulated by living as a particular person in that very community or having shared the hopes and qualities of precisely these people.

What actually came about, through the device of renewing the covenant, was something that in fact completely contradicted the theory. (We must remember that the church was, during this century, not merely something "spiritual," but the institutional center of the organized life.) Instead of the minister standing in his pulpit, saying: "I speak; you keep quiet," he found himself, bit by bit, assuming the posture of pleading with the people: "Come, and speak up." He did not know what was happening. He began to find out only in the Great Awakening, when the people at last and multitudinously spoke up.

III

The greatness of Jonathan Edwards is that he understood what had happened. But note this carefully. He was not Thomas Jefferson: he did not preach democracy, and he had no interest whatsoever in any social revolution. He was the child of this aristocratic, medieval system; he was born to the purple, to ecclesiastical authority. Yet he was the man who hammered it home to the people that they *had* to speak up, or else they were lost.

Edwards was a Puritan and a Calvinist. He believed in predestination and original sin and all those dogmas which modern students hold to be outworn stuff until they get excited about them as slightly disguised by Franz Kafka. Edwards did not submit these doctrines to majority vote, and he did not put his theology to the test of utility. But none of this was, in his existing situation, an issue. Granting all that, the question he had to decide was: What does a man do who leads the people? Does he, in 1740, say with the Winthrop of 1645 that they submit to what he as an ontologist tells them is good, just, and honest?

What he realized (lesser leaders of the Awakening, like Gilbert Tennent, also grasped the point, but none with the fine precision of Edwards) was that a leader could no longer stand before the people giving them mathematically or logically impregnable postulates of the eternally good, just, and honest. That might work in 1640, or in Europe (where to an astonishing extent it still works), but it would not work in the American wilderness. By 1740 the leader had to get down amongst them, and bring them by actual participation into an experience that was no longer private and privileged, but social and communal.

In other words, Edwards carried to its ultimate implication — this constitutes his "relation to his times," which no purely social historian can begin to diagnose — that slowly forming tendency which had been steadily pressing through enlargements of the ceremonial owning of the covenant. He carried it so far that at last everybody could see what it really did mean. Then the Harvard faculty lifted their hands in horror — because this ritual, which they had thought was a segment of the cosmology of John Winthrop, was proved by Edwards' use to flow from entirely alien principles. For this reason, his own Yale disowned him.

IV

In the year 1748 Edwards' revolutionary effort — his leadership of the Awakening must be seen as a resumption of the revolutionary thrust that had been allowed to dwindle in the halfway covenant — was almost at an end. The opposition was mobilizing, and he knew, even before they did, that they would force him out. When the fight had only begun, his patron and friend, his one bulwark in the civil society, Colonel John Stoddard, chief of the militia and warden of the marches, died. There was now no civil power that could protect him against the hatred of the "river gods." Out of all New England, Stoddard had been really *the* outstanding magistrate in that tradition of aristocratic leadership which had begun with Winthrop and had been sustained through a massive succession. As was the custom in New England, the minister gave a funeral sermon; Edwards preached over the corpse of the town's greatest citizen — who happened, in this case, to be also his uncle and his protector. Those who were now certain, with Colonel Stoddard in the ground, that they could get Edwards' scalp were in the audience.

Edwards delivered a discourse that at first sight seems merely one more Puritan eulogy. He told the people that when great and good men like Stoddard are taken away, this is a frown of God's displeasure, which indicates that they ought to reform their vices. This much was sheer convention. But before he came, at the end, to the traditional berating of the populace, Edwards devoted the major part of his oration to an analysis of the function and meaning of authority.

It should be remembered that Winthrop had commenced the New England tradition by telling the people that they had the liberty to do only that which is in itself good, just, and honest; that their liberty was the proper end and object of authority thus defined; that the approbation of the people is no more than the machinery by which God calls certain people to the exercise of the designated powers. And it should also be borne in mind that these powers are given apart from any consideration of the social welfare, that they derive from ethical, theological — a priori — considerations.

Jonathan Edwards says that the supreme qualification of a ruler is that he be a man of "great ability for the management of public affairs." This is his first and basic definition! Let us follow his very words, underlining those which carry revolutionary significance. Rulers are men "of great *natural* abilities" who are versed in discerning "those things wherein the *public welfare or calamity consists,* and the proper *means* to avoid the one and promote the other." They must have lived among men long enough to discover how the mass of them disguise their motives, must have learned how to "unravel the false, subtle arguments and cunning sophistry that is often made use of to defend *iniquity.*" They must be men who have improved their talents by — here are his great criteria — *study, learning, observation,* and *experience.* By these means they must have acquired "skill" in public affairs, "a great understanding of *men and things,* a great *knowledge of human nature,* and of the way of *accommodating* themselves to it." Men are qualified to be rulers if and when they have this "very extensive knowledge of men with whom they are concerned," and when also they have a full and particular understanding "of the *state and circumstances* of the country or people that they have the care of." These are the things — not scholastical articles — that make those in authority "fit" to be rulers!

Look closely at those words and phrases: skill, observation, men and things, state and circumstances — above all, experience! Is this the great Puritan revivalist? It is. And what is he saying, out of the revival? He is telling what in political terms the revival really meant: that the leader has the job of accommodating himself to the realities of human and, in any particular situation, of social, experience. No matter what he may have as an assured creed, as a dogma — no matter what he may be able to pronounce, in the terms of abstract theology, concerning predestination and original sin — as a public leader he must adapt himself to public welfare and calamity. He cannot trust himself to a priori rules of an eternal and uncircumstanced good, just, and honest. There are requirements imposed by the office; authority does indeed consist of propositions that pertain to it, but what are they? They are the need for knowing the people, the knack of properly manipulating and operating them, the wit to estimate their welfare, and the cunning to foresee what may become their calamity.

When we are dealing with so highly conscious an artist as Edwards, we not only are justified in submitting this crucial paragraph to close analysis, we are criminally obtuse if we do not. So it becomes significant to note what Edwards says immediately after his radically new definition of the ruler. Following his own logic, he is prepared at once to attack what, in the state and circumstances of the Connecticut Valley, constituted the primary iniquity, from which the greatest social calamity might be expected.

He says it without, as we might say, pulling punches: a ruler must, on these considerations of welfare, be unalterably opposed to all persons of "a mean spirit," to those "of a narrow, private spirit that may be found in little tricks and intrigues to promote their private interest, [who] will shamefully defile their hands to gain a few pounds, are not ashamed to hip and bite others, grind the faces of the poor, and screw upon their neighbors; and will take advantage of their authority or commission to line their own pockets with what is fraudulently taken or withheld from others." At the time he spoke, there sat before him the merchants, the sharp traders, the land speculators of Northampton; with the prompt publication of the sermon, his words reached similar gentlemen in the neighboring towns. Within two years, they hounded him out of his pulpit.

The more one studies Edwards, the more one finds that much of his preaching is his condemnation, in this language of welfare and calamity rather than of "morality," of the rising and now rampant businessmen of the Valley. It was Edwards' great perception — and possibly his greatest value for us today is precisely here — that the get-rich-quick schemes of his contemporaries were wrong not from the point of view of the eternal values but from that of the public welfare. The ruler, he said, must know the "theory" of government in such a way that it becomes "natural" to him, and he must apply the knowledge he has obtained by study and observation "to that business, so as to perform it most advantageously and effectually." Here he was, at the moment his protector was gone, when he knew that he was lost, telling those about to destroy him that the great man is he who leads the people by skill and experiential wisdom, and not by making money.

It is further revealing that, after Edwards had portrayed the ruler in this frame of utility and calculation, as he came to his fourth point, he then for the first time said that the authority ought to be a pious man, and only in his fifth and last did he suggest the desirability of a good family. For Winthrop these qualifications had been essentials of the office; for Edwards they were radically submitted to a criterion of utility. "It also contributes to the strength of a man in authority . . . when he is in such circumstances as give him advantage for the exercise of his strength, for the public good; as his being a person of honorable descent, of a distinguished education, his being a man of estate." But note — these are all "useful" because they "add to his strength, and increase his ability and advantage to serve his generation." They serve "in some respect" to make him more effective. It had never occurred to John Winthrop that the silent democracy should imagine for a moment that the elected ruler, in church or state, would be anyone but a pious, educated, honorably descended person, of adequate economic substance. Edwards (who was pious, educated, and very well descended, but not wealthy) says that in some respects these advantages are helps to efficiency.

From one point of view, then, this was what actually was at work inside the hysterical agonies of the Great Awakening. This is one thing they meant: the end of the reign over the New England and American mind of a European and scholastical conception of an authority put over men because men were incapable of recognizing their own welfare. This insight may assist us somewhat in comprehending why the pundits of Boston and Cambridge, all of whom were rational and tolerant and decent, shuddered with a horror that was deeper than mere dislike of the antics of the yokels. To some extent, they sensed that the religious screaming had implications in the realm of society, and those implications they — being businessmen and speculators, as were the plutocracy of Northampton — did not like.

Again, I would not claim too much for Edwards, and I have no design of inscribing him among the prophets of democracy or the New Deal. What he marks — and what he alone could make clear — is the crisis of the wilderness' Awakening, in which the social problem was taken out of the arcana of abstract morality and put into the arena of skill, observation, and accommodation. In this episode, the Americans were indeed participating in an international movement; even so, they came — or Edwards brought them — to sharper formulations of American experience. What the Awakening really meant for Americans was not that they too were behaving like Dutchmen or Germans or Lancashire workmen, but that in the ecstasy of the revival they were discovering, especially on the frontier, where life was the toughest, that they rejected imported European philosophies of society. They were now of themselves prepared to contend that the guiding rule of this society will be its welfare, and the most valuable knowledge will be that which can say what threatens calamity for the state.

CHAPTER VII

THE RHETORIC OF SENSATION

[Jonathan Edwards was something more than the preacher of sermons that frightened his listeners, at the height of the Great Awakening, into paroxysms of shrieking. Even the goriest of his thunderings have a fascination for the modern reader — though that reader be entirely secular-minded — which does not obtain with the printed discourses of such fellow revivalists as George Whitefield or Gilbert Tennent. Had Edwards been merely a tormentor of his people, he would be but a minor character in a long parade of American evangelists. Many later prophets studied him and strove to imitate him, but none could bend Ulysses' bow. None could approach the calm, majestic impersonality with which he stood in the center of, and seemed to dominate, the cyclone.

Therefore the secret of his power, and the immensity of his failure, have to be sought elsewhere than in the conventional pattern of a frontier revival. If he seized the opportunity of exploiting a vague spiritual discontent among the populace, at the same time he perfected a method for fanning the flames that derives from other areas of human psychology than exclusively an anxiety about salvation. In the midst of an orgy, Edwards retained conscious control — for which he had eventually to blame himself. He should, no doubt, have been easier upon himself: he could have shifted the blame onto his Puritan heritage, could have excused himself because he had foregone the consolation of the covenant. But he did not.

Many elements are combined in his oratorical achievement: his own passionate self, the traditions of the Valley (those of Hooker and Stoddard), the imagery of his society, the impression of the Valley's landscape. Yet in the final analysis, the meaning of Edwards comes down to a mastery of the word, of the word transformed from a counter in scholastic demonstration to a bare and brutal engine against the brain. He was as literate as he could be (considering how difficult it was for him to acquire the books) in European theology, but we are bound to consider that, being a child of the wilderness, he early conceived his resolution to present ideas naked. In his method more than in his content (if the two be separable), he was a radical innovator. In this way the archconservator of the Puritan past made his break with that past — in this respect the logician spoke for the wilderness.

This piece was first printed in *Perspectives of Criticism*, edited by Harry Levin (Cambridge, 1950), a volume dedicated to the memory of Theodore Spencer.]

I

"Tell me, Hylas," demands the interlocutor in Bishop Berkeley's *Three Dialogues*, the Socratic Philonous who is the transparent disguise for Berkeley himself, "hath every one a liberty to change the current proper signification attached to a common name in any language?" Can he call fire water, or trees men? The hapless Hylas, who perfectly embodies the received, enlightened, respectable opinion of 1713, is bound to answer in only one way, bound to fall into Philonous' trap, for Hylas is, inevitably, a reader of John Locke. Of course not, he replies, such conduct would not be rational, because "common custom is the standard of propriety in language." [1]

Neither Berkeley nor his alter ego had any intention — indeed they were not capable — of refuting Locke. Men of the early eighteenth century were not so much the beneficiaries of Locke as they were his prisoners. Try as he might, Berkeley could not transcend the *Essay Concerning Human Understanding*; he could only alter a few emphases and enlarge the method. So, being resolved to deny the existence of "an absolute external world," not only did he have to commence with the sensational psychology, not only did he have to borrow Locke's method even while extending the critique to primary as well as secondary qualities, but he had, still more unavoidably, to accept Locke's third book, the treatise on the nature of language, and then try to bend it to his own devices. He had to prove upon sound Lockean principles that even Locke, by persisting in his belief in material substance, was, despite his own Book III, entangled in "the embarras and delusion of Words." [2]

For two or three generations after 1690 practically all the theorizing upon language attempted by English or colonial American writers, and much of that on the Continent, was a reworking or reinterpretation of Locke. Vast differences slowly began to emerge, but the starting points remained, into what we call the romantic era, those of Book III; perhaps these are even yet the tacit assumptions of schools that are hostile to the Lockean temper. Locke's own motive for devoting a section to language (he says that he had not intended such a discussion, but that as he proceeded he found "so near a connexion" of words, which interpose themselves between the understanding and truth, with knowledge that he could not escape the challenge) [3] was simple: he blamed theological disputatiousness, the word-spinning of "schoolmen," for the commotions of Europe. If words could be reduced to what in fact they are, mere sounds, which "in their first original, and their appropriated use" do not stand for clear or distinct ideas, then the "disputing natural and moral philosophers of these latter

[1] *Dialogues*, ed. Mary Whiton Colkins (New York, 1929), 281–82.
[2] Berkeley, *Dialogues*, 123.
[3] *An Essay Concerning Human Understanding*, book III, chap. 9, par. 21.

ages" could be silenced and the soft voice of reason at last be heard.[4] "The multiplication and obstinacy of disputes, which have so laid waste the intellectual world, is owing to nothing more than to this ill-use of words."[5] More than any other influence, except perhaps sheer exhaustion, Locke's treatise brought about that cessation from acrimonious theological pamphleteering with which English Protestantism greeted the new century. But John Locke, who died in 1704, did not live long enough to see that, whereas his downright and commonsensical doctrine delivered men from the wrangling of theologians, it raised up as many problems as it solved and condemned mankind to a new, and almost as bad-tempered, warfare of rhetoricians.

After a century of it, human endurance weakened, and the reëxamination of Locke became a revulsion, identifying him and all his commentators with an era declared to have been dead to the things it knew not and wed to "musty laws lined out with wretched rule." Only in our own day, when one may safely suggest that the romantic denunciation was possibly excessive, can it be perceived that the Lockean analysis actually posed the very terms in which the romantic counterrevolution was phrased, and that, with all its fatal limitations, his was a heroic effort to come to grips with the problem of language. To the extent that our own conception of speech has become less transcendental, that the Coleridgean and Emersonian belief in the word becoming one with the thing no longer seems plausible, we find ourselves, to some extent, facing once more the issues posed by the third book of the *Essay Concerning Human Understanding*.

Locke's treatise exerted so profound an influence on the eighteenth century not only because of his felicity in phrasing the doctrine, but because the doctrine itself was the culmination and synthesis of a development that had been gathering way for a century. It was, one might say, the final recognition and acceptance of the consequences for philology of the scientific revolution. The essence of Locke's theory is that language, like government, is artificial; it rests upon contract, and neither vocabulary nor syntax have any inherent or organic rationale. By themselves, words are only noises, having no transcendental or preternatural correspondence with what they name; there is no "natural connexion . . . between particular articulate sounds and certain ideas," and a specific word serves as the sensible mark of a particular idea only "by a perfect voluntary imposition."[6] Meaning is arbitrary, the result of social convention. And therefore — to Locke's adherents this was the liberating discovery — words are *separable* from things. They are related to reality according to nothing more than their conscious designation by society, and no utterance can convey meaning to anyone who does not accept, who is too boorish or too eccentric to accept, the manners of society.

[4] *Essay*, book III, chap. 10, par. 2.
[5] *Essay*, book III, chap. 10, par. 22.
[6] *Essay*, book III, chap. 2, pars. 1, 8.

Behind this formulation lay the long effort of the partisans of nature to achieve, against the futilities of the Scholastics and the pretensions of sectaries, what they fondly expected would be the serenity of a universal and sane truth, a truth that would have the further advantage of utility in mechanics and accounting. By making words their target, they executed a flank attack on theologians. "Words," said Bacon, setting the theme his followers were assiduously to enlarge, "as a Tartar's bow, do shoot back upon the understandings of the wisest, and mightily entangle and pervert the judgment." Verbiage is the enemy, which makes it impossible for men "to follow and as it were to hound nature in her wanderings." [7] By the middle of the seventeenth century, the chorus was swelling: the "guardians and tutors" of mankind, said Cowley, have withheld him from nature's endless treasure by distracting him with painted scenes, but Bacon at last has turned his mind from words, "which are but Pictures of the Thought," to things, "the Mind's right object"; he who now would make "an exact Piece" must disregard the images of fancy, and

> before his sight must place
> The Natural and Living Face;
> The real Object must command
> Each Judgment of his Eye, and Motion of his Hand.[8]

The manifesto of the Royal Society, Bishop Sprat's *History* of 1667, was studied with condemnations of "notional wandrings," "imaginary ideas of conceptions," demonstrations "onely fitted for talk," and proudly asserted that the aim of the society was "to separate the knowledge of Nature, from the colours of Rhetorick, the devices of Fancy, or the delightful deceit of Fables." [9] In Locke, therefore, Sprat's ideal of style, freed from the domination of colors, devices, and deceits, maintaining "an inviolable correspondence between the hand and the brain," received at last a psychological and physiological justification. Locke proved by the nature of things that when men "set their thoughts more on words than things," they are employing terms learned "before the ideas are known for which they stand," and therefore could not possibly know what was being talked about.[10] Fortified by his authority, the doctrines of the separableness of words from objects and of the artificial origin of language became the dominant stereotypes of the eighteenth century. Gathering up the platitudes of the new criticism, Alexander Pope declared in 1711,

> Words are like leaves; and where they most abound,
> Much fruit of sense beneath is rarely found.[11]

---

[7] Bacon, *Works*, ed. Spedding, Ellis, and Heath (Boston, 1857), VII, 412.

[8] Preface to Thomas Sprat, *The History of the Royal Society* (London, 1667).

[9] *The History of the Royal Society*, 62.

[10] *Essay*, book III, chap. 2, par. 7.

[11] *An Essay on Criticism*, vv. 309–10.

Typical spokesmen, like Adam Smith in 1759, declared that the names of objects are merely "assigned," [12] and Hugh Blair in 1783 epitomized the whole theory in a sentence: "Words, as we now employ them, taken in general, may be considered as symbols, not as imitations; as arbitrary, or instituted, not natural signs of ideas." [13]

Hence Berkeley, who may be said to inaugurate a minority report in the "age of reason," executed a strategic maneuver when, far from calling in question the fundamental premises of Locke, as a Cambridge Platonist might or as Leibniz did, he accepted entirely the analysis of language and then proceeded to argue that from it followed consequences utterly opposite to the comfortable assurances of Locke and the popularizers of Newton. Granted that language is a social convention, as arbitrary as one wished, had not Locke, by the rigor of his own logic, been forced to assert that the correspondence was arranged not between the word and a material object, but between the word and an idea in a man's head? Locke's "new way of reasoning by ideas" had to see words as simply impacts on the senses that were artificially linked with other impacts derived from objects; what men experienced as gold they called "gold," but properly speaking, the word applied to the experience, not to the material. Locke could not see why anyone should be disturbed over this consideration. As he worked out his psychology, he found that the basic components of thought were "simple ideas," which did come directly into the mind from concrete objects; hence the elements of speech, the vocabulary of basic English, so to speak, would be attached to those mental entities "only to be got by those impressions objects themselves make on our minds, by the proper inlets appointed to each sort." [14] Since all men possess the same inlets, they would get the same impressions; gold would be experienced as gold, and the word "gold," though in itself simply a vibration of the ether, would stand securely for one, and only for one, thing. This was an adequate basis for coherent society — or for "the comfort and advantage of society," [15] which was all Locke wanted. The social compact and the rights of property rested firmly on the assurance, given by psychology, that a man can make articulate signs "stand as marks for the ideas within his mind." [16]

There was one slight danger to guard against. Even Cowley, naïvely assuming that the real object could directly command the judgment, had still confessed, although in parentheses, that we do "perversely" draw our thoughts sometimes from words. Sociable creature though he was, Locke was obliged to perceive that the process of attaching words to ideas might be reversible. A name is normally affixed to the idea derived from experi-

[12] Adam Smith, "Considerations on the First Formation of Languages," reprinted in *Essays Philosophical and Literary* (London, n.d.).

[13] Hugh Blair, *Lectures on Rhetoric and Belles Lettres* (Dublin, 1783), I, 115.

[14] *Essay*, book III, chap. 4, par. 11.

[15] *Essay*, book III, chap. 2, par. 1.

[16] *Essay*, book III, chap. 1, par. 2.

ence, but in the temporal order of experience the name may come first and so excite the idea, or some idea, before the object has even been met. By custom and education, Locke agreed, words are indeed assumed to stand for the things; the connection between "certain sounds and the ideas they stand for" becomes, by constant use, so intimate "that the names heard, almost as readily excite certain ideas as if the objects themselves, which are apt to produce them, did actually affect the senses." Obviously, children learn many words before they know the things, and adult discourse, consisting largely of general terms, actually requires that speakers do not perpetually have in mind, or put into words, all the component ideas, let alone the myriad sensations, that enter into an "abstract idea." [17] If they did, they would be bores!

Locke had no intention of augmenting boredom. In fact, by the mechanics of his psychology, an elision of detail was eminently to be expected: "ideas become general, by separating from them the circumstances of time and place, and any other ideas that may determine them to this or that particular existence." [18] The principle of separation, which accounts for the origin of language in general, also operates within language; thus a generalized name — honor, truth, regeneration, grace, matter — becomes affixed to this or that abstract idea. So far, so good; but did not Locke run the danger, at the end of his subtlety, of introducing by the back door the very "imaginary ideas of conceptions" he and the scientists had expelled by the front? Was he admitting, after all, that there are some words, the very words over which the wars had been fought, from which men might legitimately, instead of perversely, draw their thoughts?

Locke's answer was emphatically no. He protected his argument against this objection by his ingenious distinction between simple ideas and all the forms of complex ideas: mixed modes, relations, and substances. Simple ideas are the hard pellets of sensation, the irreducible atoms of impression, out of which complex ideas are built; simple ideas — this is the heart of Locke's conception — can be given a name only by those who have first had the sensation. No word alone can impart a simple idea, and therefore such ideas "are not capable of any definition"; "all the words in the world, made use of to explain or define any of their names, will never be able to produce in us the idea it stands for." He who has never tasted "pine apple" cannot get, from any number of words, "the true idea of the relish of that celebrated and delicious fruit." [19] This was Locke's major contribution to the Enlightenment, his weapon against enthusiasm, incantation, and priestcraft, his guarantee against perversity. The primary alphabet of thought simply cannot be taken from words; words can only be attached subsequently, by public agreement, to indubitable shocks of sense. This was the way to achieve what Sprat had defined as the goal of the Royal Society, the

[17] *Essay*, book III, chap. 2, par. 6; chap. 3, par. 7.
[18] *Essay*, book III, chap. 3, par. 16.
[19] *Essay*, book III, chap. 3, pars. 4, 11.

correspondence of hand and brain, the way — once and for all — to emancipate the solid knowledge of nature from the frivolous and discordant colors of rhetoric.

Thereafter the sailing was clear. Complex ideas are mechanical compositions of the simples, made not from new or unitary sensations but by "putting together those which the mind had before." They are wholly, completely "voluntary," "put together in the mind, independent from any original patterns in nature." Complex ideas do not need to correspond to real conjunctions of simple ideas in nature; they are "always suited to the end for which abstract ideas are made" — which is to say, for counters in civilized conversation — and as long as everybody is agreed, they will serve.[20] They are economical, because they collect an abundance of particulars into "short sounds," and they can never (except to enthusiasts!) become the instigators of perverse thoughts, because they are always definable. That is, they can always be resolved back into their components. Since they "depend on such collections of ideas as men have made, and not on the real nature of things," [21] there is no need to fight about them: if a dispute threatens, all we need do is to take apart the complex idea in question, see what differences appear in our respective inventories of impressions, and so come to an accommodation. "A definition is best made by enumerating those simple ideas that are combined in the signification of the term defined." [22]

That the terms of theology and ethics, the words over which Christendom had been rent, were "mixed modes," Locke was well aware; he thought he might do "some service to truth, peace, and learning, if, by any enlargement on this subject, I can make men reflect on their own use of language," because this would be to make them aware that both they and their opponents might have good words in their mouths "with very uncertain, little, or no signification." [23] They might even, he insinuated, begin to suspect that because the revealed will of God happens to be clothed in words, doubt and confusion unavoidably attend that sort of conveyance; whereas in nature, in the realm of the simple ideas, "the precepts of Natural Religion are plain, and very intelligible to all mankind, and seldom come to be controverted." [24] If the concept of predestination, for instance, is in fact nothing but a bundle of particulars, then unloosening the thongs and spreading out the collection of elements may make for pleasant discourse over the port — "for easier and readier improvement and communication of their knowledge" [25] — but surely not for the splitting of skulls.

Berkeley improved upon this logic by insisting that Locke did not go far

[20] *Essay*, book III, chap. 5, pars. 4, 7.
[21] *Essay*, book III, chap. 6, par. 1.
[22] *Essay*, book III, chap. 3, par. 10.
[23] *Essay*, book III, chap. 5, par. 16.
[24] *Essay*, book III, chap. 4, par. 23.
[25] *Essay*, book III, chap. 3, par. 20.

enough. The premise being that language is separable from reality, a word would therefore have meaning only so long as it could be attached, either immediately or by stopping to think, to an idea framed in the mind of speaker and listener; consequently, the name of a complex idea would be viable only so long as both agreed that if they took the time to investigate it they would turn up the same array of simple ideas. Thereupon Berkeley pounced upon Locke's admission that in social intercourse, men do get along without the investigation, that for indefinite periods the word serves from man to man without anybody's really entertaining the idea. If the idea can be dispensed with temporarily, need it ever be required? If it is unnecessary, does it exist? "It is one thing for to keep a name constantly to the same *definition*, and another to make it stand everywhere for the same *idea*: the one is necessary, the other useless and impracticable." [26] In other words, it is entirely logical, on the basis of the sensational psychology, to argue that the names of complex ideas, being only human constructions for social ends, for converse over the port, do not stand for any ideas at all and never have stood for any; that they are merely words and nothing but words. If a bundle has to be resolved back into its particulars in order to be defined, the particulars are the definition, and bundles are simply "fictions and contrivances of the mind." [27]

For certain words — Berkeley concentrated on "matter" — there obviously are no corresponding ideas; the whole business is a social makeshift, and Locke, for all his precaution, had failed to hound nature in her wanderings. Those indeed advise well, Berkeley continued, who tell us to attend our ideas and not the absurd opinions which grow out of words, but they have not heeded their own counsel "so long as they thought the only immediate use of words was to signify ideas, and that the immediate signification of every general name was a determinate abstract idea." [28] Locke and the Lockeans had, in short, fallen into the error of contending, in the face of their own logic, that whereas no word can engender a simple idea, a word standing for an intricate conception, if susceptible of definition, can communicate a nexus of ideas. The result was that they still tried to use such a word as "matter" as though it could summon up an idea, when to the simplest introspection it was evident that no such idea ever had existed or could exist. But Locke, we remember, had classified the concept of matter, along with all mixed modes and substances, under the head of complex ideas, which included also the propositions of Christian theology, such as resurrection, regeneration, and reprobation. Was Berkeley alone or peculiar in sensing a terrible deficiency in the very center of the rational optimism? Did he, in fact, realize how enormous the deficiency was? Was it the century's desire for stability and its want of logical acumen that induced so

[26] Berkeley, *A Treatise Concerning the Principles of Human Knowledge* (London, 1710), intro., par. 18.

[27] *Treatise*, intro., par. 13.

[28] *Treatise*, intro., par. 23.

many businessmen and divines to accept Locke with a sigh of relief, in the confidence that life could now become genial, enthusiasm unfashionable, and Christianity reasonable, that language could at last be so brought under control that it would no longer "insinuate wrong ideas, move the passions, and thereby mislead the judgment"? [29]

Suppose there were a mind as acute as Berkeley's, no less prepared to seize upon the weakness of the sensational rhetoric and yet equally convinced that the terms of the analysis were correct; and suppose that this mind, not so much concerned with the purely metaphysical issue of materialism and appreciating that there never had been an age "wherein strength and penetration of reason, extent of learning, exactness of distinction, correctness of style, and clearness of expression, did so abound," was also convinced that never was there an age "wherein there has been so little sense of the evil of sin"? If this mind, fully possessed of the doctrine of the sensational rhetoric, were also persuaded that "our people do not so much need to have their heads stored, as to have their hearts touched; and they stand in the greatest need of that sort of preaching, that has the greatest tendency to do this," [30] would he be content with refinements on the Lockean metaphysics, or would he see in the Lockean theory of language a help to that of which the people had greatest need? What would he therefore do with it? What could he do?

II

There is no evidence that Jonathan Edwards ever read Berkeley. He did read Locke, probably in 1717 when he was fourteen years of age — read him with more pleasure, he recollected, "than the most greedy miser finds, when gathering up handfuls of silver and gold, from some newly discovered treasure." [31] In 1727 he went up the river to become colleague pastor with his magnificent grandfather at Northampton, and two years later to assume the sole spiritual dictatorship of the most turbulent town in New England. He went there to preach, to touch the people's hearts and not to store their heads, but his own head was full of Newton and Locke; while Newton had impressed upon him the inviolable connection of cause and effect, Locke had taught him that in general the words used by parsons "signified nothing that really existed in nature." [32] The frontiersmen, farmers, aspiring merchants, and land speculators who made up pioneer Northampton existed in nature, and to them Edwards was to preach the New England theology, as complicated a collection of mixed modes as could be imagined. Meanwhile, he had read in Locke that the mixed modes which constitute the propositions of theology are "for the most part such whose

[29] *Essay*, book III, chap. 10, par. 23.
[30] Jonathan Edwards, *Works* (New York, 1844), III, 336.
[31] Sereno E. Dwight, *The Life of President Edwards* (New York, 1830), 30.
[32] *Essay*, book III, chap. 10, par. 16.

component parts nowhere exist together." Hence his mission was defined for him: "It is the mind alone that collects them, and gives them the union of one idea: and it is only by words enumerating the several simple ideas which the mind has united, that we can make known to others what their names stand for." [33]

As a student and tutor at New Haven, Edwards had already jotted down his *Notes on the Mind,* which to historians have seemed so to echo Berkeley that they have supposed an influence; in fact the similarity stems from Edwards' having also, and precociously, grasped the implication of the Lockean postulate. For Berkeley it led inescapably to a stylistic injunction: "Whatever ideas I consider, I shall endeavour to take them bare and naked into my view"; [34] for the young Edwards, acceptance of the sensational psychology was a commitment, for a lifetime of effort, "to extricate all questions from the least confusion of ambiguity of words, so that the ideas shall be left naked." [35]

Within a few years at Northampton he was preaching naked ideas in this fashion:

How dismal will it be, when you are under these racking torments, to know assuredly that you never, never shall be delivered from them; to have no hope: when you shall wish that you might but be turned into nothing, but shall have no hope of it; when you shall wish that you might be turned into a toad or a serpent, but shall have no hope of it; when you would rejoice, if you might but have any relief, after you shall have endured these torments millions of ages, but shall have no hope of it; when after you shall have worn out the age of the sun, moon, and stars, in your dolorous groans and lamentations, without any rest day or night, or one minute's ease, yet you shall have no hope of ever being delivered; when after you shall have worn out a thousand more such ages, yet you shall have no hope, but shall know that you are not one whit nearer to the end of your torments; but that still there are the same groans, the same shrieks, the same doleful cries, incessantly to be made by you, and that the smoke of your torment shall still ascend up forever and ever; and that your souls, which have been agitated with the wrath of God all this while, yet will still exist to bear more wrath; your bodies, which shall have been burning and roasting all this while in these glowing flames, yet shall not have been consumed, but will remain to roast through an eternity yet, which will not have been at all shortened by what shall have been past.[36]

By such rhetoric he whipped up a revival in 1734, and a still greater one in 1740, which, with the help of Whitefield, spread over all New England, became a frenzy and a social upheaval, and then burned itself out in a sullen resentment against its begetter and resulted in Edwards' expulsion from Northampton. Students have worried over how Edwards ever got from his

---

[33] *Essay,* book III, chap. 11, par. 18.
[34] *Treatise,* intro., par. 21.
[35] Dwight, *Life,* 702.
[36] *Works,* IV, 278.

early devotion to Locke, with the denunciation of "magisterial, positive, and imperious" ways of "imposing our own sense and interpretation" [37] on the Bible, to his later and indubitably imperious utterance. They have assumed that he could not have read Locke carefully; actually, he read Locke so profoundly that the progress from Book III of the *Essay* to the apocalyptic terrors of his revival sermons seemed to him not only logical but irresistible.

Edwards became a revolutionary artist in the midst of the eighteenth century because he took with painful seriousness Locke's theory that words are separable from all reality, natural or spiritual, and in themselves are only noises. "Sounds and letters are external things, that are the objects of the external senses of seeing and hearing"; therefore, he told his people, "ideas of certain marks upon paper, such as any of the twenty-four letters, in whatever order, or any sounds of the voice, are as much external ideas, as of any other shapes or sounds whatsoever." [38] Hence, "words are of no use any otherwise than as they convey our own ideas to others." [39] Out of the Lockean psychology, for instance, he could readily explain the failure of the educational methods employed by his enemies in Stockbridge upon the Indian children, who were being taught, Edwards reported, to read words merely as sensations and not as signs of ideas, "without any kind of knowledge of the meaning of what they read." They were being permanently disabled from ever getting knowledge by their "habit of making such and such sounds, on the sight of such and such letters, with a perfect inattentiveness to meaning." The proper method, "a rational way of teaching" either in the schoolroom or in the pulpit, would be to attach every word to an idea, so that eventually the words would provoke the concept: "Being long habituated to make sounds without connecting any ideas with them, they so continue until they come to be capable of well understanding the words, and would perhaps have the ideas, properly signified by the words, naturally excited in their minds on hearing the words, were it not for an habitual hearing and speaking them without any ideas." Edwards was an unbreakable, and unbendable, man; he would never admit that the methods he used to instigate the Awakening were wrong, even after they failed him; in the midst of his bitter exile, he unrepentantly insisted, "The child should be taught to understand *things*, as well as *words*." [40]

In his notebooks Edwards came back again and again to the troubling theme which was the crux, as he saw it, not only of his own problem but, in view of what the people most needed, of that of the age. The one incontrovertible and yet disastrous fact, "duly considering human nature," was simply that a great part of our discourse about things can be conducted without "the actual ideas" of the things in our mind, that "the mind makes

---

[37] *Essays*, book III, chap. 9, par. 23.
[38] *Works*, III, 80.
[39] *Works*, I, 532.
[40] Dwight, *Life*, 475–76.

use of signs instead of the ideas themselves." [41] This ability was obviously a consequence of the sensational psychology; it was immensely useful in practical affairs because it saved time; it enabled a man to run his eye down a page and take in a staggering array of abstract terms — "God, man, angel, people, misery, happiness, salvation, destruction, consideration, perplexity, sanctification" — without having to stop and frame a conception for every word. "If we must have the actual ideas of everything that comes in our way in the course of our thoughts, this would render our thoughts so slow as to render our power of thinking in great measure useless." [42] But granted these conveniences, nevertheless a terrible prospect followed: thinking can get along without being employed about things or ideas; it can operate entirely with those artificial signs which the mind habitually substitutes for reality. Profitable though the device may be for warfare, business, and speculation, what is it but the supreme manifestation of original sin? It is the negation of life, the acceptance of substitutes, of husks without the corn. Actually to know something, actually to live, is to deal with ideas themselves, for which words must remain forever the inadequate, because arbitrary, symbols:

> To have an actual idea of a thought, is to have that thought we have an idea of then in our minds. To have an actual idea of any pleasure or delight, there must be excited a degree of that delight. So to have an actual idea of any trouble or kind of pain, there must be excited a degree of that pain or trouble. And to have an idea of any affection of the mind, there must be, then present, a degree of that affection. [43]

In one of the several astonishing passages of his notebooks, Edwards worked out in a significant image the immense distinction between knowledge of the word and knowledge of the actuality for which the word is a substitute:

> When we have the idea of another's love to a thing, if it be the love of a man to a woman [whom] we are unconcerned about, in such cases we have not generally any further idea at all of his love, we only have an idea of his actions that are the effects of love, as we have found by experience, and of those external things which belong to love and which appear in case of love; or if we have any idea of it, it is either by forming our ideas so of persons and things as we suppose they appear to them that we have a faint vanishing notion of their affections, or — if the thing be a thing that we so hate that this can't be — we have our love to something else faintly and least excited: and so in the mind, as it were, referred to this place, we think this is like that. [44]

To know the love of a woman only from the *signs* displayed by another man in love, and to deduce from this that what he feels must resemble some

---

[41] Perry Miller, "Jonathan Edwards on the Sense of the Heart," *Harvard Theological Review*, XLI (April 1948), 129.

[42] Miller, 133.

[43] Miller, 131.

[44] "Miscellanies, No. 288," Jonathan Edwards Manuscripts, Yale University Library (quoted by permission).

lesser feeling of one's own, bears the same relation to one's actually loving a woman that the word bears to the idea.

When we come to the words of theology, the problem of getting from the term to the idea becomes difficult in the extreme. Instead of striving with ourselves to excite in ourselves the constituent ideas of the complex conception, "and so having actually such an abstract idea as Mr. Locke speaks of," we content ourselves with "only an idea of something in our mind, either a name, or some external sensible idea, that we use as a sign to represent that idea." [45] But in the face of this dilemma, it never occurred to Edwards, as it had to Berkeley, to solve his problem by denying the reality of the abstract idea — which is presumptive proof that Edwards was unaffected by Berkeley. He remained, on this point, faithful to Locke: the way to comprehend an abstract idea was, for him, not to deny it, but to define it. "If we are at a loss concerning a connection or consequence, or have a new inference to draw, or would see the force of some new argument, then commonly we are put to the trouble of exciting the actual idea, and making it as lively and clear as we can; and in this consists very much of that which we call attention of the mind in thinking." [46] But to excite the actual idea of certain realities, of the love of woman or the fear of God, for example, does indeed put us to "trouble." And it was precisely here that Edwards went beyond Locke, far beyond him! He reached into a wholly other segment of psychology, the realm of the passions, and linked the word not only with the idea but also with that from which Locke had striven to separate it, with the emotions.

Edwards' great discovery, his dramatic refashioning of the theory of sensational rhetoric, was his assertion that an idea in the mind is not only a form of perception but is also a determination of love and hate. To apprehend things only by their signs or by words is not to apprehend them at all; but to apprehend them by their ideas is to comprehend them not only intellectually but passionately. For Edwards, in short, an idea became not merely a concept but an emotion. Thus he could achieve, to the bewilderment of his opponents, his radical definition of grace as "a new simple idea," and thereby elevate the central Christian experience entirely above the ambiguities of the mixed modes. He went so far as to distinguish the emotional from the intellectual apprehension by calling it the truly "sensible" method, and to whisper to himself in the seclusion of his study, "Perhaps this distribution of the kinds of our knowledge into Speculative and Sensible, if duly weighed, will be found the most important of all." [47] For Edwards it was the most important achievement of his life and the key to his doctrine and practice.

Again he presents a strange parallel to Berkeley, though now with an important difference. As soon as Berkeley had proved, out of Locke's own

[45] Miller, 131.
[46] Miller, 134.
[47] Miller, 138.

principles, that words can function in communication without there being any idea involved or, as with abstractions, even existing, he was ready to suggest that words, simply as physiological stimuli, could operate not by actually communicating anything but by "the raising of some passion, the exciting to or deterring from an action, the putting the mind in some particular disposition." He entreated his readers to answer honestly if they had not, upon hearing certain discourses, experienced passions of fear or love or admiration "without any ideas coming between." Yet even with his logical destruction of abstract ideas to support him, Berkeley knew that when he claimed for language the right of working as a mere provoker of emotion, without the intermediacy of concepts, he was challenging the reigning complacency of the age: it is "commonly supposed," he noted, that "the communicating of ideas marked by words is . . . the chief and only end of language." [48] The Lockeans were positive on this point: consigning emotion to the pathology of enthusiasm, Locke explicitly limited the function of language to making known one man's thoughts or ideas to another, to doing it easily, and to conveying the knowledge of things.[49] Once more Locke was resolutely consolidating the gains of the recent scientific offensive; Sprat, for example, had lamented that tropes and figures, which originally had been intended to "bring Knowledge back again to our very senses, from when it was at first deriv'd," were in this degenerate age being used, in defiance of reason, to correspond "with its Slaves, the Passions!" [50] Locke's triumph, by restricting the validity of words to their matching ideas, seemed to preclude their ever being used again by civilized men as the goads of passion; and yet by 1710 Berkeley was soberly maintaining that, since there are words which symbolize abstract ideas, when in reality no such ideas can be conceived, at least such words must be used in the ordinary affairs of life only to "excite in us proper sentiments or dispositions to act in such a manner as is necessary for our well-being, how false soever they may be if taken in a strict and speculative sense." [51]

Edwards, as we have seen, remained a true Lockean, in that he persisted in taking abstract ideas for realities; had he in other respects remained as literal a disciple of Locke he would have frowned, as did his opponents in Boston, Lockeans like Chauncy and Mayhew, upon any use of words to arouse affections. On the other hand, had he followed the line of Berkeley and denied the existence of complex abstractions, he might have given way entirely to employing words for their emotional excitement without bothering about ideas, and so have gone along with the enthusiasts who turned the Awakening into an orgy. His greatness is that he did neither. Instead, he redefined "idea." He so conceived it that it became a principle of organization and of perception not only for the intellectual man but for the passionate man, for the loving and desiring man, for the whole man. He conceded

[48] *Treatise*, intro., par. 20.
[49] *Essay*, book III, chap. 10, par. 23.
[50] Sprat, *History*, 112.
[51] *Treatise*, part I, par. 52.

readily that a word can act as an emotional stimulus, not because like Berkeley he separated emotion from the mind, but because, having consolidated the mind with the passions, he was ready to maintain that an emotional response is also an intellectual, or that an intellectual, in the highest sense, is also emotional. A passionate grasping of meaning from a thing or a word is as much an idea — a more clear and distinct idea — as a theoretical grasping. He argued that the purport of a symbol can be appreciated not only by the human head but more accurately by the human heart. An "ideal apprehension" is not only a proposition, it is a "sense" — "whereby things are pleasing or displeasing, including all agreeableness and disagreeableness, all beauty and deformity, all pleasure and pain, and all those sensations, exercises and passions of the mind that arise from either of those." [52]

In other words, Edwards did not deny what Berkeley maintained, that the noise of a word can produce a visceral response which has nothing to do with any intelligibility. He was too rigorous a sensationalist not to see that such a phenomenon was altogether likely, and had he been doubtful, the extremists of the Awakening gave him empirical verification. What Edwards saw was that a purely physiological — or, as we might say, "aesthetic" — reaction to a word is of no use to anybody; what he denied was that the appeal to the emotions must always be made at the cost of the idea; what he insisted upon was that by the word (used in the place of a thing) an idea can be engendered in the mind, and that when the word is apprehended emotionally as well as intellectually, then the idea can be more readily and more accurately conceived. When the word sets in train a sequence of passions, out of it — not invariably, but frequently — there emerges, like Venus from the foam, a "sensible" concept. This was possible, he argued, because an idea is a unit of experience, and experience is as much love and dread as it is logic. To go from the word to a mechanical response, in preaching or in literary criticism, is a direct, natural, scientifically explicable process; but to get from the sensational impact of a word, through the emotion, to the saving, comprehending idea, there must be an indirect, a supernatural, a mysterious leap. And yet, wonder of wonders, it happens! It happens because, while the saving and comprehending idea is not an effect of which the word is the cause, still, in the marvelous order of divine providence, the preliminary application of the word is, for the producing of that idea, absolutely indispensable.

Hence it seemed obvious to Jonathan Edwards that the sounding of the word, out of which the new simple idea would or might be born, had to be of a word that stood for reality; and reality, to any objective consideration, is grim as well as beautiful. "I am not afraid to tell sinners, that are most sensible of their misery, that there case is indeed as miserable as they think it to be, and a thousand times more so; for this is the truth." [53] Edwards was the heir of a tradition which often found its happiest formulations in the

[52] Miller, 136.
[53] Works, III, 338.

terms of formal logic, and he sometimes expounded the rationale of his apocalyptic preaching by drawing upon old distinctions: the nature of a cause, he pleaded, is not always to be deduced from the nature of an effect, nor that of an effect from the cause, "when the cause is only *causa sine qua non,* or an occasional cause: yea, that in such a case, oftentimes the nature of the effect is quite contrary to the nature of the cause." [54] But Edwards could not have explained by the logic of federal Puritanism and by the scholastic psychology of the "faculties" how his naked preaching of terror could become an "occasional cause"; federal Puritanism would have suspected, as Edwards' opponents in fact did during the 1740's, that the effect was merely the efficient work of the word and so was entirely "natural." Edwards decisively departed from the old Puritanism by his appropriation of the new psychology of sensation. By defining grace in this novel frame of reference as a new simple idea, and by keeping in the center of his thinking the principle that an undefinable simple idea can be learned only from experience, he committed himself as a preacher to a rhetoric in which words were obliged to stand in the place of engendering objects, in spite of the fact that there is never any inherent reason why any particular word should stand for any specific object. He was prepared to stake his life upon the assurance that words which were disciplined into becoming "naked" embodiments of ideas could thence become, at least for those capable of receiving the concept, the source or the occasion of an ideational discovery. But if his rhetoric was to achieve such an effect, it had to be not only naked, but so passionately presented that the passions of listeners would heed it. "I should think myself in the way of duty, to raise the affections of my hearers as high as I possibly can, provided that they are affected with nothing but truth, and with affections that are not disagreeable to the nature of what they are affected with." [55] Because the terror of damnation is a truth, and fear is an affection agreeable to it, Edwards preached terror and fear.

To step for a moment outside history, let us look a century ahead of Edwards to Kierkegaard's observation that the teacher can give the learner not truth but only the condition necessary for understanding truth. By conceiving of the word as the occasional rather than the efficient cause, Edwards was maintaining, in the idiom of colonial New England, essentially Kierkegaard's position; in their different phrases both claimed that there is a fundamental limitation upon all literature, namely, that after the artist has provided the verbal environment, at this point another power must intervene if the beholder is to collect out of it the true conception.

But one who gives the learner not only the Truth, but also the condition for understanding it, is more than teacher. All instruction depends upon the presence, in the last analysis, of the requisite condition; if this is lacking, no teacher can

[54] *Works,* III, 290.
[55] *Works,* III, 335.

do anything. For otherwise he would find it necessary not only to transform the learner, but to recreate him before beginning to teach him. But this is something no human being can do; if it is done, it must be done by God himself.[56]

In Edwards' version, the statement runs that a person can indeed respond to words in terms of his knowledge of natural good or evil, but for him to react to the spiritual import of rhetoric — since spiritual good or evil will never consist in any consonancy whatsoever with human nature — "it must be wholly and entirely a work of the Spirit of God, not merely as assisting and coworking with natural principles, but as infusing something above nature." [57]

Yet this did not mean for Edwards — any more than for Kierkegaard — that the rhetorician simply builds up a wall of words around the listener, and then reclines, to let the Spirit of God work or not work. Had Edwards evaded the issue by taking so easy a way out, he too could be accused, as have most of the followers of Locke, for having surrendered to a "passive" notion of intelligence and to a naïve environmentalism. Edwards' point was that the sensory impression, and especially the sensible word, comes to the human spirit bearing significances of love or terror, and the leap to a saving understanding proceeds out of the natural. Though a sense of spiritual excellency is required for salvation, it is not the only kind of ideal apprehension that is concerned in conviction: "It also partly depends on a sensible knowledge of what is natural in religion." The mind, being convinced of the truth, "thence naturally and immediately infers from this fitness" what is originally beyond the contrivance of man.[58] So the word must be pressed, and rhetoric must strive for impression; it is a strength, not a weakness, of language that no matter how sensational it becomes, it has to depend upon something happening to the recipient outside and above its own mechanical impact. If this fact imposes a limitation upon the efficacy of art, it bestows at the same time an infallible criterion for its success: "There is a great difference between these two things, viz., lively imaginations arising from strong affections, and strong affections arising from lively imaginations." If Edwards' artistry was an accidental effect or a consequence of real passion, it would be genuine; but if it produced in the listener or reader an emotion that contained no more than what the rhetoric imparted, "then is the affection, however elevated, worthless and vain." [59] I think Edwards meant the affection of both speaker and listener, for he never spared himself. To this paradoxical and yet logical conclusion, this desperate and yet exhilarating insight, the sensational concept of language led to the reasoning of America's greatest sensationalist.

[56] Robert Bretall, *A Kierkegaard Anthology* (Princeton: Princeton University Press, 1946), 158.
[57] Miller, 141.
[58] Miller, 143, 145.
[59] *Works*, III, 124.

CHAPTER VIII

FROM EDWARDS TO EMERSON

[There can be no doubt that Jonathan Edwards would have abhorred from the bottom of his soul every proposition Ralph Waldo Emerson blandly put forth in the manifesto of 1836, *Nature*. We may be certain that he would have regarded it, as did the stalwart Calvinists at Princeton, as an inevitable outcome of that degenerate "Arminianism," the initial stirrings of which he had been the first to detect and to the destruction of which he devoted his life. Could he have lived long enough to witness the appearance in New England of "transcendentalism," he would have beheld in it the logical and predictable collapse of the "liberal" theology which, in New England, became institutionalized as Unitarianism. If Edwards ever laughed, then he would have laughed — along with the other theologians of his party, few of whom were given to laughter — over the discomfiture of the Unitarians upon discovering a heresy in *their* midst, but I suspect he would have seen even more vividly than did the Princeton pundits the threat which the gentle Emerson raised against everything Edwards stood for. In that strictly historical regard, then, there is no organic evolution of ideas from Edwards to Emerson.

This essay — let me for once call a piece by that name, using it here in the original sense of an endeavor or an exertion that does not quite reach its goal — has been unhappily construed by many readers, since it first appeared in *The New England Quarterly* for December 1940 (XIII, 589–617), as meaning that in some mystical pretension I argue for a direct line of intellectual descent, as though Edwards were a Holinshed to Emerson's Shakespeare. That notion — which would require the fatigue of a journey from the Puritans of the covenant out into the Connecticut Valley, and then back to the Harvard Divinity School — I never contemplated. That would obviously be a silly version of how ideas get transmitted, even in so confined a laboratory as New England then was. For a while I regretted ever having published this speculation.

Clearly, the sequence I strove to outline in this tentative form requires at least a volume of documentation. Possibly I may yet find the time and energy to supply it, but I welcome assistance, even though that shall prove my hunches wrong. For the moment, I must be content to let this exploration stand, with all its faults.

On the crudest of levels, I am arguing that certain basic continuities persist in a culture — in this case taking New England as the test tube — which underlie the successive articulation of "ideas." Or, I might put it, the history of ideas — if it is to be anything more than a mail-order catalogue — demands of the historian not only a fluency in the concepts themselves but an ability to get underneath them. This, certainly, is a dangerous invitation, opening the iron gates of scholarship to all sorts of obscurantist divination. However, if the safeguards of discrimination and of humor are adequately supplied, then it may be permissible to suggest that the gulf between Edwards and Emerson is not so deep nor so wide as a strictly doctrinal definition would lead us to believe. What is persistent, from the covenant theology (and from the heretics against the covenant) to Edwards and to Emerson is the Puritan's effort to confront, face to face, the image of a blinding divinity in the physical universe, and to look upon that universe without the intermediacy of ritual, of ceremony, of the Mass and the confessional.

The real difference between Edwards and Emerson, if they can thus be viewed as variants within their culture, lies not in the fact that Edwards was a Calvinist while Emerson rejected all systematic theologies, but in the quite other fact that Edwards went to nature, in all passionate love, convinced that man could receive from it impressions which he must then try to interpret, whereas Emerson went to Nature, no less in love with it, convinced that in man there is a spontaneous correlation with the received impressions.

Another way of saying this might, it is evident, be to define Emerson as an Edwards in whom the concept of original sin has evaporated. This would satisfy the textbooks: Edwards sought the "images or shadows of divine things" in nature, but could not trust his discoveries because he knew man to be cut off from full communion with the created order because of his inherent depravity. But Emerson, having decided that man is unfallen (except as his sensibilities have been blunted by civilization), announced that there is no inherent separation between the mind and the thing, that in reality they leap to embrace each other. Yes, that will do for the textbooks, or for students' notebooks. Yet true though it be, such an account leaves out the basic continuance: the incessant drive of the Puritan to learn how, and how most ecstatically, he can hold any sort of communion with the environing wilderness.]

RALPH WALDO EMERSON believed that every man has an inward and immediate access to that Being for whom he found the word "God" inadequate and whom he preferred to designate as the "Over-Soul." He believed that this Over-Soul, this dread universal essence, which is beauty, love, wisdom, and power all in one, is present in Nature and throughout Nature. Consequently Emerson, and the young transcendentalists of New England with him, could look with complacence upon certain prospects which our less transcendental generation beholds with misgiving:

> If the red slayer thinks he slays,
>   Or if the slain think he is slain,
> They know not well the subtle ways
>   I keep, and pass, and turn again.

Life was exciting in Massachusetts of the 1830's and '40's; abolitionists were mobbed, and for a time Mr. Emerson was a dangerous radical; Dr. Webster committed an ingenious murder; but by and large, young men were not called upon to confront possible slaughter unless they elected to travel the Oregon Trail, and the only scholar who did that was definitely not a transcendentalist. Thus it seems today that Emerson ran no great risk in asserting that should he ever be bayoneted he would fall by his own hand disguised in another uniform, that because all men participate in the Over-Soul those who shoot and those who are shot prove to be identical, that in the realm of the transcendental there is nothing to choose between eating and being eaten.

It is hardly surprising that the present generation, those who are called upon to serve not merely as doubters and the doubt but also as slayers and slain, greet the serene pronouncements of Brahma with cries of dissent. Professors somewhat nervously explain to unsympathetic undergraduates that of course these theories are not the real Emerson, much less the real Thoreau. They were importations, not native American growths. They came from Germany, through Coleridge; they were extracted from imperfect translations of the Hindu scriptures, misunderstood and extravagantly embraced by Yankees who ought to have known better — and who fortunately in some moments did know better, for whenever Emerson and Parker and Thoreau looked upon the mill towns or the conflict of classes they could perceive a few realities through the haze of their transcendentalism. They were but transcendental north-north-west; when the wind was southerly they knew the difference between Beacon Hill and South Boston. I suppose that many who now read Emerson, and surely all who endeavor to read Bronson Alcott, are put off by the "philosophy." The doctrines of the Over-Soul, courrespondence, and compensation seem nowadays to add up to shallow optimism and insufferable smugness. Contemporary criticism reflects this distaste, and would lead us to prize these men, if at all, for their incidental remarks, their shrewd observations upon society, art, manners, or the weather, while we put aside their premises and their conclusions, the ideas to which they devoted their principal energies, as notions too utterly fantastic to be any longer taken seriously.

Fortunately, no one is compelled to take them seriously. We are not required to persuade ourselves the next time we venture into the woods that we may become, as Emerson said we might, transparent eyeballs, and that thereupon all disagreeable appearances — "swine, spiders, snakes, pests, mad-houses, prisons, enemies" — shall vanish and be no more seen. These afflic-tions have not proved temporary or illusory to many, or the compensations always obvious. But whether such ideas are or are not intelligible to us, there remains the question of whence they came. Where did Emerson, Alcott, Thoreau, and Margaret Fuller find this pantheism which they preached in varying degrees, which the Harvard faculty and most Boston businessmen found both disconcerting and contemptible? Was New England's tran-scendentalism wholly Germanic or Hindu in origin? Is there any sense, even though a loose one, in which we can say that this particular blossom in the flowering of New England had its roots in the soil? Was it foolishly transplanted from some desert where it had better been left to blush unseen? Emerson becomes most vivid to us when he is inscribing his pungent re-marks upon the depression of 1837, and Thoreau in his grim comments upon the American blitzkrieg against Mexico. But our age has a tendency, when dealing with figures of the past, to amputate whatever we find irrelevant from what the past itself considered the body of its teaching. Certain fragments may be kept alive in the critical test tubes of the Great Tradition, while the rest is shoveled off to potter's field. The question of how much in the transcendental philosophy emerged out of the American background, of how much of it was not appropriated from foreign sources, is a question that concerns the entire American tradition, with which and in which we still must work. Although the metaphysic of the Over-Soul, of self-reliance, and of compensation is not one to which we can easily subscribe, yet if the particular formulations achieved by Emerson and Thoreau, Parker and Ripley, were restatements of a native disposition rather than amateur versions of *The Critique of Pure Reason*, then we who must also reformulate our traditions may find their philosophy meaningful, if not for what it held, at least for whence they got it.

Among the tenets of transcendentalism is one which today excites the minimum of our sympathy, which declared truth to be forever and every-where one and the same, and all ideas to be one idea, all religions the same religion, all poets singers of the same music of the same spheres, chanting eternally the recurrent theme. We have become certain, on the contrary, that ideas are born in time and place, that they spring from specific environ-ments, that they express the force of societies and classes, that they are generated by power relations. We are impatient with an undiscriminating eclecticism which merges the Bhagavad-Gita, Robert Herrick, Saadi, Swedenborg, Plotinus, and Confucius into one monotonous iteration. Em-erson found a positive pleasure — which he called "the most modern joy" — in extracting all *time* from the verses of Chaucer, Marvell, and Dryden, and so concluded that one nature wrote all the good books and one nature could read them. The bad books, one infers, were written by fragmentary individuals temporarily out of touch with the Over-Soul, and are bad because they do partake of their age and nation. "There is such equality and identity both of judgment and point of view in the narrative that it is plainly the work of one all-seeing, all-hearing gentleman." We have labored to restore the historical time to Chaucer and Dryden; we do not find it at all plain that they were mouthpieces of one all-seeing agency, and we are sure that if there is any such universal agent he certainly is not a gentleman. We are exasperated with Emerson's tedious habit of seeing everything *sub specie aeternitatis*. When we find him writing in 1872, just before his mind and memory began that retreat into the Over-Soul which makes his last years so pathetic, that while in our day we have witnessed great revolutions in religion we do not therefore lose faith "in the eternal pillars which we so differently name, but cannot choose but see their identity in all healthy souls," we are ready to agree heartily with Walt Whitman, who growled that Emerson showed no signs of adapting himself to new times, but had "about the same attitude as twenty-five or thirty years ago," and that he himself was "utterly tired of these scholarly things." We may become even more tired of scholarly things when we find that from the very beginning Emerson conceived the movement which we call transcendentalism as one more expression of the benign gentleman who previously had spoken in the persons of Socrates and Zoroaster, Mohammed and Buddha, Shakespeare and St. Paul. He does not assist our quest for native origins, indeed for any origins which we are prepared to credit, when he says in 1842, in the Boston Masonic Temple, that transcendentalism is a "Saturnalia of Faith," an age-old way of thinking which, falling upon Roman times, made Stoic philosophers; falling on despotic times, made Catos and Brutuses; on Popish times, made Protestants; "on prelatical times, made Puritans and Quakers; and falling on Unitarian and commercial times, makes the peculiar shades of Idealism which we know." Were we to take him at his word, and agree that he himself was a Stoic revisiting the glimpses of the moon, and that Henry Thoreau was Cato redivivus, we might then decide that both of them could fetch the shades of their idealism from ancient Rome or, if they wished, from Timbuktu, and that they would bear at best only an incidental relation to the American scene. We might conclude with the luckless San Francisco journalist, assigned the task of reporting an Emerson lecture, who wrote, "All left the church feeling that an elegant tribute had been paid to the Creative genius of the First Cause," but we should not perceive that any compliments had been paid to the intellectual history of New England.

Still, to take Emerson literally is often hazardous. We many allow him his Stoics, his Catos and Brutuses, for rhetorical embellishment. He is coming closer home, however, when he comes to Puritans and Quakers, to Unitarian and commercial times. Whether he intended it or not, this particular sequence constitutes in little an intellectual and social history of New England: first Puritans and Quakers, then Unitarians and commercial times, and now transcendentalists! Emerson contended that when poets spoke out of the transcendental Reason, which knows the eternal correspondence of things, rather than out of the shortsighted Understanding — which dwells slavishly in the present, the expedient, and the customary, and thinks in terms of history, economics, and institutions — they builded better than they knew. When they were ravished by the imagination, which makes every dull fact an emblem of the spirit, and were not held earthbound by the fancy, which knows only the surfaces of things, they brought their creations from no vain or shallow thought. Yet he did not intend ever to dispense with the understanding and the fancy, to forget the customary and the institutional — as witness his constant concern with "manners." He would not raise the siege of his hencoop to march away to a pretended siege of Babylon; though he was not conspicuously successful with a shovel in his garden, he was never, like Elizabeth Peabody, so entirely subjective as to walk straight into a tree because "I saw it, but I did not realize it." Could it be, therefore, that while his reason was dreaming among the Upanishads, and his imagination reveling with Swedenborg, his understanding perceived that on the plain of material causation the transcendentalism of New England had some connection with New England experience, and that his fancy, which remained at home with the customary and with history, guided this choice of words? Did these lower faculties contrive, by that cunning which distinguishes them from reason and imagination in the very moment when transcendentalism was being proclaimed a saturnalia of faith, that there should appear a cryptic suggestion that it betokened less an Oriental ecstasy and more a natural reaction of some descendants of Puritans and Quakers to Unitarian and commercial times?

I have called Emerson mystical and pantheistical. These are difficult adjectives; we might conveniently begin with Webster's dictionary, which declares mysticism to be the doctrine that the ultimate nature of reality or of the divine essence may be known by an immediate insight. The connotations of pantheism are infinite, but in general a pantheist holds that the universe itself is God, or that God is the combined forces and laws manifested in the existing universe, that God is, in short, both the slayer and the slain. Emerson and the others might qualify their doctrine, but when Professor Andrews Norton read that in the woods "I become a transparent eyeball; I am nothing, I see all; the currents of the Universal Being circulate through me; I am part or particle of God," in his forthright fashion he could not help perceiving that this was both mysticism and pantheism, and so attacking it as "the latest form of infidelity."

Could we go back to the Puritans whom Emerson adduced as his predecessors, and ask the Emersons and Ripleys, not to mention the Winthrops, Cottons, and Mathers, of the seventeenth century whether the eyeball passage was infidelity, there would be no doubt about the answer. They too might call it the "latest" form of infidelity, for in the first years of New England Winthrop and Cotton had very bitter experience with a similar doctrine. Our wonder is that they did not have more. To our minds, no longer at home in the fine distinctions of theology, it might seem that from the Calvinist doctrine of regeneration, from the theory that a regenerate soul receives an influx of divine spirit, and is joined to God by a direct infusion of His grace, we might deduce the possibility of receiving all instruction immediately from the indwelling spirit, through an inward communication which is essentially mystical. Such was exactly the deduction of Mistress Anne Hutchinson, for which she was expelled into Rhode Island. It was exactly the conclusion of the Quakers, who added that every man was naturally susceptible to this inward communication, that he did not need a special and supernatural dispensation. Quakers also were cast into Rhode Island or, if they refused to stay there, hanged on Boston Common. Emerson, descendant of Puritans, found the descendants of Quakers "a sublime class of speculators," and wrote in 1835 that they had been the most explicit teachers "of the highest article to which human faith soars [,] the strict union of the willing soul to God & so the soul's access at all times to a verdict upon every question which the opinion of all mankind cannot shake & which the opinion of all mankind cannot confirm." But his ancestors had held that while the soul does indeed have an access to God, it receives from the spirit no verdict upon any question, only a dutiful disposition to accept the verdict confirmed by Scripture, by authority, and by logic. As Roger Clap remarked, both Anne Hutchinson and the Quakers "would talk of the Spirit, and of revelations by the Spirit without the Word, . . . of the Light within them, rejecting the holy Scripture"; and the Puritan minister declared that the errors of the Antinomians, "like strong wine, make men's judgments reel and stagger, who are drunken therwith." The more one studies the history of Puritan New England, the more astonished he becomes at the amount of reeling and staggering there was in it.

These seventeenth-century "infidels" were more interested in enlarging the soul's access to God from within than in exploring the possibilities of an access from without, from nature. But if we, in our interrogation of the shades of Puritans, were to ask them whether there exists a spirit that rolls through all things and propels all things, whose dwelling is the light of setting suns, and the round ocean, and the mind of man, a spirit from whom we should learn to be disturbed by the joy of elevated thoughts, the Puritans would feel at once that we needed looking after. They would concede that the visible universe is the handiwork of God, that He governs it and is present in the flight of every sparrow, the fall of every stone, the rising and setting of suns, in the tempests of the round ocean. "Who set those candles, those torches of heaven, on the table? Who hung out those lanterns in heaven to enlighten a dark world?" asked the preacher, informing his flock that although we do not see God in nature, yet in it His finger is constantly evident. The textbook of theology used at Harvard told New England students that every creature would return into nothing if God did not uphold it — "the very cessation of Divine conservation, would without any other operation presently reduce every Creature into nothing." In regard of His essence, said Thomas Hooker, God is in all places alike, He is in all creatures and beyond them, "hee is excluded *out* of no place, included *in* no place." But it did not follow that the universe, though created by God and sustained by His continuous presence, was God Himself. We were not to go to nature and, by surrendering to the stream of natural forces, derive from it our elevated thoughts. We were not to become nothing and let the currents of Universal Being circulate through us. Whatever difficulties were involved in explaining that the universe is the work of God but that we do not meet God face to face in the universe, Puritan theologians knew that the distinction must be maintained, lest excitable Yankees reel and stagger with another error which they would pretend was an elevated thought. The difficulties of explanation were so great that the preachers often avoided the issue, declaring, "this is but a curious question: therefore I will leave it," or remarking that the Lord fills both heaven and earth, yet He is not in the world as the soul is in the body, "but in an incomprehensible manner, which we cannot expresse to you." Thomas Shepard in Cambridge tried to be more explicit: the Godhead, he said, is common to everything and every man, even to the most wicked man, "nay, to the vilest creature in the world." The same power that made a blade of grass made also the angels, but grass and angels are not the same substance, and so the spirit of God which is in the setting sun and the round ocean is not the same manifestation which He puts forth as a special and "supernatural" grace in the regenerate soul. "There comes another spirit upon us, which common men have not." This other spirit teaches us, not elevated thoughts, but how to submit our corrupt thoughts to the rule of Scripture, to the law and the gospel as expounded at Harvard College and by Harvard graduates.

The reason for Puritan opposition to these ideas is not far to seek. The Renaissance mind — which was still a medieval mind — remembered that for fifteen hundred years Christian thinkers had striven to conceive of the relation of God to the world in such a fashion that the transcendence of God should not be called in question, that while God was presented as the creator and governor of the world, He would always be something other than the world itself. Both mysticism and pantheism, in whatever form, identified Him with nature, made Him over in the image of man, interpreted Him in the terms either of human intuitions or of human perceptions, made Him one with the forces of psychology or of matter. The Renaissance produced a number of eccentrics who broached these dangerous ideas — Giordano Bruno, for instance, who was burned at the stake by a sentence which Catholics and Calvinists alike found just. The Puritans carried to New England the historic convictions of Christian orthodoxy, and in America found an added incentive for maintaining them intact. Puritanism was not merely a religious creed and a theology, it was also a program for society. We go to New England, said John Winthrop, to establish a due form of government, both civil and ecclesiastical, under the rule of law and Scripture. It was to be a medieval society of status, with every man in his

place and a place for every man; it was to be no utopia of rugged individualists and transcendental freethinkers. But if Anne Hutchinson was correct,
and if men could hear the voice of God within themselves, or if they could
go into the woods and feel the currents of Universal Being circulate
through them — in either event they would pay little heed to governors and
ministers. The New England tradition commenced with a clear understanding that both mysticism and pantheism were heretical, and also with
a frank admission that such ideas were dangerous to society, that men who
imbibed noxious errors from an inner voice of from the presence of God
in the natural landscape would reel and stagger through the streets of
Boston and disturb the civil peace.

Yet from the works of the most orthodox of Calvinists we can perceive
that the Puritans had good cause to be apprehensive lest mystical or pantheistical conclusions arise out of their premises. Anne Hutchinson and the
Quakers commenced as Calvinists; from the idea of regeneration they
drew, with what seemed to them impeccable logic, the idea that God
imparted His teaching directly to the individual spirit. With equal ease
others could deduce from the doctrines of divine creation and providence
the idea that God was immanent in nature. The point might be put thus:
there was in Puritanism a piety, a religious passion, the sense of an inward
communication and of the divine symbolism of nature. One side of the
Puritan nature hungered for these excitements; certain of its appetites
desired these satisfactions and therefore found delight and ecstasy in the
doctrines of regeneration and providence. But in Puritanism there was also
another side, an ideal of social conformity, of law and order, of regulation
and control. At the core of the theology there was an indestructible element
which was mystical, and a feeling for the universe which was almost pan-
theistic; but there was also a social code demanding obedience to external
law, a code to which good people voluntarily conformed and to which bad
people should be made to conform. It aimed at propriety and decency, the
virtues of middle-class respectability, self-control, thrift, and dignity, at a
discipline of the emotions. It demanded, as Winthrop informed the citizens
of Massachusetts Bay in 1645, that men forbear to exercise the liberty they
had by nature, the freedom to do anything they chose, and having entered
into society thereafter, devote themselves to doing only that which the
authorities defined as intrinsically "good, just and honest." The New England tradition contained a dual heritage, the heritage of the troubled spirit
and the heritage of worldly caution and social conservatism. It gave with one
hand what it took away with the other: it taught men that God is present
to their intuitions and in the beauty and terror of nature, but it disciplined
them into subjecting their intuitions to the wisdom of society and their impressions of nature to the standards of decorum.

In the eighteenth century, certain sections of New England, or certain
persons, grew wealthy. It can hardly be a coincidence that among those
who were acquiring the rewards of industry and commerce there should

be progressively developed the second part of the heritage, the tradition of reason and criticism, and that among them the tradition of emotion and ecstasy should dwindle. Even though a few of the clergy, like Jonathan Mayhew and Lemuel Briant, were moving faster than their congregations, yet in Boston and Salem, the centers of shipping and banking, ministers preached rationality rather than dogma, the Newtonian universe and the sensational psychology rather than providence and innate depravity. The back country, the Connecticut Valley, burst into flame with the Great Awakening of the 1740's; but the massive Charles Chauncy, minister at the First Church, the successor of John Cotton, declared that "the passionate discovery" of divine love is not a good evidence of election. "The surest and most substantial Proof is, *Obedience to the Commandments of God*, and the *stronger* the Love, the more uniform, steady and pleasant will be this *Obedience*." Religion is of the understanding as well as of the affections, and when the emotions are stressed at the expense of reason, "it can't be but People should run into Disorders." In his ponderous way, Chauncy was here indulging in Yankee understatement. During the Awakening the people of the back country ran into more than disorders; they gave the most extravagant exhibition of staggering and reeling that New England had yet beheld. Chauncy was aroused, not merely because he disapproved of displays of emotion, but because the whole society seemed in danger when persons who made a high pretense to religion displayed it in their conduct "as something wild and fanciful." On the contrary, he stoutly insisted, true religion is sober and well-behaved; as it is taught in the Bible, "it approves itself to the Understanding and Conscience, . . . and is in the best Manner calculated to promote the Good of Mankind." The transformation of this segment of Puritanism from a piety to an ethic, from a religious faith to a social code, was here completed, although an explicit break with the formal theology was yet to come.

Charles Chauncy had already split the Puritan heritage. Emerson tells that Chauncy, going into his pulpit for the Thursday lecture (people at that time came all the way from Salem to hear him), was informed that a little boy had fallen into Frog Pond and drowned. Requested to improve the occasion,

the doctor was much distressed, and in his prayer he hesitated, he tried to make soft approaches, he prayed for Harvard College, he prayed for the schools, he implored the Divine Being "to — to — to bless to them all the boy that was this morning drowned in Frog Pond."

But Jonathan Edwards felt an ardency of soul which he knew not how to express, a desire "to lie in the dust, and to be full of Christ alone; to love him with a holy and pure love; to trust in him; to live upon him; to serve and follow him; and to be perfectly sanctified and made pure, with a divine and heavenly purity." To one who conceived the highest function of religion to be the promotion of the good of mankind, Jonathan Edwards stood guilty of fomenting disorders. Chauncy blamed Edwards for inciting the populace, and was pleased when the congregation at Northampton, refusing to measure up to the standards of sanctification demanded by Edwards, banished him into the wilderness of Stockbridge. Edwards, though he was distressed over the disorders of the Awakening, would never grant that a concern for the good of mankind should take precedence over the desire to be perfectly sanctified and made pure. In his exile at Stockbridge he wrote the great tracts which have secured his fame for all time, the magnificent studies of the freedom of the will, of the nature of true virtue, of the purpose of God in creating the universe, in which Chauncy and Harvard College were refuted; in which, though still in the language of logic and systematic theology, the other half of the Puritan heritage — the sense of God's overwhelming presence in the soul and in nature — once more found perfect expression.

Though the treatises on the will and and on virtue are the more impressive performances, for our purposes the eloquent *Dissertation Concerning the End for which God Created the World* is the more relevant, if only because when he came to this question Edwards was forced to reply specifically to the scientific rationalism toward which Chauncy and Harvard College were tending. He had, therefore, to make even more explicit than did the earlier divines the doctrines which verged upon both mysticism and pantheism, the doctrines of inward communication and of the divine in nature. It was not enough for Edwards to say, as John Cotton had done, that God created the world out of nothing to show His glory; rationalists in Boston could reply that God's glory was manisfested in the orderly machine of Newtonian physics, and that a man glorified God in such a world by going about his rational business: real estate, the triangualr trade, or the manufacture of rum out of smuggled molasses. God did not create the world, said Edwards, merely to exhibit His glory; He did not create it out of nothing simply to show that He could: He who is Himself the source of all being, the substance of all life, created the world out of Himself by a diffusion of Himself into time and space. He made the world, not by sitting outside and above it, by modeling it as a child models sand, but by an extension of Himself, by taking upon Himself the forms of stones and trees and of man. He created without any ulterior object in view, neither for His glory nor for His power, but for the pure joy of self-expression, as an artist creates beauty for the love of beauty. God does not need a world or the worship of man; He is perfect in Himself. If He bothers to create, it is out of the fullness of His own nature, the overflowing virtue that is in Him. Edwards did not use my simile of the artist; his way of saying it was, "The disposition to communicate himself, or diffuse his own fulness, which we must conceive of as being originally in God as a perfection of his nature, was what moved him to create the world," but we may still employ the simile because Edwards invested his God with the sublime egotism of a very great artist. God created by the laws of His own nature, with no thought of doing good for anybody or for mankind, with no didactic purpose, for no other reason but the joy of creativeness. "It is a regard to himself that disposes him to diffuse and communicate himself. It is such a delight in his own internal fulness and glory, that disposes him to an abundant effusion and emanation of that glory."

Edwards was much too skilled in the historic problems of theology to lose sight of the distinction between God and the world or to fuse them into one substance, to blur the all-important doctrine of the divine transcendence. He forced into his system every safeguard against identifying the inward experience of the saint with the Deity Himself, or of God with nature. Nevertheless, assuming, as we have some right to assume, that what subsequent generations find to be a hidden or potential implication in a thought is a part of that thought, we may venture to feel that Edwards was particularly careful to hold in check the mystical and pantheistical tendencies of his teaching because he himself was so apt to become a mystic and a pantheist. The imagery in which a great thinker expresses his sense of things is often more revealing than his explicit contentions, and Edwards betrays the nature of his insight when he uses as the symbol of God's relation to the world the metaphor that has perennially been invoked by mystics, the metaphor of light and of the sun:

And [it] is fitly compared to an effulgence or emanation of light from a luminary, by which this glory of God is abundantly represented in Scripture. Light is the external expression, exhibition and manifestation of the excellency of the luminary, of the sun for instance: it is the abundant, extensive emanation and communication of the fulness of the sun to innumerable beings that partake of it. It is by this that the sun itself is seen, and his glory beheld, and all other things are discovered; it is by a participation of this communication from the sun, that surrounding objects receive all their lustre, beauty and brightness. It is by this that all nature is quickened and receives life, comfort, and joy.

Here is the respect that makes Edwards great among theologians, and here in fact he strained theology to the breaking point. Holding himself by brute will power within the forms of ancient Calvinism, he filled those forms with a new and throbbing spirit. Beneath the dogmas of the old theology he discovered a different cosmos from that of the seventeenth century, a dynamic world, filled with the presence of God, quickened with divine life, pervaded with joy and ecstasy. With this insight he turned to combat the rationalism of Boston, to argue that man cannot live by Newtonian schemes and mathematical calculations, but only by surrender to the will of God, by reflecting back the beauty of God as a jewel gives back the light of the sun. But another result of Edwards's doctrine, one which he would denounce to the nethermost circle of Hell but which is implicit in the texture, if not in the logic, of his thought, could very easily be what we have called mysticism or pantheism, or both. If God is diffused through nature, and the substance of man is the substance of God, then it may follow that man is divine, that nature is the garment of the Over-Soul, that man must be self-reliant, and that when he goes into the woods the currents of Being will indeed circulate through him. All that prevented this deduction was the orthodox theology, supposedly derived from the Word of God, which taught that God and nature are not one, that man is corrupt and his self-reliance is reliance on evil. But take away the theology, remove this overlying stone of dogma from the wellsprings of Puritan conviction, and both nature and man become divine.

We know that Edwards failed to revitalize Calvinism. He tried to fill the old bottles with new wine, yet none but himself could savor the vintage. Meanwhile, in the circles where Chauncy had begun to reëducate the New England taste, there developed, by a very gradual process, a rejection of the Westminster Confession, indeed of all theology, and at last emerged the Unitarian churches. Unitarianism was entirely different wine from any that had ever been pressed from the grapes of Calvinism, and in entirely new bottles, which the merchants of Boston found much to their liking. It was a pure, white, dry claret that went well with dinners served by the Harvard Corporation, but it was mild and was guaranteed not to send them home reeling and staggering. As William Ellery Channing declared, to contemplate the horrors of New England's ancestral creed is "a consideration singularly fitted to teach us tolerant views of error, and to enjoin caution and sobriety."

In Unitarianism one half of the New England tradition — that which inculcated caution and sobriety — definitely cast off all allegiance to the other. The ideal of decorum, of law and self-control, was institutionalized. Though Unitarianism was "liberal" in theology, it was generally conservative in its social thinking and in its metaphysics. Even Channing, who strove always to avoid controversy and to appear "mild and amiable," was still more of an enthusiast than those he supplied with ideas, as was proved when almost alone among Unitarian divines he spoke out against slavery. He frequently found himself thwarted by the suavity of Unitarian breeding. In his effort to establish a literary society in Boston, he repaired, as Emerson tells the story, to the home of Dr. John Collins Warren, where

he found a well-chosen assembly of gentlemen variously distinguished; there was mutual greeting and introduction, and they were chatting agreeably on indifferent matters and drawing gently towards their great expectation, when a side-door opened, the whole company streamed in to an oyster supper, crowned by excellent wines; and so ended the first attempt to establish aesthetic society in Boston.

But if the strain in the New England tradition which flowered so agreeably in the home of Dr. Warren, the quality that made for reason and breeding and good suppers, found itself happily divorced from enthusiasm and perfectly enshrined in the liberal profession of Unitarianism, what of the other strain? What of the mysticism, the hunger of the soul, the sense of divine emanation in man and in nature, which had been so important an element in the Puritan character? Had it died out of New England? Was it to live,

if at all, forever caged and confined in the prison house of Calvinism? Could
it be asserted only by another Edwards in another treatise on the will and a
new dissertation on the end for which God created the universe? Andover
Seminary was, of course, turning out treatises and dissertations, and there
were many New Englanders outside of Boston who were still untouched
by Unitarianism. But for those who had been "liberated" by Channing
and Norton, who could no longer express their desires in the language of
a creed that had been shown to be outworn, Calvinism was dead. Unitarianism rolled away the heavy stone of dogma that had sealed up the mystical
springs in the New England character; as far as most Unitarians were
concerned, the stone could now be lifted with safety, because to them the
code of caution and sobriety, nourished on oyster suppers, would serve
quite as well as the old doctrines of original sin and divine transcendence to
prevent mankind from reeling and staggering in freedom. But for those
in whom the old springs were still living, the removal of the theological
stopper might mean a welling up and an overflowing of long suppressed
desires. And if these desires could no longer be satisfied in theology, toward
what objects would they now be turned? If they could no longer be expressed in the language of supernatural regeneration and divine sovereignty,
in what language were they to be described?

The answer was not long forthcoming. If the inherent mysticism, the
ingrained pantheism, of certain Yankees could not be stated in the old
terms, it could be couched in the new terms of transcendental idealism, of
Platonism, of Swedenborg, of "Tintern Abbey" and the Bhagavad-Gita,
in the eclectic and polyglot speech of the Over-Soul, in "Brahma," in
"Self-Reliance," in *Nature*. The children of Puritans could no longer say
that the visible fabric of nature was quickened and made joyful by a diffusion
of the fullness of God, but they could recapture the Edwardsean vision by
saying, "Nature can only be conceived as existing to a universal and not to
a particular end; to a universe of ends, and not to one, — a work of
ecstasy, to be represented by a circular movement, as intention might be
signified by a straight line of definite length." But in this case the circular
conception enjoyed one great advantage — so it seemed at the time —
that it had not possessed for Edwards: the new generation of ecstatics had
learned from Channing and Norton, from the prophets of intention and
the straight line of definite length, that men did not need to grovel in the
dust. They did not have to throw themselves on the ground, as did Edwards,
with a sense of their own unworthiness; they could say without trepidation
that no concept of the understanding, no utilitarian consideration for the
good of mankind, could account for any man's existence, that there was no
further reason than "*so it was to be.*" Overtones of the seventeenth century
become distinctly audible when Emerson declares, "The *royal* reason, the
Grace of God, seems the only description of our multiform but ever
identical fact," and the force of his heredity is manifest when he must go
on to say, having mentioned the grace of God, "There is the incoming or

the receding of God," and as Edwards also would have said, "we can show neither how nor why." In the face of this awful and arbitrary power, the Puritan had been forced to conclude that man was empty and insignificant, and account for its recedings on the hypothesis of innate depravity. Emerson does not deny that such reflections are in order; when we view the fact of the inexplicable recedings "from the platform of action," when we see men left high and dry without the grace of God, we see "Self-accusation, remorse, and the didactic morals of self-denial and strife with sin"; but our enlightenment, our liberation from the sterile dogmas of Calvinism, enables us also to view the fact from "the platform of intellection," and in this view "there is nothing for us but praise and wonder." The ecstasy and the vision which Calvinists knew only in the moment of vocation, the passing of which left them agonizingly aware of depravity and sin, could become the permanent joy of those who had put aside the conception of depravity, and the moments between could be filled no longer with self-accusation but with praise and wonder. Unitarianism had stripped off the dogmas, and Emerson was free to celebrate purely and simply the presence of God in the soul and in nature, the pure metaphysical essence of the New England tradition. If he could no longer publish it as orthodoxy, he could speak it fearlessly as the very latest form of infidelity.

At this point there might legitimately be raised a question whether my argument is anything more than obscurantism. Do words like "New England tradition" and "Puritan heritage" mean anything concrete and tangible? Do they "explain" anything? Do habits of thought persist in a society as acquired characteristics, and by what mysterious alchemy are they transmitted in the blood stream? I am as guilty as Emerson himself if I treat ideas as a self-contained rhetoric, forgetting that they are, as we are now discovering, weapons, the weapons of classes and interests, a masquerade of power relations.

Yet Emerson, transcendental though he was, could see in his own ideas a certain relation to society. In his imagination transcendentalism was a saturnalia of faith, but in his fancy it was a reaction against Unitarianism and in his understanding a revulsion against commercialism. We can improve his hint by remarking the obvious connection between the growth of rationalism in New England and the history of eighteenth-century capitalism. Once the Unitarian apologists had renounced the Westminster Confession, they attacked Calvinism not merely as irrational but as a species of pantheism, and in their eyes this charge was sufficient condemnation in itself. Calvanism, said Channing, robs the mind of self-determining force and makes men passive recipients of the universal force:

> It is a striking fact that the philosophy which teaches that matter is an inert substance, and that God is the force which pervades it, has led men to question whether any such thing as matter exists. . . . Without a free power in man, he is nothing. The divine agent within him is every thing, Man acts only in show.

He is a phenomenal existence, under which the One Infinite Power is manifested; and is this much better than Pantheism?

One does not have to be too prone to economic interpretation in order to perceive that there was a connection between the Unitarian insistence that matter is substance and not shadow, that men are self-determining agents and not passive recipients of Infinite Power, and the practical interests of the society in which Unitarianism flourished. Pantheism was not a marketable commodity on State Street, and merchants could most successfully conduct their business if they were not required to lie in the dust and desire to be full of the divine agent within.

Hence the words "New England tradition" and "Puritan heritage" can be shown to have some concrete meaning when applied to the gradual evolution of Unitarianism out of the seventeenth-century background; there is a continuity both social and intellectual. But what of the young men and young women, many of them born and reared in circles in which, Channing said, "Society is going forward in intelligence and charity," who in their very adolescence instinctively turned their intelligence and even their charity against this liberalism, and sought instead the strange and uncharitable gods of transcendentalism? Why should Emerson and Margaret Fuller, almost from their first reflective moments, have cried out for a philosophy which would reassure them that matter is the shadow and spirit the substance, that man acts by an influx of power — why should they deliberately return to the bondage from which Channing had delivered them? Even before he entered the divinity school Emerson was looking askance at Unitarianism, writing in his twentieth year to his southern friend, John Boynton Hill, that for all the flood of genius and knowledge being poured out from Boston pulpits, the light of Christianity was lost: "An exemplary Christian of today, and even a Minister, is content to be just such a man as was a good Roman in the days of Circero." Andrews Norton would not have been distressed over this observation, but young Emerson was. "Presbyterianism & Calvinism at the South," he wrote, "at least make Christianity a more real & tangible system and give it some novelties which were worth unfolding to the ignorance of men." Thus much, but no more, he could say for "orthodoxy": "When I have been to Cambridge & studied Divinity, I will tell you whether I can make out for myself any better system than Luther or Calvin, or the *liberal besoms* of modern days." The "Divinity School Address" was forecast in these youthful lines, and Emerson the man declared what the boy had divined when he ridiculed the "pale negations" of Unitarianism, called it an "icehouse," and spoke of "the corpse-cold Unitarianism of Harvard College and Brattle Street." Margaret Fuller thrilled to the epistle of John read from a Unitarian pulpit: "Every one that loveth is born of God, and knoweth God," but she shuddered as the preacher straightway rose up "to deny mysteries, to deny second birth, to deny influx, and to renounce the sovereign gift of insight, for the sake of what he deemed a *'rational'* exercise of will." This Unitarianism, she argued in her journal, has had its place, but the time has now come for reinterpreting old dogmas: "For one I would now preach the Holy Ghost as zealously as they have been preaching Man, and faith instead of the understanding, and mysticism instead &c — ." And there, characteristically enough, she remarks, "But why go on?"

A complete answer to the question of motives is probably not possible as yet. Why Waldo and Margaret in the 1820's and '30's should instinctively have revolted against a creed that had at last been perfected as the ideology of their own group, of respectable, prosperous, middle-class Boston and Cambridge — why these youngsters, who by all the laws of economic determinism ought to have been the white-headed children of Unitarianism, elected to become transcendental black sheep, cannot be decided until we know more about the period than has been told in *The Flowering of New England* and more about the nature of social change in general. The personal matter is obviously of crucial importance. The characters of the transcendentalists account for their having become transcendental; still two facts of a more historical nature seem to me worth considering in the effort to answer our question.

The emergence of Unitarianism out of Calvinism was a very gradual, almost an imperceptible, process. One can hardly say at what point rationalists in eastern Massachusetts ceased to be Calvinists, for they were forced to organize into a separate church only after the development of their thought was completed. Consequently, although young men and women in Boston might be, like Waldo and Margaret, the children of rationalists, all about them the society still bore the impress of Calvinism: the theological break had come, but not the cultural. In a thousand ways the forms of society were still those determined by the ancient orthodoxy, piously observed by persons who no longer believed in the creed. We do not need to posit some magical transmission of Puritanism from the seventeenth to the nineteenth century in order to account for the fact that these children of Unitarians felt emotionally starved and spiritually undernourished. In 1859 James Cabot sent Emerson *The Life of Trust,* a crude narrative by one George Muller of his personal conversations with the Lord, which Cabot expected Emerson to enjoy as another instance of man's communion with the Over-Soul, which probably seemed to Cabot no more crackbrained than many of the books Emerson admired. Emerson returned the volume, accompanied by a vigorous rebuke to Cabot for occupying himself with such trash:

I sometimes think that you & your coevals missed much that I & mine found: for Calvinism was still robust & effective on life & character in all the people who surrounded my childhood, & gave a deep religious tinge to manners & conversation. I doubt the race is now extinct, & certainly no sentiment has taken its place on the new generation, — none as pervasive & controlling. But they were a high tragic school, & found much of their own belief in the grander traits of the Greek mythology, — Nemesis, the Fates, & the Eumenides, and, I am sure, would have raised an eyebrow at this pistareen Providence of . . . George Muller.

At least two members of the high tragic school Emerson knew intimately and has sympathetically described for us — his stepgrandfather, the Reverend Ezra Ripley, and his aunt, Mary Moody Emerson. Miss Emerson put the essence of the Puritan aesthetic into one short sentence: "How insipid is fiction to a mind touched with immortal views!" Speaking as a Calvinist, she anticipated Max Weber's discovery that the Protestant ethic fathered the spirit of capitalism, in the pungent observation, "I respect in a rich man the order of Providence." Emerson said that her journal "marks the precise time when the power of the old creed yielded to the influence of modern science and humanity"; still in her the old creed never so far yielded its power to the influence of modern humanity but that she could declare, with a finality granted only to those who have grasped the doctrine of divine sovereignty, "I was never patient with the faults of the good." When Thomas Cholmondeley once suggested to Emerson that many of his ideas were similar to those of Calvinism, Emerson broke in with irritation, "I see you are speaking of something which had a meaning once, but is now grown obsolete. Those words formerly stood for something, and the world got good from them, but not now." The old creed would no longer serve, but there had been power in it, a power conspicuously absent from the pale negations of Unitarianism. At this distance in time, we forget that Emerson was in a position fully to appreciate what the obsolete words had formerly stood for, and we are betrayed by the novelty of his vocabulary, which seems to have no relation to the jargon of Calvinism, into overlooking a fact of which he was always aware — the great debt owed by his generation "to that old religion which, in the childhood of most of us, still dwelt like a sabbath morning in the country of New England, teaching privation, self-denial and sorrow!" The retarded tempo of the change in New England, extending through the eighteenth into the nineteenth century, makes comprehensible why young Unitarians had enough contact with the past to receive from it a religious standard by which to condemn the pallid and unexciting liberalism of Unitarianism.

Finally, we do well to remember that what we call the transcendental movement was not an isolated phenomenon in nineteenth-century New England. As Professor Whicher has remarked, "Liberal ideas came slowly to the Connecticut Valley." They came slowly also to Andover Theological Seminary. But slowly they came, and again undermined Calvinist orthodoxies as they had undermined orthodoxy in eighteenth-century Boston; and again they liberated a succession of New Englanders from the Westminster Confession, but they did not convert them into rationalists and Unitarians. Like Emerson, when other New Englanders were brought to ask themselves, "And what is to replace for us the piety of that race?" they preferred to bask "in the great morning which rises forever out of the eastern sea" rather than to rest content with mere liberation. "I stand here to say, Let us worship the mighty and transcendent Soul" — but not the good of mankind! Over and again the rational attack upon Calvinism served only to release energies which then sought for new forms of expression in directions entirely opposite to rationalism. Some, like Sylvester Judd, revolted against the Calvinism of the Connecticut Valley, went into Unitarianism, and then came under the spell of Emerson's transcendentalist tuition. Others, late in the century, sought out new heresies, not those of transcendentalism, but interesting parallels and analogues. Out of Andover came Harriet Beecher Stowe, lovingly but firmly underlining the emotional restrictions of Calvinism in *The Minister's Wooing* and *Oldtown Folks*, while she herself left the grim faith at last for the ritualism of the Church of England. Out of Andover also came Elizabeth Stuart Phelps in feverish revolt against the hard logic of her father and grandfather, preaching instead the emotionalism of *Gates Ajar*. In Connecticut, Horace Bushnell, reacting against the dry intellectualism of Nathaniel Taylor's Calvinism just as Margaret Fuller had reacted a decade earlier against the dry rationalism of Norton's Unitarianism, read Coleridge with an avidity equal to hers and Emerson's, and by 1849 found the answer to his religious quest, as he himself said, "after all his thought and study, n‑t as something reasoned out, but as an inspiration — a revelation from the mind of God himself." He published the revelation in a book, the very title of which tells the whole story, *Nature and the Supernatural Together Constituting One System of God*, wherein was preached anew the immanence of God in nature: "God is the spiritual reality of which nature is the manifestation." With this publication the latest — and yet the oldest — form of New England infidelity stalked in the citadel of orthodoxy, and Calvinism itself was, as it were, transcendentalized. At Amherst, Emily Dickinson's mental climate, in the Gilded Age, was still Emerson's; the break-up of Calvinism came later there than in Boston, but when it had come the poems of Emily Dickinson were filled with "Emersonian echoes," echoes which Professor Whicher wisely declines to point out because, as he says, resemblances in Emerson, Thoreau, Parker, and Emily Dickinson are not evidences of borrowings one from another, but their common response to the spirit of the time, even though the spirit reached Emily Dickinson a little later in time than it did Emerson and Thoreau. "Their work," he says, "was in various ways a fulfillment of the finer energies of a Puritanism that was discarding the husks of dogma." From the time of Edwards to that of Emerson, the husks of Puritanism were being discarded, but the energies of many Puritans were not yet diverted — they could not be diverted — from a passionate search of the soul and of nature, from the quest to which Calvinism had devoted them. These New Englanders — a few here and there — turned aside from the doctrines of sin and predestination, and thereupon sought with renewed fervor for the accents of the Holy Ghost in their own hearts and in woods and mountains. But now that the restraining hand of theology was withdrawn, there was nothing to prevent them, as there had been everything to prevent Edwards, from identifying their intuitions with the voice of God, or from fusing God and nature into the one substance of the transcendental imagination. Mystics were no longer inhibited by dogma. They were free to carry on the ancient New England propensity for reeling and staggering with new opinions. They could give themselves over, unrestrainedly, to becoming transparent eyeballs and debauchees of dew.

CHAPTER IX

NATURE AND THE NATIONAL EGO

[Historical surveys customarily present Emerson as the one who floated to the top of a fermentation of ideas peculiarly limited to New England. Though in general his reputation has declined, while that of Henry Thoreau has risen, they both are presented as parochial figures. Emerson tried to avoid either sectarianism or regionalism, and commenced his youthful journal with a dedication to America; nevertheless, he is labeled the foremost spokesman for "transcendentalism," which in the American context does not mean transcendental idealism, as in Europe, but a sort of midsummer madness that overtook a few intellectuals in or around Boston about the year 1840. Actually, in the vicinity of Boston he was greeted by the majority with disdain, if not with open hostility; outside the area, most respectable journals treated him with contempt. Had he been nothing more, we might be justified in dismissing him, as several have done, for being at best the plaintive voice of a decadent Puritanism.

However, the facts are that Emerson went back and forth across the land, a voice speaking to the American people. In the decade of 1850–1860 he achieved a kind of apotheosis, and even such organs of New York Whiggery as *The Knickerbocker Magazine* had to confess that he was a power to be reckoned with. If the modern observer, noting these evidences of acceptance, can then withdraw to a sufficiently elevated altitude — from which the sectional peculiarities are lost to view and only the continent is seen — the theses of Emerson do become central to the emerging civilization of his time. As in 1836 he first proclaimed them, they all cohere about the idea of *Nature*. And Nature — not to be too tedious — in America means the wilderness.

So, if there be any validity in my unscientific version of a continuity from federal Puritans to Edwards to Emerson, then by the same token Emerson bespoke the inarticulate preoccupation of the entire community.

To regard only the literary scene, we must recognize that our first "national" novelist, James Fenimore Cooper, dramatized the obsessive American drama, that of Nature versus civilization. Cooper was simply annoyed by the metaphysics of transcendentalists, whom he regarded as one more aberration of nasal-twanging Yankeedom; Emerson had so little taste for fiction that he never could see the symbolic majesty of Cooper. Even so, we get nowhere with Thoreau, Whitman, or Melville until we recognize how they revolved around, or struggled with, the propositions of Emerson's *Nature*.

Moreover, not only writers of such sophistication as Emerson and Melville raise the theme, *the* American theme, of Nature versus civilization. You can find it in the politics of Andrew Jackson, in the observations of foreign travelers, in the legend of Abraham Lincoln, in Stephen Douglas no less than in Francis Parkman. Once possessed of that view, you see that the United States became a nation in the late eighteenth century under the aegis of rationalism, but found itself obliged to conceive of itself in the nineteenth as still running the Puritans' errand into an apparently limitless wilderness. How then it can cope with New York, Detroit, Gary, becomes its problem; but the outlines of that problem were faintly perceptible from the beginning. John Winthrop had been worried about it even in the middle of the Atlantic: is any wilderness, in God's finite creation, really illimitable?

This piece was first delivered at Yale University in October 1953, then in altered versions for the American Historical Association in New York, December 1954, and at Gonzaga University, in Spokane, April 1955. It is now reprinted, in final form, from *The Harvard Theological Review*, XLVIII (October 1955), 239–53.]

ON May 8, 1847, *The Literary World* — the newly founded vehicle in New York City for the program of "nativist" literature — reviewed an exhibition at the National Academy. The magazine had just undergone an editorial revolution and the new management was endeavoring to tone down the strident nationalism of the first few issues; still, the exuberant patriotism of the reviewer could not be restrained, for he had just beheld two exciting landscapes of Staten Island painted by J. F. Cropsey.

This artist, said the reviewer, must be ranked along with the acknowledged masters, Thomas Cole and Asher Durand — and this was high praise in 1847. And as do these masters, young Cropsey illustrates and vindicates the high and sacred mission of the American painter:

The axe of civilization is busy with our old forests, and artisan ingenuity is fast sweeping away the relics of our national infancy. What were once the wild and picturesque haunts of the Red Man, and where the wild deer roamed in freedom, are becoming the abodes of commerce and the seats of manufactures. Our inland lakes, once sheltered and secluded in the midst of noble forests, are now laid bare and covered with busy craft; and even the primordial hills, once bristling with shaggy pine and hemlock, like old Titans as they were, are being shorn of their locks, and left to blister in cold nakedness in the sun. "The aged hemlocks, through whose branches have whistled the winds of a hundred winters," are losing their identity, and made to figure in the shape of deal boards and rafters for unsightly structures on bare commons, ornamented with a few peaked poplars, pointing like fingerposts to the sky. Yankee enterprise has little sympathy with the picturesque, and it behooves our artists to rescue from its grasp the little that is left, before it is for ever too late.

Students of the history of art recognize in this passage a doctrine that had, by 1847, become conventional among landscape painters in Europe, England, and America: that of a fundamental opposition of Nature to civilization, with the assumption that all virtue, repose, dignity are on the side of "Nature" — spelled with a capital and referred to as feminine — against the ugliness, squalor, and confusion of civilization, for which the pronoun was simply "it." However, though this passage proceeds from a premise as familiar in Dusseldorf as in New York, still it takes the form of an exhortation that is seldom, if ever, encountered in the criticism of Europe. In America the artist has a calling above and beyond an accurate reporting of scenery: he must work fast, for in America Nature is going down in swift and inexorable defeat. She is being defaced, conquered — actually ravished. Civilization is leading us into a horrible future, filled with unsightly structures, resounding with the din of enterprise. All too soon we shall become like Europe. In the old world artists may indeed paint only such "garden landscapes" as are dotted here and there in a setting that man has mastered; but our noble Hudson and "the wild witchery of our unpolluted inland lakes and streams," this Nature is not man's but "GOD'S." American artists return from Europe, "their hands cramped with mannerism, and their minds belittled and debauched by the artificial stimulants of second-hand and second-rate creations." This was what America must resist, debauching artificiality. Yet if history is so irresistibly carrying the defiling axe of civilization into our sublime wilderness, will it not be merely a matter of time — no matter how furiously our Coles, Durands, and Cropseys, our poets and novelists, strive to fix the fleeting moment of primitive grandeur — before we too shall be cramped into mannerism, before our minds shall be debauched by artificial stimuli?

The reader may object that I am talking nonsense. This was the expanding, prospering, booming America of the 1840's; here, if ever in the annals of man, was an era of optimism, with a vision of limitless possibilities, with faith in a boundless future. There was indeed some fear that the strife of North and South might wreck the chariot of progress, but the more that threat loomed the more enthusiastically the nation shouted the prospects of wealth and prosperity, if only in order to show the folly of allowing politics to spoil the golden opportunity. Dickens and other foreign visitors report a republic constantly flinging into their faces preposterous vaunts about what it would shortly become, and then steadily making good its wildest boasts. Surely this society was not wracked by a secret, hidden horror that its gigantic exertion would end only in some nightmare of debauchery called "civilization"?

The most cursory survey of the period does indeed display a seemingly untroubled assurance about the great civilization America was hewing out of the wilderness. This faith, with its corollaries of belief in progress and republican institutions, might be called the "official" faith of the United States. It was primarily an inheritance from the eighteenth century: back in 1758, the almanac-maker, Nathaniel Ames, writing from Dedham, Massachusetts, dreamed that within two hundred years arts and sciences would transform nature "in their Tour from Hence over the Appalacian Mountains to the Western Ocean," and that vast quarries of rocks would be piled into cities. On the whole, despite the Jeffersonians' distrust of cities, I think it fair to say that the founders had no qualms about doing harm to nature by thrusting civilization upon it. They reasoned in terms of wealth, comfort, amenities, power, in terms which we may conveniently call, though they had not been derived from Bentham, "utilitarian."

Now in 1840, in 1850, the mighty tread of American civilization was heard throughout the Ohio Valley, across the Mississippi, and the advanced guard was rushing into California. But the astonishing fact about this gigantic material thrust of the early nineteenth century is how few Americans would any longer venture, aside from their boasts, to explain, let alone to justify, the expansion of civilization in any language that could remotely be called that of utility. The most utilitarian conquest known to history had somehow to be viewed not as inspired by a calculus of rising land values and investments but (despite the orgies of speculation) as an immense exertion of the spirit. Those who made articulate the meaning of this drama found their frames of reference not in political economy but in Scott and Byron, in visions of "sublimity." The more rapidly, the more voraciously, the primordial forest was felled, the more desperately poets and painters — and also preachers — strove to identify the unique personality of this republic with the virtues of pristine and untarnished, of "romantic," Nature.

We need little ingenuity to perceive that behind this virtually universal American hostility to the ethic of utilitarian calculation lies a religious mood — one that seventeenth-century Puritanism would not have understood, and which was as foreign, let us say, to the evangelicalism of Whitefield as to the common sense of Franklin. We note, first of all, that this aversion to the pleasure-pain philosophy became most pronounced in those countries or circles in which a vigorous Christian spirit was alive. In the long run, the emotions excited in the era we call romantic were mobilized into a *cri du coeur* against Gradgrind. A host of nameless magazine writers uttered it on the plane of dripping sentiment, of patriotic or lachrymose verse, but on higher levels the poet Bryant, the novelists Cooper and Simms, the painters Durand and Cole — and on still more rarefied heights the philosopher Emerson — denounced or lamented the march of civilization. In various ways — not often agreeing among themselves — they identified the health, the very personality, of America with Nature, and therefore set it in opposition to the concepts of the city, the railroad, the steamboat. This definition of the fundamental issue of life in America became that around which Thoreau, Melville, and Whitman organized their peculiar expression. They (along with the more superficial) present us with the problem of American self-recognition as being essentially an irreconcilable opposition between Nature and civilization — which is to say, between forest and town, spontaneity and calculation, heart and head, the unconscious and the self-conscious, the innocent and the debauched. We are all heirs of Natty Bumppo, and cannot escape our heritage. William Faulkner, notably in "The Bear," is only the most dramatic of recent reminders.

Now, in this epoch, American Protestants were especially hostile to utilitarianism, even to the conciliatory form promulgated by John Stuart Mill. In England there were elements in the general situation which supported him, which could rally to his side a few sensitive and intelligent Christians. Sensitive and intelligent Christians in America were so constantly distressed by the charge that America was utterly given over to the most brutal utilitarianism that they in effect conspired to prevent the appearance of an American Mill. The more their consciences accused them of surrendering historic Christian concerns to the rush of material prosperity, the more they insisted that inwardly this busy people lived entirely by sentiment. A review of the gift-books and annuals of the 1830's and 1840's — if one can bring himself to it — will tell how, at that pitch of vulgarity, the image of America as tender, tearful, dreaming noble thoughts, luxuriating in moonlit vistas, was constructed. These works were produced in huge numbers for the predominant middle class — if the term be admissible; they reposed on the parlor tables of wives whose husbands spent all day at the office pushing the nation on its colossal course of empire. But the more sophisticated or learned disclaimers of utility said, in this regard, about the same thing. An organ of Episcopalian scholarship. *The New York Review*, declared for instance in 1837 that utilitarianism is a "sordid philosophy." And why? Because it teaches that virtue is the creature of the brain, whereas true righteousness is "the prompt impulse of the heart." Yet this review, with no awareness of inconsistency, was at the same time rigorously preaching that because of the fall of Adam the impulses of the natural heart are suspect!

There is one truism about the early nineteenth century which cannot too often be repeated: in one fashion or another, various religious interests, aroused against the Enlightenment, allied themselves with forces we lump together as "romantic." In England the Established Church was surprised, and momentarily bewildered, to discover that Scott, Wordsworth, and Coleridge started new blood pulsating through its veins, expelling the noxious humors of indifference, deism, and skepticism. At Oxford, romantic religiosity indeed swung so far to the other extreme that it carried Newman all the way to Rome. (His conversion so shattered the ranks of Episcopalian naturalists in America that *The New York Review*, finding itself unable to speak for a united body, had to discontinue.) On the Continent there appeared a romantic Catholicism which could afford not to answer but to disregard the *philosophes* as being no longer relevant. However, this ecstasy of romantic piety did not always require institutions; it could amount simply to a passionate assertion against the Age of Reason. Carlyle and Chateaubriand might have little love for each other, but they could embrace on one piece of ground: they could dance together on the grave of Voltaire.

Everywhere this resurgence of the romantic heart against the enlightened head flowered in a veneration of Nature. Wordsworth did speak for his era when he announced that he had learned to look on her not as in the hour of thoughtless — that is, eighteenth-century — youth, but as one who heard through her the still, sad music of humanity. This was not the nature of traditional theology: neither the law of nature of the Scholastics, nor the simple plan of Newtonian apologists. It was Nature, feminine and dynamic, propelling all things. Wordsworth had no such vogue in America as had Scott or Byron, but he helped enthusiasts for both of them to find more precise, more philosophical, formulations for their enthusiasm. As early as 1840, Emerson could say, "The fame of Wordsworth is a leading fact in modern literature," because Wordsworth expressed the "idea" he shared with his coevals. Evert Duyckinck was a thorough New Yorker and thus despised Emerson's metaphysics; still, on reading *The Prelude*, Duyckinck hailed Wordsworth as one entitled to join the band of immortals "whose voices go up to Heaven in jubilant thanksgiving and acknowledgment of the Great High Priest, in whose temple they perpetually worship." And Wordsworth had taught both transcendentalist Emerson and Episcopalian Duyckinck that

> One impulse from a vernal wood
> May teach you more of man,
> Of mortal evil and of good
> Than all the sages can.

With so many Americans severally convinced that this had become ultimate truth, was not a further reflection bound to occur to a nation that was, above all other nations, embedded in Nature: if from vernal woods (along with Niagara Falls, the Mississippi, and the prairies) it can learn more of good and evil than from learned sages, could it not also learn from that source more conveniently than from divine revelation? Not that the nation would formally reject the Bible. On the contrary, it could even more energetically proclaim itself Christian and cherish the churches; but it could derive its inspiration from the mountains, the lakes, the forests. There was nothing mean or niggling about these, nothing utilitarian. Thus, superficial appearances to the contrary, America is not crass, materialistic: it is Nature's nation, possessing a heart that watches and receives.

In American literature of the early nineteenth century, this theme is ubiquitous. Social historians do not pay much attention to it; they are preoccupied with the massive expansion and the sectional tensions. Probably John Jacob Astor and the builders of railroads gave little thought to the healing virtues of the forests and swamps they were defiling. The issue I am raising — or rather that the writers themselves raised — may have little to do with how the populace actually behaved; nevertheless, it has everything to do with how the people apprehended their conduct. If there be such a thing as an American character, it took shape under the molding influence of these conceptions as much as under the physical impositions of geography and the means of transport.

So, let me insist upon the highly representative quality of an essay by one James Brooks, published in *The Knickerbocker* in 1835, which so phrased the theme that it was reprinted over the whole country. Manifestly, Brooks conceded, this country *seems* more dedicated to matter than to mind; there is indeed a vast scramble for property, and no encouragement is given the arts. But, though foreigners may sneer, we need not despair; we do not have to reconcile ourselves to being forever a rude, Philistine order. In the future we shall vindicate our culture, if only we can preserve our union. For this confidence, we have the highest authority:

> God has promised us a renowned existence, if we will but deserve it. He speaks this promise in the sublimity of Nature. It resounds all along the crags of the Alleghanies. It is uttered in the thunder of Niagara. It is heard in the roar of two oceans, from the great Pacific to the rocky ramparts of the Bay of Fundy. His finger has written it in the broad expanse of our Inland Seas, and traced it out by the mighty Father of Waters! The august TEMPLE in which we dwell was built for lofty purposes. Oh! that we may consecrate it to LIBERTY and CONCORD, and be found fit worshippers within its holy wall!

Walt Whitman had for years been drugging himself upon such prose; in him the conception comes to its most comprehensive utterance, so self-contained that it could finally dismiss the alliance with Christian doctrine which romantic Christians had striven to establish. However, he was so intoxicated with the magniloquent idea that he had to devise what to contemporaries seemed a repulsive form, and they would have none of it. Nevertheless, Whitman's roots reach deep into the soil of this naturalistic (and Christianized) naturalism. Today a thousand James Brookses are forgotten; Whitman speaks for a mood which did sustain a mass of Americans through a crucial half-century of Titanic exertion — which sustained them along with, and as much as, their Christian profession.

That is what is really astounding: most of the ardent celebrators of natural America serenely continued to be professing Christians. Or rather, the amazing fact is that they so seldom — hardly ever — had any intimation that the bases of their patriotism and those of their creed stood, in the slightest degree, in contradiction. Magnificent hymns to American Nature are to be found among Evangelicals and Revivalists as well as among scholarly Episcopalians. If here and there some still hard-bitten Calvinist reminded his people of ancient distinctions between nature and grace, his people still bought and swooned over pseudo-Byronic invocations to Nature. It was a problem, even for the clearest thinkers, to keep the orders separate. For example, *The New York Review* in January 1840, devoted an essay to foreign travelers, saying that their defect was an inability to behold in America not the nonexistent temples and statues but the "Future":

> A railroad, a penitentiary, a log house beyond the Mississippi, the last hotly-contested elections — things rather heterogeneous to be sure, and none of them at first glance, so attractive as the wonders of the old world — are in reality, and to him who regards them philosophically, quite as important, and as they connect themselves with the unknown future, quite as romantic.

For some pages the *Review* keeps up this standard chant, and then abruptly recollects its theology. Confidence in the American future, it remembers barely in the nick of time, must not betray us into the heresy of supposing man perfectible: "Tell a people that they are perfectible, and it will not be long before they tell you that they are perfect, and that he is a traitor who presumes to doubt, not their wisdom simply, but their infallibility." Assuredly, the American Christian would at this point find himself in an intolerable dilemma, with his piety and his patriotism at loggerheads, did not the triumphant ethos seem to give him a providential way out: America can progress indefinitely into an expanding future without acquiring sinful delusions of grandeur simply because it is nestled in Nature, is instructed and guided by mountains, is chastened by cataracts.

It is here that errors are rebuked, and excesses discountenanced. Nature preserves the identity and the individuality of its various races and tribes, and by the relation in which each stands to her, and the use which each makes of her, she becomes both a teacher and an historian.

So then — because America, beyond all nations, is in perpetual touch with Nature, it need not fear the debauchery of the artificial, the urban, the civilized. Nature somehow, by a legerdemain that even so highly literate Christians as the editors of *The New York Review* could not qutie admit to themselves, had effectually taken the place of the Bible: by her unremitting influence, she, like Bryant's waterfowl, would guide aright the faltering steps of a young republic.

Here we encounter again the crucial difference between the American appeal to romantic Nature and the European. In America, it served not so much for individual or artistic salvation as for an assuaging of national anxiety. The sublimity of our natural backdrop not only relieved us of having to apologize for a deficiency of picturesque ruins and hoary legends: it demonstrated how the vast reservoirs of our august temple furnish the guarantee that we shall never be contaminated by artificiality. On the prairies of Illinois, Bryant asked the breezes of the South if anywhere in their progress from the equator they have fanned a nobler scene than this.

> Man hath no part in all this glorious work:
> The hand that built the firmament hath heaved
> And smoothed these verdant swells, and sown their slopes
> With herbage, planted them with island-groves,
> And hedged them round with forests.

Goethe might insist in ancient Germany that he devoted his life to Nature, but in Europe this meant that he became an elegant genius domesticated in the highly artificial court of Weimar. What could Europe show for all of Rousseau's tirades against civilization but a band of Bohemians, congregated amid the brick and mortar of Paris, trying to keep alive a yearning for such naturalness and spontaneity as any child of the Ohio Valley indubitably flaunted without, like them, becoming outcast from society? America, amid its forests, could not, even if it tried, lose its simplicity. Therefore let Christianity bless it.

But — could America keep its virtue? As *The Literary World*'s exhortation to the artists reveals, almost as soon as the identification of virtue with Nature had become axiomatic, the awful suspicion dawned that America was assiduously erecting the barriers of artifice between its citizenry and the precious landscape. If God speaks to us in the sublimity of Nature, then was not the flood of pioneers a devilish stratagem for drowning the voice of God? In the same issue that printed Brooks's "Our Country," *The Knickerbocker* also carried an oration on the Mississippi River, declaring that no words can convey what an American feels as he looks upon this moving ocean, because he sees not only the present majesty but the not distant period when the interminable stretch of vacantness shall become bright with towns, vocal with the sounds of industry: "When the light of civilization and religion shall extend over forests and savannahs." Or, as the same magazine vaunted in 1838, "Nature has been penetrated in her wildest recesses, and made to yield her hidden stores." But how could we at one and the same time establish our superiority to artificial Europe upon our proximity to Nature, and then view with complacency the rapidity of our despoiling her? And furthermore — most embarrassing of questions — on which side does religion stand, on Nature's or on civilization's? Once the dichotomy had become absolute, as in American sentiment it had become, then piety could no longer compromise by pretending to dwell in both embattled camps.

Once more, in Europe the problem was personal, a matter of the individual's coming to terms with himself, absorbing a taste for Nature into his private culture. Here it was a problem for the society — and so for the churches. Goethe had put it for Europe: the young revel in those aspirations of the sublime which in fact only primitive and barbaric peoples can experience; vigorous youth pardonably strives to satisfy this noble necessity, but soon learns circumspection:

> As the sublime is easily produced by twilight and night, when forms are blended, so, on the other hand, it is scared away by the day which separates and divides everything, and so must it also be destroyed by every increase of cultivation, if it is not fortunate enough to take refuge with the beautiful and closely unite itself with it, by which these both become immortal and indestructible.

By recognizing that the sublime is ephemeral, for a nation as for a person, Goethe inculcated the necessity of a mature reconciliation to the merely beautiful, in order to preserve a fugitive glory, one which might, by adroit cultivation, survive into a weary civilization as a memory out of the natural sublimity of youth. But the beautiful is only ornament, amenity, decoration. A nation cannot live by it, neither can a faith. It is far removed from the voice of God thundering out of lofty ridges and roaring waterfalls. Even the painter Cole in 1841 published "The Lament of the Forest," by which, he seemed to say, he found at the end of his self-appointed task only a tragic prospect. The forest stood for centuries, sublime and unsullied, until there came man the destroyer. For a few centuries thereafter, America was the sanctuary; now, even into it comes artificial destruction:

> And thus come rushing on
> This human hurricane, boundless as swift.
> Our sanctuary, this secluded spot,
> Which the stern rocks have guarded until now,
> Our enemy has marked.

It was this same Thomas Cole, this master interpreter of the American landscape whose death in 1848 was, according to *The New York Evening Mirror*, "a national loss," who most impressed his generation by five gigantic canvases entitled "The Course of Empire." The first shows the rude, barbaric state of man; the second is a perfect symbolization of that pastoral conception with which America strove to identify itself. Presiding over each scene is a lofty and rocky peak, which patently represents Nature, but in the pastoral panel, and only in this one, the point of view is shifted so that there can be seen looming behind and above the peak of Nature a still more lofty one, which even more patently is the sublime. In the third cartoon the perspective returns to that of the first, but the entire scene is covered with a luxurious civilization, only the tip of mountain Nature peering over the fabulous expanse of marble. In the fourth, barbarians are sacking the city, and the picture is a riot of rape, fire, pillage; in the fifth, all human life is extinguished, the temples and towers are in ruin, but the unaltered mountain serenely presides over a panorama of total destruction.

The orator who in *The Knickerbocker* anticipated the civilization to arise along the Mississippi was obliged to warn the young empire to learn from the history of the past, from the follies of the old world: it must so improve the condition of the *whole* people as to "establish on this continent an imperishable empire, destined to confer innumerable blessings on the remotest ages." Yet like so many vaunters of American confidence in this ostensible age of confidence, by admitting the adjective into his exhortation he indirectly confesses the lurking possibility of the perishable. Cole's "Course of Empire" was exhibited over and over again to fascinated throngs of the democracy; the series ought, said George Templeton Strong in 1838, "to immortalize him." Cole made explicit what the society instinctively strove to repress: the inescapable logic of a nationalism based upon the premises of Nature. (Many, even while forced into admiration, noted that the drama as Cole painted it, he being both a pious Christian and a devout Wordsworthian, left out any hint of Christianity; the "Empire" is wholly material, and there is no salvation except for the mountain itself.) The moral clearly was that a culture committed to Nature, to the inspiration of Nature and of the sublime, might for a moment overcome its barbarous origins, take its place with the splendor of Rome, but it was thereby committed to an ineluctable cycle of rise and fall. The American empire was still ascending, rising from Cole's second to his third phase. But if this rationale explained America, then was not the fourth stage, and after it the fifth, inescapable?

The creator of Natty Bumppo and of Harvey Birch (who was a vestryman and a close friend of Cole) grew worried. As Cooper reissued *The Spy* in 1849, he could only marvel at the immense change in the nation since 1821, when the book had first appeared. America had now passed from gristle into the bone, had indeed become a civilization, and had no enemy to fear — "but the one that resides within." In his mingling of anxieties and exultations, Cooper is indeed the principal interpreter of his period; even while glorifying the forest-born virtue of America, he had also portrayed the brutal Skinners in *The Spy* and the settlers in *The Pioneers* who wantonly slaughter Nature's pigeons.

It would not be difficult to show how widespread, even though covert, was this apprehension of doom in the America of Jackson and Polk. Of course it was so elaborately masked, so concertedly disguised, that one may study the epoch for a long time without detecting it. Yet it is there, at the heart — at what may be called the secret heart — of the best thought and expression the country could produce. So much so, indeed, that some patriots sought escape from the haunting course of empire by arguing that America was no more peculiarly the nation of Nature than any other, that it had been civilized from the start. For instance, in 1847 *The Literary World* noticed a work on the prairies by Mrs. Eliza Farnham which once more appealed to the piled cliffs, the forest aisles, the chant of rushing winds and waters in the West against the decadence of eastern civilization. The New York journal, conscious of the city's daily growth, had to ask if this tedious declamation was not becoming trite. After all, the *World* demanded, when men go deeper and deeper into wild and sublime scenes, do they in fact put off false and artificial ways? Do they become spontaneously religious? Unfortunately, we must admit that some of the fairest portions of the earth are occupied by the most degraded of mankind; even sublimity works no effect on the rude and thoughtless, and so, instead of following a fatal course from the primordial to the metropolitan, perhaps we should try to stabilize this society at the merely decent and sane. "Moral and aesthetic culture require something more than the freest and most balmy air and mellow sunshine."

The *World* did not quote Goethe to justify this escape from the cycle of naturalism, but Emerson, who did know his Goethe, could never successfully resolve within himself the debate between Nature and civilization, solitude and society, rusticity and manners. In fact, something of the same debate went on through most of the fiction and poetry, and markedly among the architects and landscape gardeners, of the time. Very few of those who found themselves impelled in both directions consciously tried to find their way into civilization because, thanks to Cole, they had peered into the frightful prospect of Nature. Still, I think it can be demonstrated that some vague sense of the doom was at work in all of them, as it surely was in both Cooper and Simms. As the implications of the philosophy of natural destiny forced themselves upon the more sentient, these were obliged to seek methods for living in civilization, all the more because civilization was so spectacularly triumphing over the continent. A growing awareness of the dilemma informed the thinking of Horace Bushnell, for instance, and he strove to turn American Protestantism from the revival, associated with the lurid scenery of Nature, to the cultivation of "nurture" which could be achieved only in a civilized context.

Of course, there was also the possibility of escape from the cycle of empire in another direction, opposite to that chosen by Bushnell. The nation could resolutely declare that it is invincibly barbaric, that it intends to remain so, and that it refuses to take even the first step toward civilization. Or at least, if the nation as a whole shrank from such audacity, if Christians fled for protection to older sobrieties they had come near to forgetting, a few brave spirits might seek the other spiritual solution, though they had to defy the palpable evidence of economic life and to renounce a Christianity that was proving itself incapable of mediating between forest and city. They would refuse to be content with the beautiful, they would defiantly wear their hats indoors as well as out, and would sound a barbaric (and American) yawp over the roof of the world. Possibly there were, in sum, no more than three Americans who chose this violent resort, and in their time they were largely ignored by their countrymen. Yet Whitman, Thoreau, and Melville speak for this society, and to it, in great part because, by making their choice, they thrust upon it a challenge it cannot honestly evade. In 1855 Melville pictured John Paul Jones in Paris as a jaunty barbarian in the center of the very citadel of civilization; exclaiming over his incorruptibility amid corruption, Melville apostrophized: "Intrepid, unprincipled, reckless, predatory, with boundless ambition, civilized in externals but a savage at heart, America is, or may yet be, the Paul Jones of nations."

Possibly the fact that America came to its first essay in self-analysis and self-expression in the period we call romantic is only fortuitous. But perhaps there is a deeper conjunction. The suspicion that we are being carried along on some massive conveyor belt such as Cole's "Course of Empire" is hard to down. It is more nagging today than it was around the year 1900, when for the moment America could give up the dream of Nature and settle for a permanently prosperous civilization. It more pesters the religious conscience in our time, when a leading theologian expounds the "irony" of American history, than it did when the most conscientious were absorbed in "the social gospel." So, it is no longer enough to dismiss the period of romantic America as one in which too many Christians temporized their Christianity by merging it with a misguided cult of Nature. No scorn of the refined, no condescension of sophisticated critics toward the vagaries of romance, can keep us from feeling the pull: the American, or at least the American artist, cherishes in his innermost being the impulse to reject completely the gospel of civilization, in order to guard with resolution the savagery of his heart.

In that case, the savage artist poses for the Christianity of the country a still more disturbing challenge, as Thoreau, Melville, and Whitman posed it: if he must, to protect his savage integrity, reject organized religion along with organized civilization, then has not American religion, or at any rate Protestantism, the awful task of reëxamining, with the severest self-criticism, the course on which it so blithely embarked a century ago, when it dallied with the sublime and failed to comprehend the sinister dynamic of Nature?

CHAPTER X

THE END OF THE WORLD

[Can an errand, even an errand into the wilderness, be run indefinitely?
To this question, it seems, Americans must constantly revert. Can it forever
be carried on, as mere automation, forever disclosing new meanings, forever
holding out the hope of ultimate completion? Can a culture, which chances
to embody itself in a nation, push itself to such remorseless exertion without
ever learning whether it has been sent on its business at some incomprehensible behest, or is obligated to discover a meaning for its dynamism in
the very act of running?

Historically speaking, mankind have lived in several wildernesses. Tra-
ditionally, they have called these deserts. In all of them, before the American, men received a particular satisfaction, a positive stimulation, from their
inward assurance that the scene of their exertions would, sooner or later,
come to a glorious, even though a violent, conclusion. There would be a
consuming chord of rest and of resolution.

In the civilizations that emerged out of the primordial wildernesses of
Europe, this assurance solidified into the Christian eschatology; in that form
it was brought to America, most energetically by the Puritans. Officially the
doctrine of an end to the world has, of course, been professed by every
denomination within the country, even when, as lately, some have striven
to interpret it metaphorically. What will America do — what *can* America
do — with an implacable prophecy that there is a point in time beyond
which the very concept of a future becomes meaningless? Protestant America, as well as Catholic, has an implicit commitment to this event. What
then happens to the errand?

Originally given as an address at Rutgers University, this piece was re-
written for *The William and Mary Quarterly* (VIII, April 1951), and
is here reproduced with permission, though I have in several places modified
that text.]

WE find it hard to comprehend how men in medieval towns
could go cheerfully, as evidently they did, about their daily business when
constantly before their eyes, sculptured on the fronts of their churches and
cathedrals, were extended terrifying realistic scenes of the last judgment.

Still harder to comprehend is that they could live, as certainly they did, with any degree of cheer when they all, learned or unlearned, could see no scientific reason why the awful blow should not fall at any moment. In their physics, the universe was not self-sustaining. Motion was given by God and all movement was propelled by Him, so that clearly He might at any moment call a halt. Then the trumpet would sound, motion would cease, the moon turn to blood, the stars fall like withered leaves, and the earth would burn to the accompaniment of horrible thunders and lightnings. In the midst of this scene, the dead would rise: out of the flames would speak absolute justice and by the lurid light of universal conflagration, speedily and unerringly, the one supreme court of law would pronounce sentence on each and every transgressor. In this cosmic setting, village gossips and usurers would get their just deserts.

It would be not only the last, but also the finest show on earth, because it would be the perfect combination of aesthetic and moral spectacle. The elect would discuss it endlessly down the vistas of eternity and jubilantly extol this ideal mixture of destruction and retribution. The ecstasy of the anticipation sounds in the very cadences of the *Dies Irae*:

> Mors stupebit et natura
> Quum resurget creatura
> Judicanti responsura.

Precisely because, one is obliged to conclude, the end of the world was identified with the fitting of punishment to crime and of reward to virtue, it was entirely plausible to the medieval artist; it was both so physically realizable and so ethically satisfying that he could treat it with familiarity and precision of detail, and could even enliven the dreadful scene with figures of sheer slapstick.

The Puritans who settled the wilderness of Massachusetts Bay were medieval men, for all that they were Protestants, and cherished still the vision of a glorious consummation. Hence the first best seller in the annals of the American book trade was a versified story of the judgment written by a gentle pastor in Malden and published in 1662. For a century it was read in every household in New England, and as far south as the Shenandoah. Commentators sometimes suppose that Michael Wigglesworth's *The Day of Doom* drove Puritan children crazy, but it did nothing of the sort: they loved it. (Tourists are not terrified by Michelangelo's baroque judgment on the wall of the Sistine Chapel; even Popes have been so little perturbed that they found leisure to call for emendations in the interests of modesty.) In the ballad meter that made memorizing easy, Wigglesworth told how on the night of judgment, when

> Virgins unwise, who through disguise
> Amongst the best were number'd,
> Had clos'd their eyes; yea, and the wise
> Through sloth and frailty slumber'd,

the apocalypse came upon the wise and the unwise in the wholly traditional manner, in the form that several centuries ago had become stylized:

> For at midnight brake forth a Light
>   Which turn'd the night to day,
> And speedily an hideous cry
>   Did all the world dismay.
> Sinners awake, their hearts do ake,
>   Trembling their loynes surprizeth;
> Amazed with fear, by what they hear,
>   Each one of them ariseth.

The end of the world, in this standardized version, was to come in the guise of a terrific pyrotechnical display, which would commence with light, be followed by a blast and then become universal fire. But the reason for these displays was evident: they were necessary in order to strike the terror of the judgment into all souls:

> They cry, no, no: Alas! and wo!
>   Our Courage all is gone:
> Our hardiness (fool hardiness)
>   Hath us undone, undone.

Devastation would be a preliminary to regeneration, and not only would it rectify all injustices, but it would herald the era when never again would there be any iniquities. Wrong once righted, there would begin the unending reign of right — and of the righteous:

> Where with long Rest they shall be blest,
>   And nought shall them annoy:
> Where they shall see as seen they be,
>   And whom they love enjoy.

Surely destruction would be a small price to pay! That then would be found "no hiding place," either in mountain or in cave, was actually a comforting reflection.

To our disinterested view, there remains in Wigglesworth's apocalypse one fascinating omission: what happens to this miserable little earth? Sinners go "down" to the pit of woe, saints "ascend" to a glorious place. Certainly Wigglesworth, like all educated Puritans, was aware of the Copernican revolution; nevertheless, there is no slightest hint in his version of the catastrophe that "down" and "up" had become relative, unspatial terms. The earth seems to stand, as for centuries it had stood, at the center, so ideally situated as to be the scene both of the Judgment and of the ultimate conflagration.

Just how delicately Michael Wigglesworth, pretending to be the simple bard, was evading a problem that had already become a bother to Puritan theologians we may gauge from a work published in the very year, 1630, when Winthrop led his band to an exodus that was supposed to liberate them from all merely "traditional" annoyances. George Hakewill's *An Apologie or Declaration of the Power and Providence of God in the Gouernment of the World* is an aggressively modern book, addressed to refuting "the Common Errour Touching Natures Perpetuall and Universall Decay." Puritan theology was resolutely determined that no fantasy of some merely natural decay, within the composition of the created universe, should bring it to a predictable standstill. As long as God sees fit providentially to govern it, the universe will function as it has from the beginning. Hence these Puritans welcomed, as did most orthodox Christians, Hakewill's demonstration that God, "by His powerfull Hand, . . . holdeth backe the Sythe of Tyme from destroying or imparying the Universe," until, an astute Hakewill added, "the same Hand shall at last destroy the Whole by Fire." Still, the equally astute might have been, and in fact were, disturbed by the way in which Hakewill, after 477 folio pages arguing that neither man nor nature has deteriorated since the creation, had to attach his contention that everything shall be consumed in the form of an afterthought. In a fashion which Hakewill could not make altogether clear, the thesis for uniform preservation could be maintained only on the assumption (which he said was so obvious that not even the most abandoned of heretics ever called it in question) that the unalterable perfection of nature would some day come to an abrupt end. Behind this uneasy confidence Hakewill was trying to conceal the fact that a new sort of heretic — hitherto unprecedented in the chronicles of deviation — was indeed calling in doubt the ancient consolation: natural scientists were raising the specter of a universe which, though it might have been created in time, would remain indestructible! While they seemed to be approaching an accord, it remained a scandal, Hakewill had to confess, that even the best of divines could reach no agreement "touching the manner of the Consummation of the world." For himself, he believed simply that it would be totally annihilated, but his rueful tone admits that such assurance had become personal, what we might call subjective. Nevertheless he boldly continued, whistling to keep his courage up, that however the world's end was to be engineered, the day of annihilation would certainly be the same as the Day of Judgment.

American Puritans in the seventeenth century knew of John Milton principally as the advocate of subversive ideas about marriage. By gradual steps (which have not yet been traced) *Paradise Lost* became, around the middle of the eighteenth century, not so much a secondary Book of Genesis as a substitute for the original — at least as far as the pictorial imagination was concerned.[1] This process of assimilation was so far completed for Jonathan Edwards that he could see in Milton an author whose "inimitable excellencies" demanded an uncommon force of mind to be appreciated — a force so uncommon that it was virtually one with the "new simple idea"

[1] The effect of Milton upon American "primitive" paintings of the late eighteenth and early nineteenth centuries is especially striking. Cf. my "The Garden of Eden and the Deacon's Meadow," *American Heritage*, VII (December, 1955), 55–61, 102.

imparted by supernatural grace. Now it is interesting that Edwards, who most explicitly in his generation rejected the Aristotelian or Ptolemaic cosmos, should thus have rated Milton, who, as commentators never weary to point out, willfully retained the medieval setting. Of course, the angel Raphael reveals Milton's awareness that this system was highly suspect. Still, it remains difficult to explain why the magnificent heretic, who barely concealed inside his epic his blasphemous voyages into the nature of the Trinity, who spectacularly demanded a virtue so uncloistered as to confront without trepidation any form of temptation, took what looks like special pains to advise Adam, after informing him that God circumscribed the world (the Empyrean) with golden compasses, not to worry about Copernicus:

> Sollicit not thy thoughts with matters hid,
> Leave them to God above, him serve and feare.

It may be — this is mere speculation — that among the considerations which induced John Milton to persist in dramatizing the fall of man within an obsolete cosmology was his anxiety lest the Copernican universe cast doubts upon the possibility of an end which could also be a Judgment. If so, then Milton sheltered himself under an ambiguity which the old astronomy conveniently offered. No less than Michael Wigglesworth — to whom, once we overlook the fact of towering genius, he is strangely analogous — Milton could remain undecided about whether the apocalypse meant an annihilation or a transformation of the physical earth. The great heresiarch chose to remain, on this crucial issue, uncommitted, and to that extent abjectly orthodox.

In the second book of *Paradise Lost* God foretells the general doom, and in the third specifies that the earth shall burn. But Milton seems primarily concerned with presenting flames as purgation. Christ the judge will first

> dissolve
> Satan with his perverted World, then raise
> From the conflagrant mass, purg'd and refin'd,
> New Heav'ns, new Earth, Ages of endless date
> Founded in righteousness and peace and love,
> To bring forth fruits Joy and eternal Bliss.

Nothing in the seventeenth century more dramatizes the impact of the revolution wrought by the new physics than the fact that no religious thinker after Milton was again able to say with such magisterial indifference that the precise character of the conflagration was irrelevant. The arresting fact about this profound break with the Christian centuries is that it manifested itself not in explicit statement but in evasion. Yet the question stared all thinkers full in the face: is an end of the world any longer thinkable, or artistically conceivable, if the world be only a minor planet in a vast Copernican system? Suppose that this mote is adjudged: do not the enduring stars continue undisturbed upon their silent courses? Of what avail, throughout those spaces, the tiny tumult of an earthly bonfire? One might learn to accept the new astronomy, and then the new physics, and still fondly imagine that Almighty God had created the stellar universe as a theater for the human drama; but the dignity of man, let alone of the Christian religion, did seem thereupon reduced to an arrogant pretension. Thus Milton took the one way to preserve the importance of his theme: he placed Eden in the symbolical center, so that the parallelism of descent and ascent might still have meaningful relations to the Judgment. If this globe is *not* the center of the universe, then the measure of all things can no longer be man or man's conception of retributive justice; instead, the rule must be an inexorable (and never ending) principle that the squares of the periodic times which the planets take to describe their orbits are proportional to the cubes of their mean distances from the sun. Could it any longer be assumed that the heavens would be rolled up like a scroll in order that adulterers and tavern-sots be judged? How was God Himself to intervene if motion, once started, continued eternally in a straight line? Would the mere blast of trumpet be able to halt the atoms, to stupefy this kind of wilderness?

Back of these questions lurked a still more worrisome problem, as Milton's Raphael rather unangelically hints: as long as motion in the universe was conceived as the rotation of concentric spheres, the more readily the Word of God, or the echoes of a trumpet, could be imagined as a check to the whirl, whereupon friction would ignite the earth. But gradually the realization dawned on Western man in the seventeenth century that so simple a fiat, so crude a spoke in the wheel, could not bring the rotating earth to a poise. Cessation could come only by a smash.

Motion, in other words, had become not a reversible revolution of the spheres, but an impetus, transmitted by immediate contact. Wherefore the conflagration could not be produced by a commandment, even the command of God, but only by some explicable collision. A qualitative relationship of earth to Heaven and to Hell had made a dramatic Judgment possible even while the mechanism of destruction was left unspecified. But once a quantitative relation among objects became the reason for any object's being, then the only method by which the end of a world might even be imagined was actual blocking of a planet's motion. Concussion in space might serve, or else an eruption from hidden geological depths. The essential requirement was explosion: arbitrary interference was no longer satisfactory.

This consideration was more than a challenge to scientific ingenuity: it was a threat to the very being of Christianity, especially to Puritan forms of Christianity, because it implied that the Judgment must henceforth be preached as depending upon the feasibility of destruction. In the new physics, the end of the world as an explosion had to take precedence over the separation of saints from sinners. There is no more curious phenomenon in the history of our civilization than the fact that the triumph of modern physics over the imagination of mankind was achieved by a sustained effort to prove that such a triumph was not only compatible with the cherished hope but that actually it was a confirmation, a veritable guarantee, of an approaching, colossally violent catastrophe.

In English literature the first attempt to come to grips with the problem in scientific terms was *The Sacred Theory of the Earth* by Thomas Burnet, Master of Charterhouse, published in 1681. Burnet, a rhetorician whom Addison and Steele admired and whom Coleridge tried to rescue from oblivion, was astute enough to perceive that after Kepler and Copernicus all theorists would be obliged not only to account for the apocalypse by some physical scheme, but by the same token, and within the same cosmology, to give a scientifically coherent version of the deluge. This too would have to be convincingly expounded as the effect not of mere brute power but of natural law. Deluge and end, they stood or fell together: if humanity was to retain its precious confidence in the last devastation, it had to be persuaded that, in the time of Noah, there had been a near miss.

Burnet calculated closely that a minimum of eight oceans were necessary to cover the entire globe and to float the Ark. "The next thing to be done," he told himself, "is to enquire where this Water is to be found." For a long and trying time he could imagine no sources that would produce enough, not all the clouds and rivers and seas put together. By using all of them, he could "upon a moderate Account" collect barely an eighth part of what was necessary to supply a universal inundation. "Those eight Oceans lay heavy upon my thoughts, and I cast about every way, to find an Expedient, or to find some way, whereby the same Effect might be brought to pass with less Water, and in such a manner that the Water might afterwards conveniently be discharg'd." Seldom has ingenuity been so well rewarded. The original chaos, Burnet reasoned, must have been a mass of atoms swirling about a center. (Here for the first time the word "atom" appears in the voluminous literature of eschatology, but of course it could appear only at the moment when scientific thought had been surreptitiously conquered by the concept of the atom.) Gradually — and naturally — the heavy atoms sank to the center, while liquid atoms were hurled to the surface, the oily ones floating to the top, where eventually they formed a crust, as smooth and as round, and also as fragile, as the shell of an egg. When it came time to float the Ark, the sun had already baked this shell so dry that it cracked, and thus, at the providential second, the waters from under the abyss flooded the surface. After all, this is the very language that Moses, centuries before Copernicus or Gassendi's atomic theory, had used to describe the phenomenon! Forty days later the fragments of crust settled, some upraised on end to become our present mountains, the rest sinking to valleys, into which the water rolled, forming our oceans. Thus everything was beautifully accounted for: at precisely that moment 1656 years after the creation, when the depravity of man had become so insupportable that God would have wanted in any event to wipe out the species and start afresh with the sons of Noah — at precisely that moment the crust crumbled.

The deluge being thus expounded, the end becomes easily explicable. During the long period since the flood, atoms at the center of the earth have been subjected to an unrelenting pressure, except for such releases as they have enforced through occasional volcanic eruptions. By now, they are thoroughly heated, and are smouldering with fire. The sun will cause a terrible draught, the waters of the surface will dry up: then the now irregular crust will crack once more. By this time, instead of water, fire will come up through the crevices. "From this external and internal Heat acting upon the Body of the Earth, all Minerals, that have the Seeds of Fire in them, will be open'd, and exhale their Effluviums more copiously." Just as spices give off odors when they are warmed, "so the Particles of Fire that are shut up in several Bodies, will easily fly abroad, when, by a further degree of Relaxation, you shake off their Chains, and open the Prison Doors." This boiling point will be reached at exactly the hour when the sins of men require final adjudication. For reasons which were, at least to a Protestant, wholly understandable, the most sulphurous soil and the most fiery mountains (*viz.* Vesuvius) exist in Italy: "so both our lines" — the scientific and the theological — "meet in this Point," and it was fair to conclude — on both accounts — that "at the glorious Appearance of our Saviour, the Conflagration will begin at the City of *Rome,* and the Roman *Territory.*"

Both lines meet! The providence of God and the march of natural causation will converge, the only difference from the picture in the medieval sculptures being that, whatever had been their physical detail — the contorted muscles and the meticulous agony on the faces — the order of natural causation is now under control. Hence we no longer need for religious reasons to reject a scientific particularization of the end of the world, nor for scientific reasons to deprive it of religious significance. The dead will still claw their way out of the earth, as they did in Signorelli's murals at Orvieto or in Roger Van der Weyden's polyptych. This naturally produced event will not be less terrifying than those naïvely supernatural conceptions: "One must be very much a Stoic, to be a cold and unconcerned Spectator of all this." The earth will still be consumed: there will still be the traditional sequence of light, then explosion, and then the stupefaction of nature. Man-made constructions will universally collapse: "The Cities and the Towns, and all the Works of Man's hands, will burn like Stubble before the Wind." As an instrument of terror and as a prologue to Judgment, this "mixt Fatality" will have the effectiveness — even more — of the light that was once supposed to break uncaused at midnight. As Burnet succinctly put it, "A World is sooner destroyed than made."

There is this to be noted about Burnet's "mixt Fatality": it is scientific, but it is not merely mechanical; it is ingenious but not inhuman. It is not a mathematical calculus. The agents that produced the deluge, and will bring about the end, are not abstract laws of physics, not formulas, but the familiar and, in a sense, the cozy elements of fire and water. The source

of destruction, which he located after so much search of soul, lies not in
some bleak and blank region outside physics, but is of the earth and in the
earth, so that it is not alien to the imagination of mankind. God is still
present throughout history, and though He operates within such processes
as liquefaction and solidification, still these are organic, and require constant
supervision. Motion is still something imparted to the physical universe by a
penetration of matter, and what God has given He may take away. The
physical and the divine are still so intermingled as to make the analyst
suppose — or half suppose — an innate power or an occult quality within
the elements themselves, wherefore they can really play parts in a moral as
well as a physical drama. The breaking of the crust, both at the deluge and
at the end, has the quality of an intentional act, and can therefore serve —
really serve — both as a detonation and a judgment. Blending with the
light of the fires from beneath will be the light of the descending host of
Heaven, "till, by nearer Approaches, this bright Body shews it self to be an
Army of Angels, with this King of Kings for their Leader."

Burnet's central thesis was that this double vision, this mixed fatality, did
not mitigate but rather enhanced the spirituality of the prospect, and that
the end was no less terrifying for being subject to physical regulation. We
do not, he said, make or contrive these things of ourselves, but we find and
discover them: *ergo*, "when they are clearly discover'd, well digested, and
well reason'd in every Part, there is, methinks, more of Beauty in such a
Theory, at least a more masculine Beauty, than in any Poem or Romance;
and that solid Truth that is at the Bottom gives a Satisfaction to the Mind,
that it can never have from any Fiction how artificial soever it be." Satisfaction, yes, because there is at one and the same time the greatest glory
that ever was visible upon earth and the greatest terror; but as for the
"romantick" beauty of Signorelli and Roger Van der Weyden, the beauty
of Chartres — the beauty of the unmixed and wholly God-administered
fatality — was it still with us? Burnet protests too much. He could not
pretend that the destruction, magnificent though it might be, would include
more than this one planet. A scientific version might, in some respects, claim
to show more genuinely masculine beauty than a romance, but it did make
one fact clear: man is no longer the center of a cosmic drama, he is at best a
side show. "We must not by any Means admit or imagine that all Nature
and this great Universe was made only for the sake of Man, the meanest
of all intelligent Creatures that we know of; nor that this little Planet,
where we sojourn for a few Days, is the only habitual Part of the Universe."
(Where now was the dogma, with all its crushing weight, of original sin?)
This doubt eats at the heart of Burnet's hypothesis: do flames that arise
from natural fissions of matter give quite as much satisfaction to the mind
as those that rain arbitrarily from Heaven? Is a God who must bake the
earth in order to inflict His vengeance quite as formidable as the God who
simply avenges? Is the fatality, in this modernized version, really mixed
of fire and terror, or does it become merely a terror of the fire? Burnet

contended with fervor: "What Trifles are our Mortar-Pieces and Bombs, when compared with these Engines of Nature!" Still — an engine is not an angel. After all his eloquence and his ingenuity about the oceans, had Burnet managed to construct no more than an engine, simply a bigger and better bomb?

Burnet had the misfortune to publish only six years before the most efficient brain of modern times gave to the world the result of his profound meditations upon the engines of nature. A few years later, and an Oxford mathematician would be making fun of poor Burnet's physics in the name of "the great Philosopher of this age, the most Ingenious and Incomparable Mr. Newton." Burnet's rhetoric, which is superb, could not save his hypothesis from the ash heap, nor can it today shield the book from ridicule. Henceforth the apocalyptic vision was entrusted to the disciples of Sir Isaac Newton and to the philosophers of mechanical motion.

They had their work cut out for them. Burnet could construct the drama out of elements and not worry about motion; for him there was no power so innate to matter as to be thought without beginning or end. But Sir Isaac, to the dismay of common sense, proved that a sphere of matter attracts outside bodies as though all its mass were mysteriously concentrated at the pinpoint of its center, with the result that the planets become chained to their slightly elliptical orbits. Each attracts the other with a force proportional to the product of the masses and inversely proportional to the squares of the distances: — what then are water and fire? Motion is now encased in rigidity, not the rigidity of a divine decree which Divinity may repeal, but of irreversible continuity, from the sweep of a planet to the fall of the apple. In such a machine how — and how in the name of God — could the sun get close enough to the earth, or the earth to the sun, to bake the surface and so bring about either the flood or the conflagration which only six years before appeared so beautifully and unromantically simple to the now discredited Burnet? If the universe is a perpetual motion, of which the basic stuff is not tangible elements like fire and water but an abstract mathematical equation, how can beginning and end constitute a drama of retribution?

A host of poets, theologians, pamphleteers rushed forward to quiet these anxieties. Their first and most pressing task was to prove that catastrophe was still possible. Naturally, considering the pressures they were under, they tried to prove, and indeed did prove, that it was actually more probable and more imminent than ever. Provincial New England, where children still read their Wigglesworth, breathed a long sigh of relief. "The admirable Sir Isaac Newton," sang Cotton Mather, will rule henceforth as "the Perpetual Dictator of the learned World," for he had so expounded physics that men must forever confess "that Philosophy is no Enemy but a mighty and wondrous Incentive to Religion."

Of course, as we read these Newtonians, we may wonder whether they were as confident as they professed to be. Listening carefully, we detect them, like Don Giovannis awaiting a Commendatore, straining to catch the approaching tread of Laplace, in whose system there would be no place for God. Cotton Mather's father, the mighty Increase, had learned his physics in the happy pre-Newtonian era. Even to the day of his death, Increase could cheerfully exhort his congregation to repentance by reminding them of that "most awful day," and ornamented his appeals by an imagery which only the medieval astronomy would supply. A Christian who walks abroad and looks at the stars should think within himself that someday this very body of his shall "walk above the Starrs: For so it shall when after the Resurrection it shall be in that Heaven which is far above them." But son Cotton could no longer locate Heaven with quite such geographical precision, and he found it wiser to excite piety by a more intellectual reflection: "These are Laws of the Great GOD, who formed all things." But there the trouble began: God ruling alone can command an archangel to blow a trumpet, but if He has entrusted the universe to the conduct of laws, can man rely on them to bring about the consummation? Would a Creator, having set the laws in motion and having perceived that they continue of themselves, intervene from the outside of the system in order to wreck them? If He did, would He not have to behave with gross inconsistency, simply have to bring His fist down upon the contrivance? Would not the end of the world then have to be not so much a Judgment as a hammer on anvil? Would it not have to be some sort of collision?

Even while Cotton Mather was fumbling with the problem, a schoolboy from the back-country of New England, a student at the newly organized and still struggling Yale, had penetrated to the awful conclusion. Jonathan Edwards confided to his notebooks what the foremost scientists of Europe could not yet bring themselves to admit: "Solidity is gravity, so that, in some sense, the Essence of bodies is Gravity." So, the innermost secret of bodies and elements and of even the human psyche is unalterably mechanical, "and is philosophically to be solved, and ought no more to be attributed to the immediate operation of God, than every thing else which indeed arises from it." Cotton Mather was desperately clinging to a lost hope when he said in Boston, at the very same time, that gravity "must be religiously resolv'd into the immediate Will of our most wise Creator, who, by appointing this Law, . . . keeps all Bodies in their proper Place." Mather was trying to keep alive the mixed fatality by thinking of gravity as nothing more than God's will in operation, so that God could still interrupt it when He chose. If Edwards had drawn the correct deduction, what power on earth or in Heaven could withdraw the power of gravity without annihilating the essence of bodies? What then would be left to be judged? If space itself, in the language of Newton, was no longer the stage for a drama but God's own "sensorium," how could He descend into it, surrounded with angels, to play the role of destroyer? What agent, in such a mathematical orrery, could possibly wreak such havoc? Could Newton himself tell us?

The great man never answered. Said the sphinx, "Hypotheses non fingo." He did not know the cause of gravity. But his biography makes us wonder: in 1693 he suffered a mysterious psychic depression, and soon thereafter went to London, where he became Master of the Mint, a great diner-out and a gentleman, no longer the professor. He occupied this elegant leisure with an intensive study of the books of Daniel and of Revelation. Apparently — there is no other conclusion to be drawn — he wanted to find out how close he was to the end of the world! He went about it in the true Newtonian spirit, at no time in his life more resembling, except for the costume, Blake's drawing of him. The most unpoetical of men, he drew up a key for translating the poetic imagery of the prophets into the prose of history; then he calculated the prophecies, checked off those that had been fulfilled, subtracted these from the total, and had as a result the number yet to be accomplished. It was not large. "I seem to gather that God is opening these mysteries," wrote the author of the *Principia*, "The last age is now approaching."

Voltaire could account for these foibles only on the theory that Newton, out of mercy for the rest of mankind, deliberately tried, for once in his life, to be as silly as they. Later biographers are generally men of science, and they pass by, with averted gaze, the years in which Sir Isaac Newton was occupying himself with determining precisely which historical events were signified by the ten horns of the fourth beast and which by the little horn with the eyes like the eyes of a man. I think these scientific-minded biographers have failed to give us the true Newton, and I can only guess at what was driving him. We must remember that he was a Puritan by inheritance and a theologian by temperament, that he studied physics in order to know God. So I dare to say, abetted by the authority of Lord Keynes, that Newton was frightened. He had become very lonely, voyaging out there on strange silent seas of thought, dreadfully alone. The mute spaces finally terrified him, as they had already frightened the more impressionable Pascal and as they almost succeeded, to use the common phrase, in scaring the hell out of Jonathan Edwards. Newton needed to find human significance — something more satisfying to the soul, if not to the mind, than the inhuman formula that force acting on a body is proportional to the mass of the body and the acceleration produced. He had proved that beauty lay, not in remorse or in romance, but in simplicity and symmetry; what then had become of the ecstatic beauty which the saints would enjoy when they came to tread upon the stars as upon a jeweled pavement? In the history of human thought there is no spectacle more poignant: the architect of the modern cosmic machine spent his last years refiguring the assurance that, while it might in theory last forever, in historical fact it would not.

But Newton's ways were secret and peculiar unto himself; few could penetrate the labyrinth of his last meditations, of which his fragments on prophecies are tantalizing hints. Among his followers, whose insights were cruder, the problem seemed open to an easier solution. Gravity did appear to make motion an infrangible system, but might there not still be some

mix-up of particular motions, all according to law, that would engineer a
collision which would, for all practical purposes, be the end of the world?
No less a person than Newton's successor in the Lucasian Professorship at
Cambridge was ready to assure the world that all hope need not be abandoned. William Whiston stepped into the breach with a book called *A New
Theory of the Earth*, published in 1696, proclaiming the happy intelligence
that, to destroy the earth, comets are every bit as serviceable as Gabriel's
trumpet or Burnet's fires, and what is more, that in a predictable future,
some comet would oblige.

This was welcome news, the more so because it seemed to preserve, on the
best scientific bases, certain elements of the oldest tradition. Comets had
always figured prominently in the panorama of conflagration, if only because for centuries they had been the most charmingly lawless of actors in
the cosmos. In *Henry VI* the Duke of Bedford spoke the admiration of
Shakespeare (or of whoever wrote the play) for these creatures who could
"scourge the bad revolting stars." According to the Gospel of Matthew, the
return of the Son of Man shall be announced by the darkening of the sun
and by stars that fall from heaven; although false prophets may delude us
by their predictions — as both Whiston and Edwards were aware — an
approaching comet would surely be an answer to the disciples' question in
the third verse of the twenty-fourth chapter: "And what shall be the sign
of thy coming, and of the end of the world?" Burnet had not really required comets in the mechanism of his destruction, but he dared not omit
them: "For I do not doubt but the Comets will bear a Part in this Tragedy."
In 1680, in colonial Boston and still enjoying, as we have seen, the imagina-
tive prerogatives of the old astronomy, Increase Mather "improved" the
then appearing comet into a portent of "Droughts, Catterpillars, Tempests,
Inundations, Sickness." A comet, he said, was a kind of "warning piece"
that a merciful God discharges "before his Murdering pieces go off." In the
presence of this apparition, therefore, the women of Boston should stop
wearing false locks in their hair, and the men should ask themselves whether
there ought to exist "such a multitude of Licensed Drinking Houses (and
Town dwellers frequenting them) to the Shame of Boston and to the
Infamy of New England?"

But other eyes besides Mather's had watched that comet: Halley plotted
its curve, and from his data Sir Isaac Newton, swift as the hawk swoops,
extracted the law out of it. The last free and arbitrary motion in the universe
was tamed, and admirers, chanting in chorus Newton's genius, vaunted
that he had

> Persu'd the Comets where they furthest run
> And brought them back obsequious to the Sun.

Did this mean that the women of Boston might now sport their false locks
in security while the men frequented taverns with no fear of retribution?
Whiston said that it did not, and so good men on both sides of the Atlantic,

and even out in the Connecticut Valley, hastened to study his book, all the more eagerly because it was supposed to have been blessed in manuscript by the inaccessible Sir Isaac.

Whiston like Burnet strives to erect a single scientific principle which will serve as cause for both the deluge and the end, which yet, in the very consistency of its operation, will explain why the effect in one case was water and in the other is bound to be fire. He too seeks for a theory of the deluge that will engage for the performance of the conflagration. But his book offers none of Burnet's rhetoric; it is a brain child of the *Principia* (it is dedicated to Newton), furbished with an apparatus of mathematical diagrams, and argued through a series of "Lemmata," "Corollaries" and "Solutions." Along the way, in the course of this Euclidian Q. E. D., Whiston explains just about everything on earth — geology, geography, climate, history, and the distribution of races. The central problem, he said, is that by now the conception of an end to the world has given rise to so many "Perplexities and Contrarieties" (how far we have come from the tympana of the cathedrals!) that mankind threaten to fall into two irreconcilable schools: those who dogmatize "without any Consideration of Nature, Reason, Philosophy, or just *Decorum* in the several Parts of it," and those who decide that the entire business is a "meer Popular, Parabolick, or Mythological Relation." By pursuing the comets, and specifically the revolutions of Halley's comet, Whiston proposed to unite all men of good will once more, whether dogmatists or skeptics, within a new and incontrovertible mixture of fatality.

A comet — evidently Halley's — passing near the primitive chaos, by exerting upon it the power of gravity, drew it into coherence; thus the world was created, a process of which Moses gives a sufficiently accurate report. Although this hypothesis meant that Whiston — and so Moses — could speak only of what "extends no farther than this Earth and its Appendages," he was much more ready than had been the reluctant Burnet to accept this delimitation, because thereafter he could solve every perplexity by purely mechanical methods, without the slightest embarrassment of "some innate Power or *occult Quality*" resident in bodies. (The pious Newtonians, assuming that otherwise they would be forced to deny the existence of God, clung fanatically to Newton's denial that gravity is an "inherent Power really existent within," an admission which the still more pious Edwards was perfectly prepared to allow.) Thus freed of concern about the rest of the universe, Whiston was able to concentrate upon the earth, where, by calculating the Biblical chronology alongside the schedules of the comet, he could demonstrate that on the first day of the deluge this body, "cutting the Plane of the Ecliptick, in its Descent towards its *Perihelion*," passed so close to the earth as to draw the waters upward by the force of gravity, high enough, at any rate, to drown every living thing that was not already stowed away on the Ark. He would not merely suppose; he could positively demonstrate "the exact Coincidence of the Particulars

with the sacred History, and the *Phaenomena* of Nature." Whiston was in
such full possession of the facts that he could go even further than this, and
out of the coincidence of Scripture and physics solve what even for Newton
had been a puzzle: the comet that raised the deluge pulled so hard upon the
earth that it drew the whole planet slightly out of line, since when the orbit
of the earth has remained elliptical — which makes certain that it will come
close to the path of the comet on the first day of the predestined conflagration.

In the end, as in the deluge, we may contemplate the miraculous at the
same time that we, "like *Philosophers*, shall attempt to consider and remark
his Vicegerent Nature in her *Mechanical* Operations therein." At the deluge, the comet was descending toward the sun, and was cold: hence it
merely aroused the seas. But when the two ellipses once more become nearly
tangent, and the two bodies are again in close proximity, the comet will be
ascending from the sun, still glowing with solar heat; it will empty the
rivers and oceans, and will so ignite the atmosphere that "no more, I suppose, will be necessary to a general Conflagration." The same comet serves,
in either event, as sufficient cause: the only difference — which is the difference in effect — being that at the flood it was descending, whereas on the
day of doom it will be ascending:

The Vapoars acquir'd from the Comet's Atmosphere, which at the Deluge
were, by reason of their long Absence from the *Sun* in the remote Regions beyond
Saturn, pretty cool; at this Time must be suppos'd by reason of their so late and
near Approach to the *Sun* about the *Perihelion*, exceeding hot and burning; and
that to so extraordinary a Degree, that nothing but the *Idea* of the Mouth of a
Volcano, just belching out immense Quantities of liquid and burning Steams, or
Torrents of fiery Matter, can in any measure be suitable to the Violence thereof.

Mechanism has done it, mechanism will do it!

Then a curious thing happens. Whiston does indeed succeed, out of "the
Theory of Comets," in setting the earth on fire exactly as "both Sacred and
Profane Testimonies conspire to forewarn us of," but he can not provide for a simultaneous descent of the avenging Messiah and His angelic
host. In Whiston's account, they do not appear; there is no Judgment at
all. He has done enough by contriving, out of the logistics of the comet, a
catastrophe, and to him this in itself is all that a purgation should be. Thereafter he refuses to desert the earth: with all wickedness rooted out by this
celestial flamethrower, Whiston declares that the globe will be so altered and
meliorated that it shall at last be fit "to receive those Saints and Martyrs
for its Inhabitants, who are at the first Resurrection to enter, and to live
and reign a Thousand Years upon it, till the second Resurrection, the
general Judgment and the final Consummation of all Things." There does
not need to be a specific judgment, because the explosion itself will produce
a social and political millennium on earth.

In no department of human speculation or dreaming will you find a more incisive dramatization of what happened to the mind of Western man at the end of the seventeenth century than in the contrast between Burnet's book of 1681 — six years before Newton's masterpiece — and Whiston's of 1696 — nine years after it. For Burnet the end of the world was end-all, and only Heaven remained; for Whiston the end was rectification of error, to be followed by utopia. In one sense, Whiston was only the fulfillment of Burnet's and of the century's effort to spell out, in concise detail, a method by which the natural fatality could be mixed with the moral; but the difference — the epoch-making difference — was in the conception of the natural. For Burnet the end of nature could come out of its own radiant energy and power, which somehow left a place — or rather demanded a place — for the visitation of the Heavenly host; for Whiston, the conflagration of the world, becoming something "almost as agreeable to Reason, and the most solid Mechanical Philosophy, as any new Discoveries, built on the exactest Observations of present Nature whatsoever," was to be followed, not by eternity, but by a calculus of earthly felicity. The moral judgment was separated from the physical, and the two were related only sequentially. The world was still to be purged by fire, but by fire that would follow an external collision of earth and comet; by its very nature this catastrophe was mechanical and without further significance in and of itself, so that it had to be made the efficient — although really no longer the essential — prologue to a millennium of social justice, beyond which no one needed to concern himself.

Of course, by introducing the notion of a millennium into his mechanical hypothesis, Whiston was smuggling into physics, in the name of Newton, an old and furtive conception that for centuries had tried to force its way into the theology of the end. Where Whiston picked it up need not concern us, although there is abundant evidence that the doctrine was much abroad in the confusion of the Civil Wars, and that the scientists, who generally came from Puritan backgrounds, found it fascinating. What is important is that the mechanical hypothesis, although seemingly as preoccupied as Burnet's with inducing a coincidence of nature and Revelation, was actually striving to state the proposition in such a way that a wholly physical event — the blast and the fire alone — would be all that was needed for the regeneration of mankind. Confident that his comet could destroy civilization, Whiston was prepared to contend that anything so magnificently explosive was bound, after destroying millions, to introduce the millennium.

He staked everything on the comet. In a few short decades, that hope was gone. Further research and more careful evaluation of the data diminished the chances of collision. By 1759 Professor John Winthrop, lecturing in Holden Chapel at Harvard College, felt obliged to insinuate, as gently as possible, that pious New England, in which Whiston's book had enjoyed a considerable vogue, should not bank too much upon comets. He suggested that piety would do better to reflect upon "that consummate WISDOM which presides over this vast machine of nature, and has so regulated the several movements in it, as to obviate the damage that might arise from this quarter." Evidently the last natural agency capable of producing destruction on a scale large enough to constitute a respectable finish was disarmed. Did this mean that there was to be no explosion and never any day of doom?

In the early eighteenth century another theorist, contemporary with Newton, listened to Whiston, and suggested that it was just possible that a mechanically contrived end of the world might not bring a millennium but rather have quite another effect upon men, they being what they are. According to the sober report of Jonathan Swift, purporting to be "A True and Faithfull Narrative of what Passed in London, During the General Consternation of all Ranks and Degrees of Mankind, on Tuesday, Wednesday, Thursday, and Friday Last," William Whiston, commencing his lecture to an audience of fourteen tradesmen and five apprentices, announced that on Friday the world would be smashed by a comet, and as evidence of his sincerity gave back to the apprentices the shilling fee he had charged for admission. The news spread: shoplifters stole cambrics, bankers thought only of their credit, politicians clung to office, maids at court were delighted with the prospect of appearing naked and ordered a bathing tub, two colonels fought a duel, and the clergy lost their heads. The only persons really to rejoice were three malefactors condemned to be hanged on the following Monday.

In America, the greatest artist of the apocalpyse was, of course, Jonathan Edwards. To him the fire was very real; every student knows, even if nothing else about Edwards, that his God held men over it as one holds a spider or some loathsome insect over the flames. Yet Edwards understood Newton at least as well as Professor Winthrop, and he had read both Burnet and Whiston. Hence it is of the greatest significance that he took elaborate pains to avoid every suggestion of a mechanical cause for the last judgment. The day of doom will be that moment when deceits shall be removed, when the secret springs of every man's action shall be laid bare, when every person must acknowledge his real motives: "Our own consciences shall speak plain and loud, and each of us shall be convinced, and the world shall know; and never shall there be any more mistake, misrepresentation or misapprehension of the affair, to eternity." As a scientist, Edwards loved the masculine beauty of Newtonian nature, but in human society he found something less: "The affairs of the world, so far as they are in the hands of men, are carried on in a most irregular and confused manner." The need for a Judgment, he insisted, had not been removed by philosophical discoveries built on an exact observation of nature; in his view, as in Swift's, the moral had not been absorbed into the mechanical. "It will come as a cry at midnight," he said with deliberate defiance.

Nevertheless, in his secret meditations, which he would never admit to the eyes of others and would lock up in the *Miscellanies*, Edwards toyed with the prospect of mechanical devastation. Those comets were almost as seductive to him as to Whiston: without the exact care of their Creator, Edwards mused, "It could not but have come to pass before now that they should have clashed or crossed one another so often as to have destroyed the motion of one another," and eventually the motion of the earth. However, since it seemed evident that not for eons had any of them collided, Edwards put aside the temptation of the comets. Still, their very existence, taken along with the ceaseless revolutions of stars and planets, suggested that sooner or later the universe might wear itself out. But precisely how? Edwards was too sensitive a mind to vulgarize the drama; the most he would permit himself was a tentative thought that mere motion is in its very self a prognostication: "Does God make the world restless, to move and revolve in all its parts, to make no progress, to labor with motions so mighty and vast, only to come to the same place again, to be just where it was before?" But the moment one surrenders his mind to even so vague a mechanism, troubles begin. Suppose simple motion should grind the universe to an end, where would man figure in such a disaster? For unless man somehow survives, despite Burnet, an end of the world becomes pointless:

And therefore, if he don't remain after the revolutions have ceased, then no end is obtained by all those revolutions. Because nothing abides as the fruit of 'em after they are finished but all comes to no more than just what was before any of those revolutions, or before this world itself began, *viz.* an universal nonexistence.

That was always the charm and the danger of eschatology: destruction must be seen as a positive act, increasing the fund of existence; but what if it should prove a reversion to nonexistence?

Fully aware of the agony of his problem, Edwards spared his people as much as possible, giving them simplifications that might suit their limited intelligences without, in the technical sense, exactly falsifying scientific integrity. This is another of those half-deceptions he cumulatively practiced, until the weight of them broke the patience of his people and they sent him on his errand into the wilderness of Stockbridge. In 1739 he preached at Northampton a series of sermons which, twenty-eight years after his death, were published as *A History of the Work of Redemption*. Assuming that the surviving text is at least an approximation of what he actually said, we may note the cunning by which he confined his causal explanation to some unspecified but gigantic blow from outside the field of gravity. There will have to be an exertion of that Power who "manages all this vast universe, holds the globe of the earth, directs all the motions of the heavenly bodies." Only such an One can "shake all to pieces." Uninitiated listeners might suppose that Edwards was preaching only conventional doctrine; to the initiated, the imagery revealed the Newtonian. It is ruthlessly physical — the stroke will crunch both rocks and mountains: "They are tossed hither and thither, and skip like lambs." Because he had, in his hidden manuscripts, identified gravity and matter, Edwards had no choice but to summon a force from outside the physical coherence of a Newtonian universe in order to wreck it. To annihilate a self-sustaining machine, there must come a power not so much divine as simply external. Only from without could come such a force as might "shatter the whole universe, and dash it to pieces at one blow."

So, if one listens carefully to Edwards' choice of words — bearing in mind those of Burnet and Whiston — these casual emphases speak volumes, and the hidden point of a book that has generally been considered mere obfuscation becomes clear. How consciously Edwards was working may be surmised — I admit that I am surmising — from the strategy he employed to refute the apocalyptic physicists, although he never called them by name: he carefully and publicly, indeed one can say again defiantly, accepts the whole suspect doctrine of the millennium, which Whiston had fastened upon the conception by making it the reward of destruction. But Edwards puts it historically on this side of the apocalypse, allowing the thousand years of earthly virtue to be produced through natural causes; only thereafter does he call in the Judgment. He gives humanity all that Whiston and the mechanists demanded: he gives them their millennium, and lets it be shown that even with so long a conditioning in righteousness, mankind will still fall back into depravity, from which there can be no escape except the cry at midnight. "And if the wickedness of the old world, when men began to multiply on the earth, called for the destruction of the world by a deluge of waters, this wickedness will as much call for its destruction by a deluge of fire." By then the saints will know — as indeed they know even now — that they must ascend into Heaven, leaving this world, with all its beauty, to the flames, "there being no further use for it." Then the world shall be set on fire. How? He says contemptuously, "some way or other." Perhaps "by fire from heaven, or by fire breaking out of the bowels of the earth, or both, as it was with water in the time of the deluge" — it is not worth while to specify.

"Orthodox" Protestants in the early nineteenth century continued to give lip service to the conception of a catastrophic end of the world, but obviously their hearts were no longer behind it. On the lower levels, in America, such panics as that produced by Father Miller's predictions in the 1840's served only to discredit traditional imagery. As the cult of Nature captured what we may call the higher levels of the American mind, an image of infinite progress bit by bit blotted out the ancient expectation. Reinforced in the second half of the century by Darwinism — or rather, by what optimistic and liberal theologians made out of *The Origin of Species* — the dominant Protestant mind so yielded itself to the vision of an unchecked progress which was, of itself, to bring about the Kingdom of Christ on earth, that eschatology became virtually a lost art. A few souls, like Thomas Cole, may still have nourished a lingering hankering after destruction, but the best they could imagine, filled as they were with

Wordsworthian piety, was a man-made wreck of artificial civilization, within the frame of an eternal and unscarred, an inviolately "sublime," Nature. For most Americans, no doubt, the course of empire meant no such cycle of rise and fall, but the steady advance of American farmers and artisans across the continent. Thus the nineteenth century was completing the seventeenth's errand into the wilderness: the meaning was at last emerging, the meaning hidden from Winthrop and from the Puritan pioneers. After all, it now appeared, they had been dispatched into the forests not to set up a holy city on some Old World model but to commence the gigantic industrial expansion which, launched upon a limitless prospect, would demonstrate the folly of anxieties about, or even of a lust for, the end of this physical universe.

Whatever the case might be in complex Europe, in simplified America there were few to dissent, and these were promptly dismissed as cranks. Nobody in 1848, for instance, took Edgar Allan Poe's *Eureka* as anything but the disordered maunderings of a mind rushing toward disintegration. "Poe on the universe," the critics sneered. Assuredly, it is an insane book. A weird hodgepodge of Newton, Laplace, and Humboldt, none of whom Poe was equipped to understand, and constructing a senseless incantation out of the formula that the attraction of bodies for each other is "a force varying *inversel* as the squares of the distances," *Eureka* may indeed be dismissed as beneath scientific contempt.

Only in recent years, however, have students found the wit to note that Poe explicitly offered the book as a "Romance," or if he might so dignify it, as a "Poem." "It is as a Poem only," he said, "that I wish this work to be judged after I am dead." Furthermore, he makes clear that he is writing "unempirically," out of an "intellectual belief" that presupposes a mental conception embedded not in Nature but in the mind of man. Poe is actually arguing that dogmatic retention of this belief, in the face of science, is the essential badge of humanity. "The finest quality of Thought is its self-cognizance," and only self-cognizance can cope with an indefinite extension of "a perpetually atomic and inconsequential Universe" — which is the best science can offer — by insisting upon the need for delimitation. "It may be said that no fog of the mind can well be greater than that which, extending to the very boundaries of the mental domain, shuts out even those boundaries themselves from comprehension." Consequently, the thesis of Poe on the universe is that, just as the cosmos arose out of unity into the multiplicity that now bewilders us, so by an inner logic of the conception itself, the universe must seek a return to primeval unity — and that is, nor can be, nothing less than "annihilation." The dream of an endless creation, of an infinite progression of matter from center to circumference, is humanely intolerable: it is, in truth, "the veriest *cowardice* of thought." At the end, revealing from what sources his vision came, Poe shouts for joy: "In the construction of *plot*, for example, in fictitious literature, we should aim at so arranging the incidents that we shall not be able to determine, of any one of them, whether it depends from any one other or upholds it." But no mortal work of art can attain to such absolute perfection. One creation alone demonstrates it: "The Universe is a plot of God."

For our purposes, then, it is remarkable that Poe too confronted the temptation to let the death of his cosmos be brought about by some mechanical agency, some force of the wilderness, and that he too rejected the lure. In his era the welcome power was no longer a comet but the "ether." Even more concisely than Edwards discarded the comets did Poe dismiss the retarding pull of the ether. Could astronomy and physics demonstrate a collapse from so purely "collateral" a factor, he declared, man's instinct would rebel against the engine:

We should have been forced to regard the Universe with some such sense of dissatisfaction as we experience in contemplating an unnecessarily complex work of human art. Creation would have affected us as an imperfect *plot* in a romance, where the *dénouement* is awkwardly brought about by interposed incidents external and foreign to the main subject; instead of springing out of the bosom of the thesis — out of the heart of the ruling idea — instead of arising as a result of the primary proposition — as inseparable and inevitable part and parcel of the fundamental conception of the book.

Restored thus to dignity and humanity, belief in an end to the world, as an inescapable conclusion to the perfect "symmetry," is purely "inevitable": "The symmetry of principle sees the end of all things metaphysically involved in the thought of a beginning." In his last hectic months, Poe was intoxicated with an ecstatic assurance. We may well ask whether it was this rather than drink or debility that killed him: "The inevitable catastrophe is at hand."

The human brain, Poe surgically noticed, has a leaning toward the infinite; but, he arrogantly rejoined, there may be "superior intelligences" (which intelligence was here the superior was left to obvious implication) to whom this "human bias alluded to may wear all the character of monomania." If monomania it was, then out of it the American nineteenth century proclaimed that the meaning of America's errand into the wilderness had disclosed itself as an errand without an end. Henry Adams strove to liberate himself from the obsession by putting the second law of thermodynamics in the place of Whiston's comets, but that device proved little acceptable to the structure of the human brain, which a dying Poe could have told him and a dying William James did in fact tell him. A few sensitive spirits were depressed because they could perceive how only a deed of sheer violence could do it, and yet they saw little hope. Sir Frederick Pollock wrote Holmes that the ancient cosmographies had always pointed to a destruction of some sort: "It is the difference between being knocked on the head and dying of old age," but his tone was wistful. In cultured circles the theme became a joke. Professor Lovering, of the Harvard Physics Department, a hundred years after Professor Winthrop, had a famous lecture he used to deliver for one hundred dollars on the lyceum circuit; in the first half he described a stellar collision, but in the second half sent his audiences home persuaded that the mathematical probabilities were slight. He came to Plymouth, where the lyceum was poor and could pay only half the fee. He gave the first part, and sat solidly down. "Can you offer us no comfort?" asked the terrified chairman. "Not for fifty dollars!" said Professor Lovering.

The latest contribution to the literature of the apocalypse marks an innovation: the narrative for the first time becomes historical. This makes for certain stylistic difficulties, but these are so well overcome that the account otherwise conforms punctiliously to tradition. Events fall into the conventional sequence of light, blast, heat, whirlwind, and conflagration:

An intense flash was observed first, as though a large amount of magnesium had been ignited, and the scene grew hazy with white smoke. At the same time at the center of the explosion, and a short while later in other areas, a tremendous roaring sound was heard and a crushing blast wave and intense heat were felt.

After centuries of calculation, the date and moment become precise: it was 0815 hours — not 2400 — on 6 August, 1945, and the place was not Rome after all. But as theologians had always predicted, it did catch the people unprepared: "Because of the lack of warning and the populace's indifference to small groups of planes, the explosion came as an almost complete surprise, and the people had not taken shelter." (We have, of course, long been told that there really is no hiding place.) No student of the literature is surprised to learn that at the moment of the blast the populace were particularly vulnerable because of their careless pursuit of worldly ends: "Many were caught in the open, and most of the rest in flimsily constructed homes or commercial establishments." Destruction was especially severe among fire-fighting associations; this point also had been elaborated in tradition and was grudgingly retained even by Whiston. Man-made devices for protection are bound to prove inadequate:

It is unlikely that any public fire department in the world, even without damage to equipment or casualties to personnel, could have prevented the development of a conflagration in Hiroshima, or combated it with success at more than a few locations along its perimeter. The total fire damage would not have been much different.

The authors of the highly official *United States Bombing Survey* are not, I am persuaded, theologians or poets, and they probably did not know that they were falling into the pattern of a literary form more ancient, and more rigid, than the sonnet. Yet a hundred artists of the apocalyptic vision would envy them the stark simplicity, as well as the perfect tense, of their summation: "The atomic bomb shattered the normal fabric of community life and disrupted the organizations for handling the disaster." Edwards had predicted, not letting himself become too specific before the event, that there would be no help in these.

Jonathan Edwards, the American Puritan, and Jonathan Swift, the Anglican Dean, were late-comers to the apocalyptic tradition, who approached it at the moment when the scientists were bent upon appropriating it into the area of causation. They were very different men, but both of them saw one fact as clearly as the light of conflagration itself: men cannot be scared into virtue. Edwards discovered the paradox, to his pain, in the wilderness of Massachusetts, and Swift in the streets of London. In Northampton, a congregation of upstanding Americans, having yielded momentarily to terror in the Great Awakening, celebrated their return to sanity by expelling the terrorist who had goaded them. In London, when the populace realized that Whiston's comet had let them off, they expressed their gratitude by going into taverns and breaking up whole hogsheads for joy: "They drank, they whored, they swore, they lied, they cheated, they quarrelled, they murdered. In short, the world went on in the old channel."

These disparate notes upon a great tradition amount to a query: can engines, comets, or bombs teach the nations to sing the *Dies Irae?* Men have always desired the assurance of an end, and there is good reason to suppose that Christ Himself won the audience which has swelled into Christendom by assuring His disciples that the end of the world was at hand. It would be understandable, therefore, that men should press their cosmologies to yield up a machinery of destruction; yet when the mechanism becomes merely plausible — even though experts must expound it — they suddenly bethink themselves that this was not, during all the centuries, what they had in mind. When the end of the world was a descent from Heaven, it was also a Judgment; if it becomes more and more a contrivance, it has less and less to do with good and evil. Humanity lusts after the conflagration, even after nature seems unlikely to provide it. The human finger actually itches for the trigger. But then, if humanity has to do the deed itself, can it bring about more than the explosion? Can it also produce the Judgment? Explosion, in its stark physical simplicity, although satisfying the most venerable requirements for stage effects, turns out to be — like Burnet's engines and Whiston's comets — not what was wanted after all. Not for this was the errand run into a wilderness, and not for this will it be run. Catastrophe, by and for itself, is not enough.

INDEX